"Some people live an entire lifetime and wonder if they have ever made a difference to the world, but the Marines don't have that problem."

—President Ronald Reagan

"My experience as a Marine was a very positive thing. As an enlisted man, I learned real self-discipline . . . It has been immensely important to me in my business career." —J. Richard Munro, chairman, Time-Warner Inc.

"It's a funny thing, but, as years go by, I think you appreciate more and more what a great thing it was to be a United States Marine . . . I am a U.S. Marine and I'll be one till I die." —Ted Williams, Baseball Hall of Famer

"The deadliest weapon in the world is a Marine and his rifle."

—General John J. Pershing, U.S. Army

"The Marine Corps has just been called by the *New York Times*, 'The Elite of this country.' I think it is the elite of the world."

—Admiral William Halsey, U.S. Navy

"Those of us who have had the privilege of serving in the Marine Corps value our experience as among the most precious of our lives. The fellowship of shared hardships and dangers in a worthy cause creates a close bond of comradeship. It is the basic reason for the cohesiveness of Marines and for the pride we have in our corps and our loyalty to each other."

—Senator Paul H. Douglas, in his introduction
to *The United States Marines: A Pictorial History*

MARINE PRIDE

A SALUTE TO AMERICA'S ELITE FIGHTING FORCE

Scott Keller, Captain,

United States Marine Corps

CITADEL PRESS
Kensington Publishing Corp.
www.kensingtonbooks.com

CITADEL PRESS BOOKS are published by

Kensington Publishing Corp.
850 Third Avenue
New York, NY 10022

All Kensington titles, imprints, and distributed lines are available at special quantity discounts for bulk purchases for sales promotions, premiums, fund-raising, educational, or institutional use. Special book excerpts or customized printings can also be created to fit specific needs. For details, write or phone the office of the Kensington special sales manager: Kensington Publishing Corp., 850 Third Avenue, New York, NY 10022, attn: Special Sales Department; phone 1-800-221-2647.

CITADEL PRESS and the Citadel logo are Reg. U.S. Pat. & TM Off.

First printing: August 2004

10   9   8   7   6   5   4   3   2   1

Printed in the United States of America

Library of Congress Control Number: 2004100517

ISBN 0-8065-2603-3

CONTENTS

FOREWORD

"Semper Fi" is a shout every Marine, past and present, knows. Short for *Semper Fidelis*—"Always Faithful," it is a Latin phrase that sums up the beliefs and actions of the United States Marine Corps. Throughout the Corps' history, Marines have always been in the forefront of America's attempts to defend freedom throughout the world. Whether performing at the White House as part of the Marine band, the "President's Own," providing security at our embassies across the globe, or watching the enemy in the Gulf or at Guantanamo Bay, or, most important, fighting the enemies of our country, in every corner of the world, every Marine can take pride in the efforts of his comrades to safeguard our nation.

On November 10, 1775, the Continental Congress in Philadelphia passed a resolution ordering that "two battalions of Marines be raised" for service as landing forces with the fleet. This resolution, sponsored by John Adams, established the Continental Marines and marks the birth date of the United States Marine Corps. From that day to the present, "our flag's unfurled to every breeze, from dawn to setting sun." Each of America's conflicts have given the Corps fresh opportunities to add to its laurels, and those opportunities have been taken advantage of—just ask those whom they have fought against.

A small, elite force, the Marines are subjected to some of the most rigorous training in the world, and as a result have fought in some of the most grueling combats. Through it all, we have remained faithful—Semper Fidelis—and built a legacy of pride that inspires not only serving and retired Marines, but patriotic Americans everywhere. The Corps have always been the envy of the world.

In this book, I set forth 101 reasons for Marine pride: men like Smedley Butler and Dan Daly, both two-time Medal of Honor winners; battles like Bladensburg and Belleau Wood, where the Semper Fi spirit came to the fore; items of the uniform, like the Blood Stripe and the Mameluke Sword, which serve to remind us of our heritage in a modern, mechanized world; and even movies like *Sands of Iwo Jima*, which show Hollywood's attempts to capture the Marine spirit on film.

Non-Marines will learn what makes the Corps unique, and how much the nation owes it. Retired Marines will relive the glories they have read about or participated in. Serving Marines will be inspired by the past as they go about defending our country, adding their own reasons to be proud for future Marines. In a dangerous and crisis-filled world, these are things we will all need as we face the conflicts awaiting us.

MARINE PRIDE

MARINE SYMBOLS
AND TRADITIONS

Traditions—where would we be without them? In an ever-changing and confusing world, traditions, whether family, religious, civic, or whatever, provide anchors for us to hold on to. In the military, where both the risk of death and the speed of technological transition provide innumerable sources of fear and confusion, traditions become all the more important; nowhere is this truer than in the United States Marine Corps. Marine traditions are not merely museum pieces preserved for tourists! Rather, they help the Marine of today keep his head while trying to equal or excel the deeds of his predecessors in vastly changed conditions. This overt/covert pressure is always in the back of one's mind as a Marine. This will to succeed is what sets the Marines apart from other services.

The greatest importance of these traditions is that they inspire esprit de corps, that hard-to-define "group spirit," without which no organization can succeed, especially one ultimately dedicated to combat. This vastly important concept is beaten into each and every Marine . . . by the hour. In the heat of battle, men fight for each other, as well for personal survival; this is impossible to do effectively without esprit de corps. Because of their effectiveness in promoting this esprit, USMC traditions have proven their worth time after time, in battlefields across the globe. Moreover, most are products of those battlefields, uniting in one cause Marines of every era. Here, then, are some of the best known.

"And St. David." During the 1900 Boxer Uprising in China, the Marine Battalion at Tientsin and Peking in the international relief column was quartered with the Royal Welch Fusiliers (23rd Foot), one of Britain's most famous regiments. The resulting fellowship between the two organizations is symbolized each year on St. David's Day (March 1, the Welsh national holiday), when the Commandant of the Marine Corps and the Colonel of the Fusiliers exchange by dispatch the traditional watchword of Wales: ". . . And St. David."

Army–Navy Game. One major occasion of interservice rivalry is the Army–Navy football game, played between the cadets of West Point and the midshipmen of Annapolis. The Marines, given their maritime origins and continuing naval connections, always root for Navy. The first such game was played in neutral Philadelphia on December 2, 1899. The Army–Navy game is the most important game of the year to the two academies, as well as to millions of other Americans. This is so, despite the fact that neither Army nor Navy rarely makes a bowl bid. Held in Philadelphia for most of its career, the game will take place there from 2003 to 2006; Baltimore will host it in 2007, as she did in 2000.

The Corps of Cadets and the Brigade of Midshipmen march onto the field several hours prior to the game. Fans come into the stadium to witness this tradition and are allowed to leave and reenter the stadium afterward. The stadium is completely filled at kickoff, and no one gets in late.

At Divine Service. When attending divine service in uniform, or present in uniform at an occasion when prayer is offered (as at a military funeral), Marines uncover (if they have not already done so) and assume the old pre-1939 position of "Parade Rest without Arms"—right foot carried six inches to the rear, left knee slightly bent, weight equally distributed on both feet; hands clasped without constraint in front of the body, left hand uppermost; and in the case of prayer, head slightly bowed. This position enables them to appear reverent and military at the same time, and was used as the traditional position for prayer at sea throughout the old Navy.

Birthday Ball—Celebration of Birthday . . . November 10, 1775. One of the most famous Marine customs is the observance of the Marine Corps birthday. Since 1921, the birthday of the Marine Corps has been officially celebrated each year on November 10, the date in 1775 when the Continental Congress resolved, "That two Battalions of Marines be raised." Since then, the day has been celebrated in a wide variety of ways, depending on Marines' location and circumstances. The celebration involves the reading of an excerpt from the Marine Corps Manual and a birthday message from the Commandant; the cutting of a birthday cake by the commanding officer; and the presentation of the first and second pieces of cake to the oldest and youngest Marines present. Recently, the ceremony for the observance of the Marine Corps birthday by large posts and stations has been incorporated into written directives. At a large base, a band begins the ceremony with ruffles and flourishes, while a guest of honor and the senior Marine present pass through a line of saluting escorts. A color guard presents the colors, and the National Anthem is played.

The cake is then presented to the company, guarded by its own escort. A historical message by General Lejeune, the 13th Commandant, is read. The guest of honor's bio follows, and he is presented to the attending crowd. The oldest and youngest Marines present come forward; the senior Marine present is handed a sword by the senior cake escort. He cuts the cake with it, handing a piece to the guest, another to the oldest Marine, and third to the youngest. The cake escorts and the youngest and oldest Marines depart.

The color guard then retires the colors. After them, the guest of honor and senior Marine rejoin the audience, receiving a salute en route by the sword detail. Then they leave as well; after the last has gone, the band stops, and a narrator declares "Ladies and Gentlemen, this concludes our ceremony. Enjoy the ball. Happy Birthday, Marines." In most places the ball is the social highlight of the base's year.

The Blood Stripe. One of the most noticeable features of the blue dress uniform worn by the Marines is the red stripe on the side of the trousers worn by officers and noncommissioned officers (NCOs). This is the famous "blood stripe." It commemorates the blood shed by the Marines in November of 1847.

A Marine detachment accompanied Gen. Winfield Scott's army as it battered its way across central Mexico from Vera Cruz. Arriving at the fortress of Chapultepec, key to the defenses of Mexico City (the "Halls of

Montezuma" mentioned in the Marine Hymn), the Marines were assigned the task of seizing the fortress. They did so with great loss of life, which bloodshed the stripe commemorates.

It is true that the current form of the stripe was adopted only in 1904, a fact that has led revisionists to claim that it has no connection with Chapultepec. But generations of Marines have been reminded by it of the great sacrifices of their predecessors at the Halls of Montezuma.

Blue-White Dress. In summer, for many years, Marine officers wore "Dress Whites," for formal and ceremonial events; staff NCOs continued to wear Dress Blues at such times. However, Dress Whites have been abolished, and replaced with the Blue-White dress, which consists of the blue uniform jacket and white trouser, formally reserved to bands and ceremonial units during the summer. In 2001, it was decided to extend the use of Blue-White dress to NCOs, so as to accentuate the solidarity between commissioned and non-commissioned officers during summer parades and the like. One point repeatedly made by USMC leadership: black and not white socks are to be worn with this uniform.

Bulldog—Mascot of the USMC. The name of the bulldog is always . . . Chesty, after Korean War hero Gen. Lewis (Chesty) Puller. Sgt. Chesty XI is the current official mascot of Marine Barracks, Washington, D.C. The canine leatherneck is affectionately referred to as "Molly" by her fellow Marines at the "oldest post of the Corps." Molly gets her name from the term "Molly Marines," the name given to the first women in the United States Marine Corps. A brindle-and-white pedigreed English bulldog, she enlisted in the

United States Marine Corps August 24, 1995, during a ceremony at Marine Barracks, Washington, D.C. Her duties include serving as official mascot at that location and appearing weekly at the renowned "Friday Evening Parade" held at the barracks during the summer months.

Molly is part of a long tradition of English bulldogs as mascots for the Marine Corps. It began during World War I, at Belleau Wood, when German soldiers called the Marines "devil dogs," after the wild mountain dogs of Bavarian folklore. Soon afterward, a Marine recruiting poster, painted by artist Charles B. Falls, appeared depicting a dachshund, attired in a spiked helmet and Iron Cross, fleeing from an English bulldog wearing a helmet with the globe and anchor insignia. The inscription read, "Teufelhunden— German nickname for U.S. Marines . . . Devil Dog Recruiting Station." Not long after that, Brig. Gen. Smedley D. Butler, then–commanding officer of the Marine Barracks, Quantico, Virginia, enlisted Private Jiggs into the Marine Corps on October 14, 1922. Jiggs, formally King Bulwark, was sired by the once-famous pedigreed English bulldog Rob Roy and whelped in Philadelphia on May 22, 1921. Jiggs received rapid promotions, becoming a Sergeant Major on July 17, 1924. He traveled extensively (legend has it that he traveled more than 100,000 miles by sea, land, and air), made numerous public appearances, and even shared movie stardom with Lon Chaney in the 1926 Hollywood production of *Tell It to the Marines*. Since then, a succession of bulldogs has acted as mascot for the Corps, culminating in today's Sgt. Chesty XI.

The Canton Bell. Visitors to the Marine Corps Historical Center will see a weathered bronze Chinese bell hanging. This is the "Canton Bell," a gift from the Royal Marines. Taken by "the Royals" after they stormed the Canton Forts in South China in 1856, for years it occupied a place of honor in the Royal Marines Officers' mess at Chatham Barracks. When Chatham was decommissioned after World War II, the officers of the mess voted to present their trophy to the U.S. Marines as a symbol of the camaraderie between the two Corps during the Canton Forts attack and later.

Colors, Flags, and Standards. Traditionally, in most European armies, the colors have been the heart of the unit, alongside the national flag. Unlike many of these, however, the Marines still carry their colors into combat. It is often recounted by Marines that a recruit once asked his drill instructor, "Sergeant, who carries the flag into battle?" The DI replied, "Son, every Marine carries the flag in battle!" A Marine proverb says, "The flag is a jealous mistress"—every Marine is prepared to fight and die rather than allow the National Colors or a Marine Corps Color to be dishonored. The official commentary states that "Colors or standards MUST never fall into enemy

hands. If capture seems inevitable, they should be burned. Unserviceable colors or standards, or those from disbanded units, are turned into the supply system. The latter in turn forwards flags of historical value to the Marine Corps Historical Center, which is the Corps repository for historical flags, as well as for flags and war trophies captured by Marines. Soiled, torn, or badly frayed flags, if not historical, are destroyed privately by burning."

A good example of the importance of these flags was illustrated for this author one night, while attending the viewing of the Marine Drill Team at Marine Corps Barracks 8th and I, back in 1985, as a brand new 2nd Lieutenant. An older retired Marine I was talking to, at the sight of the Battle Standards marching by, started to tear up. At my noticing this, the older distinguished Marine told me, in a very somber yet compassionate way, "Behind every one of those Standards, are many dead comrades of mine." That episode sticks out in my "Brain Housing Group." To this day, I, too, feel the same emotions at times, because, I, too, unfortunately, have buried friends . . . "brothers in arms." Spending time with a deceased member's family is not an experience I will ever forget. Even while writing this, it brings a swell of emotion (yes, tears) that is unexpected. Going through hell/time with someone, as happens in a very unique way in the Corps, tends to bring out the camaraderie and genuine love for your fellow Marine, that love which motivates one to lose one's life for a fellow human being. It's something much deeper than what this book allows to expound upon, but needs to be mentioned anyway. The memory of friends like Capt Trey Wilbourne III, an AV-8B pilot who died in Desert Storm, are indicative of the caliber of "America's Best" who have lost their lives, so "Selfish Pukes" can reap the benefits. May his soul rest in peace.

"Come on, You Sons of Bitches, Do You Want to Live Forever?" Yet another tradition to come out of Belleau Wood is this one. Sgt. Maj. Dan Daly's platoon, part of the 6th Marines, was pinned down by grazing fire. Daly (possessor of two Congressional Medals of Honor—one for heroism during the China Relief Expedition in 1900 and the other received during the Haitian Campaign of 1915) ran up and down the line trying to motivate his Marines to attack. Finally, the story goes, he yelled "Come on, you sons of bitches, do you want to live forever?" He then leaped out of the trench and led his men in the attack.

The Commandant's License Plate. In Washington, D.C., the license plate "1775," is set aside for the official sedan of the Commandant of the Marine Corps.

Commandant's Own—Drum and Bugle Corps. The United States Marine Drum and Bugle Corps is renowned for its performance of martial and popular music before hundreds of thousands of spectators each year. Renowned the world over as a premier musical marching unit, the Corps boasts more than eighty Marine musicians, in splendid ceremonial red and white uniforms. Throughout the summer months, they perform in the traditional Friday Evening Parades held at the Marine Barracks, Washington, D.C., and every Tuesday evening in the Sunset Parades at the U.S. Marine Corps War Memorial (Iwo Jima Monument) in Arlington, Virginia.

The roots of the Corps lay deep in the history of the USMC. The eighteenth- and nineteenth-centuries' military musicians, or "field musics," passed commands—via their music—to Marines in battle formations. The sound of various drum beats and bugle calls were easily heard over the battlefield noise, signaling Marines to attack the enemy or retire for the evening. As late as the 1930s, Marine Corps posts were still authorized a number of buglers and drummers to play the traditional calls and to ring a ship's bell to signal the time.

But twentieth-century technology doomed this tradition in the field, as it would so many other proud practices. To preserve the USMC unique style in this area, the United States Marine Drum and Bugle Corps was formed in 1934, at Marine Barracks, Washington, D.C. Envisioned as a supplement to the United States Marine Band, the unit provided musical support to ceremonies around the nation's capital and, during World War II, provided additional presidential support duties. For this extra service, they were awarded the scarlet and gold breast cord by President Franklin Delano Roosevelt, which they now proudly display on their uniform. The war having ended, the Drum and Bugle Corps resumed performing at various military and public ceremonies.

After the war, in the early 1950s, the unit's fame grew in civilian circles. Music was composed specifically for their unique selection of instruments, and helped to establish their reputation. This led to the unit's formal designation as "the Commandant's Own"—a designation indicating that they were musicians for the Commandant of the Marine Corps. Although the members of this Corps are excellent musicians, they are also fully trained combat Marines.

Conduct in Action. As an elite force, the USMC has a definite code of conduct in action. Quite apart from the ability and bravery that each Marine is expected to show in the face of the enemy, it is a firm code of the Corps that no wounded or dead Marine will ever be left on the field or unattended, regardless of the cost of bringing him in. Napoleon's maxim sums up perfectly the Marine attitude toward surrender: "There is but one honorable mode of becoming prisoner of war. This is, by being taken separately; by which is meant, by being cut off entirely, and when we can no longer make use of our arms."

The Crucible. The recruit must pass this final test before being welcomed into the Marine Corps' enlisted ranks. Designed to emphasize the importance of teamwork in overcoming adversity, the Crucible is a rigorous fifty-four-hour field-training exercise demanding application of everything a recruit has learned in the previous thirteen weeks of recruit training, or "boot camp." Throughout the Crucible, recruits are faced with continuous physical and mental challenges that must be accomplished before advancing further. Although a fairly recent innovation, it has been a great success. Following the Crucible, the new Marines are treated to a "warrior's breakfast" and look forward to graduation ceremonies whereby they are formally recognized as Marines in front of their family and friends.

Devil Dogs. During World War I, when the Marines fought the Germans at Belleau Wood, the Germans thought that their position could not be taken. However, they had not planned on the fierce fighting ability of the Marines. The persistent attacks, delivered with unbelievable courage, soon had the Germans calling the Marines *Teufelhunden* (Devil Dogs). This is the origin of the use of a bulldog to symbolize (and later, as a mascot for) the Corps, as well as the title of the Young Marines, the Devil Pups.

The Enlisted Oath.

> "I do solemnly swear (or affirm) that I will support and defend the Constitution of the United States against all enemies foreign and domestic; that I will bear true faith and allegiance to the same. That I will obey the orders of the President of the United States and the orders of the officers appointed over me, according to regulations and the Uniform Code of Military Justice. So help me God."

Evening Parade. Another contribution of the Marine Corps to the capital's ceremonial life is the "Evening Parade," conducted from May through October, each Friday evening at 8:45, at the Marine Barracks, Eighth and I. Performed under searchlight illumination, this colorful ritual features the Marine Band, Marine Corps Drum and Bugle Corps, a special exhibition drill platoon, and a Battalion of Marines from the barracks. The present-day Evening Parade was first conducted on July 5, 1957. The parade's heritage is entwined with former military rituals such as tattoo, retreat, and lowering of the colors ceremonies.

The Field Hat—DI Campaign Hat. Marine recruits, whether at San Diego or at Parris Island, encounter the campaign hat on the heads of their drill instructors. But it has a distinguished history both inside and out of the Corps.

This hat, or, rather, cover (as Marines say, "Hats are for women, Covers are for Marines!"), developed out of various broad-brimmed hats worn by the Army and Marine Corps in the late nineteenth century. Standardized as the "Montana Peak" in 1911, it was extremely popular in both branches with officers and enlisted alike. In the Army it boasted a cord with acorns circling the crown, and colored according to service. It is often associated with the AEF in World War I, but many Doughboys wore the flat, easily folded overseas cap—which was much easier to store than the campaign hat.

Between the wars, the service hat changed little, except it now became thicker in density and the high peak of earlier years was reduced to a dome shape peak about five and a quarter inches. At the opening of World War II, The Army (also known as Doggies) decided to replace the campaign hat for good. While the hat saw service in the Pacific theater and Alaska, only the mainland Cavalry were still issued it 1942–1945. With the end of the Cavalry, the hat left Army ranks.

Despite its popularity in the Corps, its use in the USMC was abolished in 1943, save by shooting teams who liked the broad brim. After World War II, General Cates, the 19th Commandant, officially authorized its use on the rifle range in 1948 and took steps to issue field hats to all medalist shooters in Marine Corps matches. Then, in 1956, General Pate, the 21st Commandant, directed that field hats be worn by all recruit drill instructors, and the hat has since become *the* symbol of Marine Corps recruit training. Female DIs have worn the hat only since 1996. Prior to this, they were issued scarlet shoulder cords to show their authority.

Inspired by the Marines' example, the Army revived the campaign hat for their drill sergeants in 1964. Those gentlemen currently wear the "This We'll Defend" drill sergeant's cap badge, while Marine DIs wear the emblem of the Corps.

The campaign hat is still worn by many U.S. State Police forces, and of course, park rangers. It also retains an attraction in parts of the British Commonwealth. The Royal Canadian Mounted Police retain it for their ceremonial uniform, as do the Legion of Frontiersmen. Called the "lemon squeezer" in New Zealand, it was worn by Kiwi troops in World War I and went on to become their distinguishing symbol. Although dropped from the NZ Army's service uniform in 1962, it has since been resurrected and is now used as the ceremonial headdress.

"First on Foot, and Right of the Line." Marines form at the place of honor—at the head of column or on right of line—in any naval formation. This privilege was bestowed on the Corps by the Secretary of the Navy on August 9, 1876.

"First to Fight." The slogan "First to Fight" has appeared on Marine recruiting posters ever since World War I. Due to the deployment of the Corps on the front line of American interests in peacetime—at sea, in embassies, and providing security for government property abroad, the Marines have traditionally been both a trip wire in the way of anyone who would attack the United States and, due to their constant state of readiness, they are also generally the first response used by the government when such wires are tripped.

The Marines were raised at Tun Tavern, Philadelphia, in 1775, even before the Declaration of Independence was signed. They helped defend the USS *Chesapeake* against the British, before the War of 1812 broke out. At the commencement of the Mexican War, they helped raise California's Bear Flag. Just prior to the Civil War, Marines captured John Brown after his attack on the Federal Arsenal. In 1898, Huntington's Fleet Marines were the first U.S. troops to occupy Cuban soil, and Admiral Dewey's Marines were the first to land in the Philippines. At Woodrow Wilson's order, Marines landed at Vera Cruz (1914). In World War I, the 5th Marines formed part of the first American Expeditionary Force (AEF) contingent to sail for France. In World War II, Pearl Harbor, Ewa, Wake, Midway, Johnston Island, and Guam saw the Marines forming our Pacific outpost line. In the Korean War, the first reinforcements to leave the continental United States were the 1st Provisional Marine Brigade. The first American troops to land in Lebanon in 1958 were Marines. At Santo Domingo, in 1965, Marines were again the first to fight, while in Vietnam, the first U.S. ground unit to be committed to the war was the 3rd Marine Division. As we have seen recently, Marines were in the forefront of the liberation of Iraq.

By this record, "First to Fight" is a just description of the Corps.

French Fourragère. On the shoulders of their service uniforms, Marines of the 5th and 6th Regiments wear a green knotted and braided cord of which they are particularly proud. This is the French Fourragère, a decoration granted these two units by the French government for their valor during World War I.

Originally, the fourragère was a sign of shame. The Duke of Alva, a Spanish general sent by sixteenth-century King Philip II of Spain to suppress the Dutch revolt of that period, employed a unit of Flemish troops. At one battle, the Flemings retreated contrary to their orders. In response, the Duke ordered "that any further misconduct, on the part of these troops, should be punished by hanging, without regard for rank or grade." The Flemish troops, as a sign of penitence, wore coiled around one shoulder a rope in the shape of a hangman's noose, at the end of which dangled a long spike. Their subsequent bravery transformed this gear into a sign of honor. The emperor Napoleon I awarded it to units that distinguished themselves in battle. The French War Ministry revived it during World War I and gave it to formations cited more than once in the French Orders of the Army.

The three classes of the Fourragère are as follows: First—Légion d'Honneur—Scarlet; Second—Médaille Militaire—Yellow and Red; Third—Croix de Guerre (with palm)—Green and Red. The Fourragère becomes part of the uniform of the unit cited and all members of the organization are authorized to wear the cord on the left shoulder of the uniform as long as they remain members of the organization.

The presence of British, and later American, units fighting by their side in the trenches inspired the French to award the Fourragère and other decorations to foreign troops. The French government awarded them to 156 American units varying in size from a section to a brigade. But the only regiments in the American Expeditionary Force to be so decorated were the 5th and 6th Marines. Three times they won the Croix de Guerre; the third was given in reward for their bravery at Belleau Wood. Ever since, these two units have proudly worn the Fourragère. And to this day, Americans are still deploying with units attached to Expeditionary Forces throughout the world, especially in the Middle East and Korea, and a host of other countries where duty calls.

Gold Wings—Aviators Wings. The basic naval aviator wings—or as Marines call them, "Wings of Gold"—date from World War I, while the other wings originated during World War II or later. Airborne wings are issued after the Marine completes training at the Army airborne school at Fort Benning, Georgia.

Green Uniforms. The Continental Marines wore a uniform coat of moss green. If not wearing their green regimental coat, they would wear a green linen hunting shirt. In 1833 President Andrew Jackson decreed that the services would revert to the uniform colors they had worn during the Revolution. This meant green for the Marines who had been garbed in blue since 1798. Green dyes of this era were not durable under sunlight and exposure, so the green uniform, constantly fading during the tropical rigors of the Seminole War, was replaced in 1840. The blue was again the uniform color until 1912, when a forest green uniform was adopted; its cut was similar to the army uniforms of the period, although they were olive drab. In 1926, reflecting British World War I officer uniforms, the service green uniform standing collar was transformed into a rolled lapel with which a khaki shirt and tie were worn. This uniform, with minor modifications, has continued to present day.

Grog Bowl. A traditional feature of Mess Nights, the grog bowl is a large container of alcoholic drink. In origin, of course, "grog" was a mixture of rum, lime juice, and water; today, the first two may make their appearance, but generally a wide variety of other liquors will join them. Just as a ship's officer mixed up the Royal Navy grog of yore, at some mess nights today either the President or Mister Vice will do the honors, narrating their procedure as they do so. At other messes the bowl is premixed. Either way, a "trip to the grog bowl" is one of the punishments for infractions of mess etiquette. Should the President mete out such judgment, the malefactor proceeds to the bowl immediately. The bowl is usually located on Mister Vice's table. Upon arriving at the grog bowl, the defendant does an about face; saluting the President, he turns to the bowl and fills the cup. Doing another about face, he toasts the mess. He then drains the contents of the cup without removing it from the lips, and places it inverted on his head to show that it is empty. He next replaces the cup, again salutes the President, and returns to his seat. With the exception of the toast, "To the Mess," the violator is not permitted to speak during this ritual.

Iwo Jima Memorial. The "island-hopping" campaigns of World War II were particularly bloody affairs, pitting U.S. (often Marine) forces against dug-in Japanese soldiers; these latter preferred death to surrender, and they were tenacious in trying to blunt the American drive toward their home islands. The attack on Iwo Jima was particularly bloody.

One of the more inspiring images to come out of that horrific battle was the February 23, 1945, raising of the American flag on Mount Suribachi by Sgt. Michael Strank, Conemaugh, Pennsylvania; Cpl. Harlan H. Block, Weslaco, Texas; PFC Franklin R. Sousley, Ewing, Kentucky; PFC Rene A. Gagnon, Manchester, New Hampshire; PFC Ira Hayes, Bapchule, Arizona; and Navy Pharmacist's mate John H. Bradley, Appleton, Wisconsin. Strank, Block, and Sousley were killed later during the battle for Iwo Jima, but the

photo of the six raising the flag (Associated Press photographer Joe Rosenthal won a Pulitzer Prize for it) went on to the cover of *Life* magazine, and from there became a part of the national consciousness.

On November 10, 1954, the 179th birthday of the United States Marine Corps, a bronze monument modeled after the famous photo was unveiled at the Arlington National Cemetery. President Dwight D. Eisenhower dedicated the U.S. Marine Corps War Memorial to all Marines who had died to keep their country free. The names of all of the military conflicts Marines have participated in are inscribed in the black granite base of the memorial. The statue is the largest bronze statue in the world at seventy-eight feet tall and weighing one hundred tons. The five Marines and one sailor depicted on the memorial are each approximately thirty-two feet tall. The memorial is one of a select few places where the American flag is authorized to be flown twenty-four hours a day by virtue of a presidential proclamation. It is the setting every Tuesday in summer at 7:00 P.M. for the Sunset Parade (see page 39).

Jodi Calls. These cadences are used in Marine (and Army) training, whether on the march or (with a quicker speed) for double-timing. They are done as a call and response between the drill instructor or other leader, and the troops. They actually improve one's fitness by increasing the oxygen capacity of the lungs (quite ingenious of the Corps). More important, they build pride and comradeship in the face of adversity. Jodi Calls are often crude, talk a great deal about fighting and death, and are an indispensable part of PT (physical training). The tunes are often catchy, and the sentiments are sometimes poignant. But poignant or crude, they tend to remain in the memory forever—although they do alter, generation to generation. Here are a random sampling of some of the cleaner ones:

> Left Right your Left
> Lefty Right your Left
> Lefty Right your Left.
>
> I left the sky in the middle of the night
> I hit the deck and I'm ready to fight.
> A grease gun and Kabar by my side
> These are the tools that make men die.

★ ★ ★

> Hail, hail, infantry
> Queen of battles, follow me
> Marine Corps life is the life for me
> Cause nothing in this life is free.

Here I lie in this foreign land
Bleeding on this foreign sand
Ground around me turning red
By the time they find me, I'll be dead.

Hail, hail, infantry
Queen of battles, follow me
Marine Corps life is the life for me
Cause nothing in this life is free.

★ ★ ★

In the middle of the night in the drizzle and rain,
I packed my chute and I ran to the plane.
Mission top secret there's a mission unknown,
We don't know if we're ever comin' home.
Stand up buckled up shuffled to the door,
Jumped right out and shout MARINE CORPS!
If my chute don't open wide,
I've got another one by my side.
If that chute don't open round,
I'll be the first one on the ground.

Orraaahhh!
Blood and Guts
Orraaahhh!
That's all right

Blood and Guts
Everywhere
Orraaahhh!

Tell my mama not to cry
In the Marine Corps you will do or die.
Pin my wings upon my chest
Tell my girl I've done my best.
Place a Kabar in my hand.
I'll fight my way to the promised land.
Orraaahhh!
Blood and Guts
Everywhere
That's us
That's us
Lean and mean
US Marine
Orraaahhh!
Orraaahhh!

Last to Leave the Ship. When a ship is being abandoned or decommissioned, the Marine detachment is traditionally, save for the Captain, the last to leave. While the practice owes its origins to the Royal Marines and so was done by the nascent USMC, it first appears in Navy regulations of 1865: "When a vessel is to be put out of commission, the Marine Officer with the guard shall remain on board until all the Officers and Crew are detached and the ship regularly turned over to the Officers of the Navy Yard or station."

Leatherneck.   This word is listed in *Webster's* as a term for Marine. "Leatherneck" owes its origin to a leather stock once worn around the neck by both American and British Marines—and also soldiers. It is disputed whether the term originated among the American or the Royal Marines (both are called "leathernecks," although the latter are also called "roughnecks"). Commenting on its use by the British, though, some authorities maintain that the Royal Navy sailors called their Marines leathernecks not because of their collars, but because they washed only their faces, ignoring the rest of their bodies; this resulted in an unwashed and "leathery" neck.

However that might be, starting in 1798, "one stock of black leather and clasp" was issued annually to each U.S. Marine. The intention was to help hold their heads erect and protect them from slashes by sabers and cutlasses. Nearly three and a half inches high, this collar prevented the neck movement necessary for sighting along a barrel. It was supposed to improve military bearing, by forcing the chin high; Gen. George F. Elliott, recalling its use after the Civil War, said it made the wearers appear "like geese looking for rain." The stock was dropped as an article of Marine uniform in 1872, having survived the uniform changes of 1833, 1839, and 1859. But the word has survived until today, and every Marine proudly calls himself a "leatherneck."

"Looking Out for Your Men."   Marine officers are expected to "look after their men." This means more than just supervision. An officer puts his men's interest over his own—always. They are fed first, clothed first, and thought of first. If any of his men are dead or wounded, the officer insures that none are left behind.

Mameluke Sword. One of the proudest possessions of any Marine officer is his Mameluke sword, a scimitar with an ivory hilt topped by an eagle. Worn with the blue dress uniform, it commemorates the sword given by Hamet Bey (the rightful ruler of Tripoli) to Marine Lt. Presley O'Bannon in 1805. This sword was in thanks for the service given by Lieutenant O'Bannon in restoring Bey to his throne—which is remembered in the second line of the Marines' Hymn: "To the shores of Tripoli." By 1825, all Marine officers were ordered to wear the Mameluke sword. Except for the period from 1859 to 1875, commissioned Marine officers have carried it. The sword is utilized to this day, in parades and other official functions.

Marine Corps Collar Emblems. Although officers have worn collar emblems since the 1870s, Enlisted Marines did not rate this privilege until August 1918 when Franklin D. Roosevelt, then–Assistant Secretary of the Navy, visited the 4th Marine Brigade in France, shortly after Belleau Wood. In recognition of the Brigade's victory, FDR directed on the spot that Enlisted Marines would henceforth wear the emblem on their collars.

Marine Corps Colors. The colors of the Corps are scarlet and gold. Although associated with the United States Marine Corps for many years, these colors were not official until General Lejeune, the 13th Commandant, approved them.

In addition to scarlet and gold, forest green enjoys at least semiofficial standing as a Marine color. During the years since 1912 when forest green was adopted for the winter service uniform, it has become standard for such equipment as vehicles, weapons, armor, and organizational chests and baggage.

Marine Corps Emblem—Eagle, Globe, and Anchor. These three symbols represent the USMC's service under the American eagle by air, land, and sea, defending U.S. interests "in every clime and place" across the planet.

The symbol was adopted in 1868 and is perhaps the best-known insignia in the world. Its use without prior approval of the Commandant of the USMC requires, by law, the following disclaimer: "Neither the United States Marine Corps nor any other component of the Department of Defense has approved, endorsed, or authorized this product/service/activity."

The oldest components of the design—the eagle and the foul anchor (an anchor with one or more turns of chain around it)—first appeared on Marine uniform buttons in 1800; these are virtually unchanged from their original form. It was not until 1868 that the globe was added by Brig. Gen. Jacob Zeilin, the 7th Commandant. As with many aspects of our traditions, the globe was borrowed from Great Britain's Royal Marines, whose "globe and laurel" emblem was already world renowned. Whereas the British globe shows the Eastern hemisphere, the Western is in front on the USMC's insignia. In both cases, however, the globe symbolizes worldwide service. The crested eagle shows the Corps' allegiance to the United States. The foul anchor, which first appeared alone as the Marine Corps insignia in 1775 (there was no eagle, as independence had not yet been declared), shows both the amphibious nature of Marine duties and the Corps' maritime origins. On printed versions of the emblem, the eagle is clenching a ribbon inscribed with the Latin motto, *Semper Fidelis* (Always Faithful). This is lacking in the uniform ornaments, however.

The Marine Corps Hymn. It is claimed that the first verse of the Marine Corps Hymn was written by a Marine veteran of the Mexican War who sang it to a Mexican folk tune. The words "From the Shores of Tripoli to the Halls of the Montezumas" appeared on Marine Corps standards shortly after the war, but the author reversed them. The Civil War then gave the hymn wide circulation.

In 1878, a member of the Marine band reported that his wife remembered the melody as a folk song heard during her childhood in Spain. Marine band leader John Philip Sousa identified the tune as a song in Jacques Offenbach's comic opera, *Genevieve de Brabant*, first performed in Paris in 1859. It is known, however, that Offenbach often used Spanish folk music as a basis for his melodies. A variety of verses were added to the first one through the years—each Marine campaign inspiring new ones—but by 1890, the first verse, at least, had become standard. The words remained settled until 1919 when the commandant approved a revision of the last four lines, which were previously as follows:

Admiration of the Nation
We're the finest ever seen,
And we glory in the title of
United States Marine.

In 1942, as a tribute to Marine aviation, the line "On the land as on the sea" was changed to "In the air, on land, and sea." Former–Gunnery Sgt. H. L. Tallman, veteran observer in Marine Corps Aviation who participated in many combat missions with Marine Corps Aviation over the Western Front in World War I, first proposed the change at a meeting of the First Marine Aviation Force Veterans Association in Cincinnati, Ohio.

All current and former Marines stand to attention whenever it is played or sung, and it often is used at the end of Marine Base chapel services, regardless of denomination.

From the Halls of Montezuma
to the Shores of Tripoli,
We fight our country's battles
In air, on land, and sea.
First to fight for right and freedom,
And to keep our honor clean,
We are proud to claim the title
of United States Marine.

Our flag's unfurl'd to every breeze
From dawn to setting sun;
We have fought in every clime and place
Where we could take a gun.
In the snow of far-off northern lands
And in sunny tropic scenes,
You will find us always on the job
The United States Marines.

Here's health to you and to our Corps
Which we are proud to serve;
In many a strife we've fought for life
And never lost our nerve.
If the Army and the Navy
Ever look on Heaven's scenes,
They will find the streets are guarded
By United States Marines.

Marine Corps Seal. The Official Seal of the Corps, designed by General Shepherd, 20th Commandant, consists of the Marine Corps emblem in bronze with the eagle holding in his beak a scroll inscribed Semper Fidelis, a scarlet and blue background for the emblem, and the words, "Department of the Navy" and "United States Marine Corps" encircling the background.

A Marine's Prayer. The following is the text of A Marine's Prayer, adopted in 1967 by the Navy Chief of Chaplains for use by all faiths:

Almighty Father, whose command is over all and whose love never faileth; let me be aware of Thy presence and obedient to Thy will. Keep me true to my best self, guarding me against dishonesty in purpose and deed, and helping me so to live that I can stand unashamed and unafraid before my fellow Marines, my loved ones, and Thee.

Protect those in whose love I live, give me the will to do the work of a Marine and to accept my share of responsibilities with vigor and enthusiasm. Grant me fortitude that I may be proficient in my daily performance. Keep me loyal and faithful to my superior officers; make me considerate of those entrusted to my leadership and faithful to the duties my country and the Marine Corps has entrusted to me. Help me always to wear my uniform with dignity, and let it remind me daily of the traditions of the service of which I am part. If I am inclined to doubt, steady my faith; if I am tempted, make me strong to resist; I should miss the mark, give me courage to try again. Guide me with the light of truth and grant me wisdom by which I may understand the answer to my prayer. AMEN.

A less formal version recited at bootcamp is "Goodnight Chesty . . . wherever you are!" The Marine says this at attention while lying in his rack (bed).

Marine Haircut. Called "high-and-tight," the standard Marine haircut is close to the sides, with a quarter inch or so on top. Its unique appearance probably accounts for the Marine nickname, "jarhead." It can be very painful getting that first sunburn when they shave the hair off. This is where Marines also came up with the term "grape," which describes the new recruit's sunburned head, with the sunburn following the outline of the hat, or "cover," which is worn throughout training. Thus, the recruit's shaved head looks like a purple grape.

Marine One. Just as Air Force One is the President's private jet, so Marine Helicopter Squadron One consists of the USMC-provided helicopters placed at his disposal. The squadron was established in December 1947 as an experimental unit to test and evaluate helicopters and tactics, and provides all helicopter transportation for the President both overseas and within the continental United States. Marine One does the same for the Vice President, members of the President's Cabinet, and foreign dignitaries as directed by the White House Military Office. HMX-1 also provides helicopter emergency evacuation and other support as directed by the Commandant of the Marine Corps. The nickname "Marine One" is the call sign used when the President is on board one of the squadron's Marine helicopters. The primary presidential helicopter is the Sikorsky VH-3D (Sea King). The crewmen of HMX-1 must maintain spit-shined shoes and flawless dress blue uniforms for presidential lifts.

Mess Night. Yet another Marine tradition borrowed from the British armed forces is Mess Night. But this custom has been received from the British Army, rather than the Royal Marines. Its origin among the USMC goes back to 1920s Shanghai, when both the 4th Marine Regiment, and the 2nd Bn., Scots Guards, shared duty defending Shanghai's International Settlement.

At that time, a member of the 4th Regiment, Capt. Lemuel Shepard (later to become Commandant of the Marine Corps) was invited to attend the "dining in," a formal dinner in the Guards' mess. He and his commanding officer, Col. Henry Davis, were so impressed with what they saw that they soon instituted their own mess night. Later the tradition spread throughout the rest of the Corps.

But where a mess night or "dining in" in the British Army was strictly an affair for officers or for NCOs (who would nevertheless have a separate one of their own), Marine Mess Night is a night for a whole unit, regardless of rank, to get to know one another, to remember the exploits of past Marines, and to have fun.

Mess festivities begin with a cocktail reception, wherein the Marines drink with one another and meet the guests. But the heart of the mess night is a formal dinner; a Marine is selected as President of the Mess, and he will serve as master of ceremonies. The Vice President of the mess, "Mister Vice," enforces the president's decisions and decides who may speak to him. Invited guests are a key part of the event, and are seated at the head table with the President. The remaining Marines make up the mess, and are expected to pay fines as the President sees fit for infractions of the mess rules by the diners.

During the formal meal portion of the mess night, members of the mess have the opportunity to charge another mess man with a fine if he thinks he has a legitimate reason. The complaining mess man stands at attention, asking Mister Vice's permission to address the mess. Mister Vice has the option to turn the request away or to forward it to the president. If the president grants permission, the mess member must state his case as to why his comrade must be fined. If the mess member makes a good case, the President may fine the guilty party a certain amount, force the defendant to entertain the mess, or he will be sent to the grog bowl (see page 17). Frequent punishments of the latter sort tend to greatly affect the atmosphere of the evening.

The formalities begin when the mess marches in, followed by the head table guests. The Marines of the mess then sit down to dinner, usually prime rib. Before this can be started on, however, the President must test the meat in a ritual called "bringing forth the beef." Often this will have been specially covered by the mess men with such things as hot sauce and horseradish. When able to speak, the President will declare the meat "fit for human consumption."

An intermission follows dinner, followed by toasts offered by members of the mess. Tributes are given to Marine battles past, present, and future. Other portions of the mess night may include a guest speaker's presentation, recognition of the Prisoner of War/Missing in Action table, and a parade of the beef by the head chef.

Nautical Terms. Due to their naval heritage, Marines—even when ashore—customarily use nautical terms. Floors are "decks"; walls, "bulkheads"; ceilings, "overheads"; corridors, "passageways." The order "Gangway!" is used to clear the way for an officer ashore just as it is afloat. Among other terms in use are: "two-block"—to tighten or center (as a necktie); "square-away"—to correctly arrange articles or to take in hand and direct an individual;

"head"—a bathroom; "scuttle-butt"—a drinking fountain, as well as an unconfirmed rumor. "Aye, aye, sir" is used when acknowledging a verbal order. "Yes, sir" and "No, sir" are used in answer to direct questions. "Aye, aye, sir" is not used in answer to questions since this expression is reserved solely for acknowledgment of orders.

NCO Sword. The sword issued today to Marine NCOs was originally adopted by the War Department on April 9, 1850, as the regulation saber for Army infantry soldiers. Nine years later, the commissioned officers of the Marine Corps adopted the Model 1850 foot officer's sword. They found it more serviceable than their lighter Mameluke swords and welcomed its leather scabbard that was dented aboard ship like their former brass ones.

But such considerations vanished after the American Civil War, when the development of the repeating rifle doomed the use of the sword in Infantry combat (the saber would still play a part in U.S. Cavalry fighting until after World War I). As their swords became more ceremonial than tactical, Marine officers desired to revert to the Mameluke sword. Their wishes were met in 1875.

But the sabers the commissioned officers renounced were not discarded. Instead, they were turned over to the NCOs, who have used them (with slight alterations to the pattern) ever since. This was an unprecedented mark of respect to the NCOs of any branch; they still use it in parade formations and are the only noncommissioned officers in any branch of the regular United States Armed Forces who retain the privilege of carrying swords. (Certain units of the National Guard still authorize NCO swords for ceremonial use when wearing the distinctive uniform of their particular regiment.) Although banished from the modern battlefield, the sword continues to symbolize the military virtues and traditions that Marine NCOs are supposed to maintain. Each NCO is taught the centuries-old sword drill.

OoRah! Any conversation with a post-Vietnam-era Marine will be punctuated with a strange word—Oorah! It can be used to say an emphatic yes, or to indicate enthusiasm for a project. It started with the Marine Recon, who used it to motivate themselves for the extraordinarily difficult kinds of work they have to do. From them it spread throughout the Corps, and has become general, as much a part of Marine life as the globe and anchor.

President's Own. The United States Marine Band has been an integral part of the ceremonial life of the nation for over two hundred years. Established by Congress in 1798, the Marine Band is America's oldest professional musical organization. Its primary mission is to provide music for the President of the United States and the Commandant of the Marine Corps. President John Adams invited the Marine Band to make its White House debut in the unfinished Executive Mansion on New Year's Day 1801; in March of that same year, the band performed for the inaugural of Thomas Jefferson. It has performed for every presidential inaugural since that time. It was Jefferson who proudly proclaimed the U.S. Marine Band "the President's Own." They first performed "Hail to the Chief" for a President when John Quincy Adams attended the ground breaking of the C&O Canal; it has since become the official presidential march.

Marine Band musicians appear at the White House about three hundred times each year, for such functions as South Lawn arrival ceremonies, State Dinners, or receptions. Further, the band appears in more than five hundred public and official performances annually; these include concerts and ceremonies throughout the Washington, D.C., metropolitan area, and an autumn tour through some region of the United States, in accordance with the tradition started by John Philip Sousa, the band's legendary seventeenth director. The band's musicians are selected at auditions like those of major symphony orchestras, and they enlist in the Marine Corps for duty with the Marine Band only. Most of today's members are graduates of the nation's finest music schools, and nearly 60 percent hold advanced degrees in music.

Pugil Sticks. Pugil sticks, used like the old medieval quarterstaffs, are an important part of the Marine Close Combat Training Program, which consists of fighting techniques recruits may need to use to survive in combat. These include, in addition to the pugil sticks, the practical application of bayonet fighting as well as an offensive and defensive skills training program.

Quatrefoil. This braided cross of gold cord is only found on the cover worn by officers (or "zeros," as enlisted men like to call them). It was originally worn by Marine sharpshooters during the Revolutionary War to distinguish friend from foe. They would climb into the rigging of American ships; when the Marines boarded an enemy ship, the sharpshooters would fire upon the enemy while sparing the Marines who wore the cross of rope upon their covers. After the war, the quatrefoil vanished, reappearing on top of officers' caps in 1859. It was actually copied from contemporary French uniforms.

Reporting Your Post. The way in which a sentry reports his post. The customary procedure is for the sentry to salute or come to present arms and say, "Sir, Private _____ reports Post Number _____ all secure. Post and orders remain the same. Nothing unusual to report." This custom has become almost universal throughout the Marine Corps.

"Retreat, Hell. We Just Got Here." This line epitomizes the Marine view of combat. According to legend it was uttered during the third great German breakthrough of 1918, when the 4th Marine Brigade and its parent 2nd Infantry Division were thrown in to help halt the Germans at Belleau Wood. The 2nd Battalion, 5th Marines, had only just arrived at its position when an automobile skidded to a stop and a French officer dashed out and approached the commanding officer. He explained that a general retreat was in progress and that orders were for the Marines to withdraw. The Marine officer exclaimed in amazement, "Retreat Hell! We just got here." The battalion deployed, taking up their firing positions. The skilled firing of the Marines halted the Germans.

Salutes. Saluting is a universal naval and military custom throughout the world; it is believed to have its origins in the lifting of their visors by medieval knights. There are certain aspects of the custom peculiar to the USMC. For example, in the Marine Corps, a greeting is exchanged when saluting an individual. When saluting an officer, the Marine might say, "Good morning, sir," or "Good evening, sir," as appropriate. The officer in returning the salute would say, "Good morning, Sergeant (Private, Corporal, Lieutenant, etc.)."

Marines in civilian clothes and wearing a hat nevertheless conform to the rules for saluting in uniform. When a Marine recognizes another Marine, they normally greet each other, whether or not either or both are in civilian clothes (this custom is not observed by women Marines). If one or both of these Marines were an officer, the hand salute accompanied by a greeting is proper. During the playing of the National Anthem, at morning and evening colors, and at funerals, if in civilian dress, Marines uncover and hold the hat over the left breast at such times as those in uniform salute. And, of course, NOBODY salutes like Marines!

Saluting the Quarterdeck. When boarding a ship, sailors and Marines alike turn and face the quarterdeck and then salute it. This is often interpreted as a sign of courtesy to the officer commanding the vessel. In reality, the origin of the custom lies in the Pre-Reformation English Navy. The quarterdeck sheltered a statue of the Virgin Mary in those Catholic times, and this is what seamen saluted. After England became Protestant, the statues vanished, but the salute remained, traveling from the Royal Navy and Marines to the Americas, where it continues.

"Send Us More Japs." This phrase commemorates one of the most stirring episodes in the history of the Corps. After the attack on Pearl Harbor, the Japanese planned to take the tiny outpost of Wake Island—an outpost which logic dictated would fall quickly. But neither the Japanese nor logic understood the Marines. The initial attempts by the invaders to seize the island were quickly fended off. Late in December, the enemy returned with an even more powerful fleet. The Japanese launched attack after attack, shot down all the Marine planes, and watched as American casualties mounted. Despite the increasing hopelessness of their position, the Marine garrison maintained radio contact with Pearl Harbor. After naval weakness provoked cancellation of a relief expedition, Pearl Harbor queried Wake, "Is there anything that we can provide?" One of the last messages from Wake was "Send us more Japs!"

Serenading the Commandant. Every New Year's Day since 1804, the Marine Band has serenaded the Commandant at his quarters, receiving a tot of hot rum punch in return. This is the last surviving ration of "grog" in the Armed Forces.

Ship's Bell. All Marine posts as well as some field camps have their ship's bell, generally from a decommissioned warship. This bell is mounted at the base of the flag pole, and the guard has the duty, between reveille and taps, of striking the bells and also of keeping the bell in a high polish.

Silent Drill Team. Drill, as we know it, originated on the battlefield as a way of controlling the movements of large bodies of men; it became universal with the development of regular armies in the seventeenth century. Drill teams of all kinds have developed in various armed forces to show off their precision and skill. The United States Marines Silent Drill Platoon is timing and discipline at its best; this is shown at tours throughout the country performing at special events.

The Silent Drill Platoon first performed in 1948 and received such an overwhelming response that it soon became part of the routine parades at Marine Barracks, Washington, D.C. The Platoon executes a series of calculated drill movements and precise handling of their hand-polished ten and one-half pound M-1 Garand rifles with fixed bayonets. The routine concludes with a unique rifle inspection involving elaborate rifle spins and tosses.

Its members are selected from the Schools of Infantry located in Camp Pendleton, California, and Camp Lejeune, North Carolina, via interviews conducted by barracks personnel. Drill Platoon candidates undergo special training in a four-month Silent Drill School in Yuma, Arizona. They maintain their rhythm with no verbal commands or cadence. After drill school, candidates must try out before attaining a position with the team. Once selected, they are assigned to Marine Barracks, Washington, D.C., to serve a two-year ceremonial tour. Throughout the year, they continue to train at Marine Corps Air Station, Yuma, Arizona, sharpening their infantry skills at the Marine Corps Combat Development Command, Quantico, Virginia, and other bases. Experienced members of the Silent Drill Platoon have the opportunity to audition to become rifle inspectors. They must go through inspection try-outs graded by rifle inspectors of the previous year. Only two become rifle inspectors.

Make no mistake, though, all Marines are very proficient in drill, which is one of the reasons they work so well as a team. The importance of acting as one unit is beaten into Marines. This is illustrated quite well by the emphasis on drill.

Sunset Parade. An important feature of the Washington summer is the Marine Sunset Parade at the Iwo Jima Memorial near Arlington National Cemetery. The parade was held the first time in September 1956, two years after the memorial's dedication. Since then, every summer Tuesday has witnessed the event. Nearly two hundred—two companies—take part. A handful of musical selections by the U.S. Drum and Bugle Corps are played, the colors are presented, the Silent Drill Platoon performs, and at last, the troops "pass in review" before a guest of honor. The parade never fails to impress its audience.

"Tell It to the Marines." This is one more traditional saying that owes its origin to the Royal Marines. Charles II founded the Royal Marine Regiment in 1664; they quickly repaid his faith in them. Ever interested in maritime affairs, he was questioning a sea captain at Whitehall Palace. When that worthy told the King about flying fish, Charles replied, "Fish that fly like birds? I have my doubts!" But close by His Majesty's side was Sir William Killigren, colonel of the Royal Marine Regiment. "I have myself seen flying fish many a time in southern waters. I vouch for the truth of this strange tale, Your Majesty." Meditating on this statement, Charles turned to Samuel Pepys, the Secretary of the Admiralty. "Mr. Pepys," he said, "no class of our subjects hath such knowledge of odd things on land and sea as our Marines. Hereafter, when we hear a yarn that lacketh likelihood, we will tell it to the Marines. If they believe it, then we shall know it is true."

Wetting-Down Parties. Whenever an officer is promoted, it is the custom to hold a "wetting-down party." At this event, the new commission is said to be "wet down." When several officers are promoted at the same time, they frequently have a single wetting-down party together. The celebration consists of the promoted officers spending their first pay raise on fellow Marines at a favorite tavern. It is claimed that the new grade insignia is placed in the bottom of a glass of spirits, and the Marine drinks the glass dry.

Wishes of Commanding Officer. When the commanding officer of a Marine says, "I wish" or "I desire," these expressions have the force of a direct order and should be acted upon as if he had given a direct order.

MARINE PLACES

As with any organization, there are places that are very dear to every Marine. Some are important for their historic origins, some because of their importance to the Corps' current mission, and some because of the large numbers of Marines who have been through them.

Camp Pendleton. Camp Pendleton is the West Coast training camp for enlisted, and location of many Marine units. Officially called "Marine Corps Base Camp Joseph H. Pendleton," it is thirty-eight miles north of downtown San Diego, California. Covering over 250,000 acres and approximately two hundred square miles of terrain, the base boasts a seventeen-and-a-half-mile section of beach which is the largest undeveloped portion of coastal area left in southern California.

Here there are training facilities for many active-duty and reserve Marines, Army and Navy units, as well as national, state, and local agencies. Over sixty thousand military and civilian personnel work aboard the base every day. The base is home to I Marine Expeditionary Force, 1st Marine Division, 1st Force Service Support Group and many tenant units, including elements of Marine Aircraft Group 39 and Marine Corps Tactical Systems Support Activity (MCTSSA).

Marine involvement with the former Spanish Royal land grant dates back to the early 1940s, when both the Army and the Marine Corps sought land for a large training base. The Army lost interest in the project, but in April of 1942 it was announced that the rancho was about to be transformed into the largest Marine Corps base in the country. It was named for Maj. Gen. Joseph H. Pendleton who had long advocated the establishment of a West Coast training base. After five months of furious building activity, the 9th Marine Regiment marched from Camp Elliot in San Diego to Camp Pendleton to be the first troops to occupy the new base. On September 25, 1942, President Franklin D. Roosevelt arrived for the official dedication.

Camp Upshur (Also known as Camp Rupture). This Marine Officer Candidate Training Camp is one of several in Quantico, Virginia.

Marine Corp Barracks Eighth and I—Address of Commandant's House. In March of 1801 President Thomas Jefferson and the second Commandant of the Marine Corps, Lt. Col. William Ward Burrows, toured through the new city of Washington, D.C., on horseback. Their goal was to find a proper site for the Marine barracks and a home for the Commandant. They settled upon Square 927, a short walk from the Washington Navy Yard in easy marching distance of the Capitol. The 3rd Commandant of the Corps, Lt. Col. Franklin Wharton, had the honor of completing the house and the barracks in 1806. Still used for its original purpose, the Home of the Commandants has been home to all but the first two commandants, and is said to be the oldest, continuously occupied public building in Washington, D.C.

The Georgian-Federalist-style house was one of the few public buildings not burned by the British (they spared private homes) when they sacked the Capitol in 1814. This was due to the Marines' desperate stand at the Battle of Bladensburg (see page 83). They so impressed General Ross that he ordered the house and the barracks spared as a gesture of soldierly respect.

The early-nineteenth-century barracks was arranged in a quadrangle as it is today; areas on the south and east side of the quadrangle were used for offices, maintenance facilities, and living spaces for troops, and a building on the west was the location of the officers' quarters. The Commandant's House at the north end of the barracks was completed in 1806 and is the only original building still standing. Serving as Marine headquarters until 1901, the Marine Barracks has been home to the United States Marine Band since 1801.

Marine Corps Memorial Chapel, Quantico, Virginia. The Post Chapel at Quantico serves, in addition to its regular functions, as the Memorial Chapel of the Marine Corps. Here is kept a "Book of Remembrance" listing the names, rank, and date of death for Marines and members of the Navy serving with the Marine Corps who have given their lives in action. The book includes by name every Marine or eligible sailor recorded as killed in action since the Revolution to present.

Marine Corps Museums. Foremost of these museums is certainly the Marine Corps Historical Center, Washington Navy Yard, "the scrapbook of the Marine Corps," as it often called. Here may be found an astonishing collection of awards, battle honors, historical flags, and other objects of lasting sentimental significance to the Corps. The collection documents Marine Corps history from 1775 to present day. On display is an extensive array of uniforms, weapons, artifacts, equipment, prints, and painting reflecting the proud traditions of the Corps. Among these are numerous historical flags, such as the famous Colors planted by the 28th Marines atop Suribachi Yama on Iwo Jima. In addition to the museum at Washington Navy Yard, there is the Aviation Museum at Quantico, Virginia, and Post Museums at Quantico, Virginia; Parris Island, South Carolina; MCRD San Diego, California; and the Navy and Marine Museum at Treasure Island, San Francisco. In Philadelphia, at New Hall (a restored building from pre-Revolutionary days) may be found an outstanding collection of material dealing with the early days of the Corps.

MCRD San Diego. The Marine Corps Recruit Depot, San Diego, has undergone many changes since its origin in the early 1900s. In 1924, the Depot was named Marine Corps Base, Naval Operating Base, San Diego. This title stood until 1927, when the base was re-designated Recruit Depot, San Diego. The number of recruits remained constant until 1941, when World War II spurred enormous growth in the Corps. From 1939 to 1945, new barracks, twenty-seven warehouses, an exchange, and new dining and medical facilities were constructed. Hundreds of sixteen-man Quonset huts were built to accommodate the thousands of new recruits; the First Sergeants' School and Drill Instructor School were added. As a result of the Korean War, Recruit Training Command grew from three to eight battalions and over seven hundred Quonset huts were constructed to house the additional recruits.

In 1963, President John F. Kennedy visited the Depot and inspected the Sea School Honor Guard. He stood on the yellow footprints outside Recruit Training Regiment Support Battalion—the set he stood on was later plated in gold. After the Vietnam War began two years later, more expansion took place at the Depot. Between 1965 and 1979, a one-hundred-tent encampment was set up to handle the overflow of recruits. The Depot was redesignated in 1976. This time, it was named MCRD, San Diego and Western Recruiting Region. To distinguish them from the Parris Island Graduates, San Diego products are popularly called "Hollywood Marines." Unlike the isolation of Parris Island, recruits at San Diego have the planes from nearby San Diego airport flying overhead: as many a recruit there has said, "every time one of them takes off, it takes me with it."

OCS—Officer Candidate School. For Marine officers who do not attend the U.S. Naval Academy, commissioning as a lieutenant in the Corps begins with one of several programs at Officer Candidates School: The Officer Candidates Class, the Platoon Leaders Course, or the Naval Reserve Officer Training Corps. Each course is a screening process, with the mission to motivate, train, evaluate, and screen potential officers. And, while many people associate change with progress, the methods at OCS have not changed appreciably since they were first developed.

Before World War I, Marine officers primarily came from the Naval Academy or from the enlisted ranks. The first officer's training school at Quantico can trace its beginnings to 1891 when Marine Corps General Order No. 1 established the first formal resident school for Marine officers, the "School of Application" at Marine Barracks, Washington, D.C. This shifted in 1909 to the Marine Barracks at Annapolis, Maryland; it was renamed the "Marine Officers' School." A year later, it moved again to Norfolk, Virginia. With U.S. intervention in World War I, the Marine Corps expanded enormously. In the face of the growing need for officers that resulted, the officers' school moved to Quantico, where individual replacements and new units were being formed for the war.

Since 1955, Camp Upshur has been the location with Quantico for officer training. The last reorganization occurred in 1977 when women officer training was placed under the cognizance of the Commanding Officer of Officer Candidates School.

Parris Island. Dear (or otherwise) to countless Marines who have passed through its gates, Parris Island, South Carolina, is the East Coast Enlisted Boot Camp. The USMC first arrived at Port Royal in 1861. At that time, Marine activity was limited to Hilton Head and Bay Point, but the federal government began to consider acquiring a military base in the region. Nothing substantive happened until 1883, when the government bought Parris Island with the intention of building a naval station that would function as a coaling and supply depot. Though the base opened in this capacity in 1889, the Navy expanded the station's mission in 1891 and began construction on a wooden dry dock. During construction, Parris Island's first Marine detachment arrived. In 1909, almost all Navy activities ceased, and the base went on to house an officer's training school (1909), a recruit depot (1910), and a disciplinary barracks; a second recruit training depot relocated from Norfolk in 1915. Parris Island's unique career as a recruit depot was begun.

When the United States entered World War I, the Marine Corps numbered only 13,000 men; Parris Island trained a mere 835 recruits. By 1918, the Marine Corps had reached the staggering enlistment of 75,000 men. This required the Parris Island Depot to train more than 13,000 recruits at a time. As a result, more than 500 temporary buildings were constructed, providing additional space for over 10,000 men with another 2,000 recruits living in tents. During this time, an impressive 50,000 recruits graduated from Parris Island with most of them doing service in France. From that time, the island never looked back. It received its first black and female recruits in 1949. During the Korean War approximately 138,000 U.S. Marines passed through Parris Island, with 24,000 recruits undergoing training at any given time. Following the Korean War, the number of battalions at Parris Island was reduced and training was revised. At this time, the Recruit Training Command (later the Recruit Training Regiment) was established and all Marine Corps training was standardized. This was the period in which Jack Webb opened the island for Hollywood in *The D.I.*

Vietnam is the longest war fought by the USMC to date. With over 200,000 recruits trained at Parris Island during its eleven years, some 730,000 men and women served in the Marine Corps during this conflict. Instead of adding new platoons to accommodate these numbers, training was cut from twelve to ten weeks. Since the Vietnam War, Parris Island has continued to grow and change, but it remains the nation's most famous military training facility. Today, an estimated 4,500 recruits—4,000 male and 500 female—call Parris Island home. In addition, the facility employs roughly 2,000 permanent personnel and nearly 400 civilians. Each year, approximately 20,000 recruits graduate from Parris Island.

Pensacola, Florida. Called "P-Cola" in Marine slang, the town is the location for initial training for Marine aviators. The Marine Aviation Training Support Group (MATSG) provides administrative support to assigned personnel in addition to other tasks as directed by the commandant. Marine aviation itself started on May 22, 1912, when 1st Lt. Alfred A. Cunningham, USMC, reported to the Naval Aviation Camp at Annapolis, Maryland, where naval aviation remained for the next four years. In 1916, Roy Geiger, who started flying at Pensacola that year, began the association of USMC aviation with the city.

PLC—Platoon Leaders Course. Still another route to becoming a Marine officer. While it is similar to OCS, it is done before college graduation. College students can enroll in PLC when they are freshmen, sophomores, or juniors in college. Those who enroll as freshmen or sophomores attend two six-week summer training programs at the Marine Corps Officer Candidate School, located at Quantico, Virginia. Students who enroll in the program as juniors attend one ten-week summer course. The course of instruction is much the same as Marine Corps Officer Candidate School. Following commission, Marine Corps officers attend the Basic School, six months (also in Quantico) of training in leadership, land navigation, weapons, small-unit tactics, and communications.

Quantico, Virginia. Home of MCDEC; Marine Corp Development and Education Command. All officer-candidate and follow-on education for officers of the Marine Corp takes place here. Since its founding in 1917, Marine Corps Base, Quantico, has been the "front line of innovation."

Marine concepts, doctrine, training, and equipment of the future are initiated aboard the base. The techniques of amphibious warfare, for which the Corps is renowned, were conceived and perfected here. The tactics of close-air support and vertical envelopment using helicopters were also developed within its borders. Tactics for the battlefield of tomorrow are being developed here.

But Quantico also serves as the focal point for professional military education. The Marine Corps University provides the academic setting the Corps uses to prepare its leadership. In addition to the Officer Candidate School and the Basic School, enlisted marines receive additional leadership training at the university's Staff Non-Commissioned Officers Academy. Here too are the Marine Corps War College, School of Advanced Warfighting, and Amphibious Warfighting.

TBS—The Basic School. Six-month initial training for newly commissioned officers. All Marine officers have to complete this, regardless of their chosen field. Every officer is a Grunt first.

Tun Tavern, Philadelphia. This brew house was built by Samuel Carpenter in 1685. It was located on Philadelphia's historic waterfront at the corner of Water Street and Tun Alley, leading to Carpenter's Wharf near what is today known as "Penn's Landing." The site has been obliterated under Interstate 95.

Carpenter built the tavern to stimulate the development of the Philadelphia waterfront. The tavern developed a reputation for fine beers and maintained it for more than a century. Its name comes from the old English word "tun" meaning a measured cask, barrel, or keg of beer. The tavern soon reached social prominence in Philadelphia, which by the time of the Revolution was the largest city in the thirteen colonies. As a result, a number of firsts occurred here. In 1720, the first meetings of the St. George's Society (forerunner of today's "Sons of the Society of St. George") were held at the tavern. The society's goal was to assist needy Englishmen arriving in the new colony. Twelve years later, the first meetings of the St. John's No. 1 Lodge, a Grand Lodge of the Masonic Temple, were held at the tavern. The election of the first Worshipful Grand Master of the Grand Lodge of Pennsylvania was held at the tavern; subsequently Benjamin Franklin was its third Grand Master. The Masonic Temple in Philadelphia recognizes the tavern as the birthplace of the Masonic teachings in this country. The Masonic Order has played an important role in American history.

Not to be outdone by their English colleagues, in 1747 Tun Tavern was the site for the founding of the St. Andrews Society in order to help poor settlers from Scotland settle in Philadelphia. Nine years later, in face of the threat of French and Indian invasion, and the reluctance of the local Quakers to allow the assembly to raise troops, Col. Benjamin Franklin organized the Pennsylvania Militia and utilized the tavern as a gathering place to recruit the area's first regiment of soldiers—the "Associators"—to suppress Indian uprisings. The unit he founded survives today as the 111th Infantry Regiment of the Pennsylvania National Guard.

But it was what happened at the tavern on November 10, 1775, which concerns Marines. That was the day that Robert Mullan, proprietor of the tavern, was commissioned by Congress to raise the first two battalions of

Marines, under the leadership of Samuel Nicholas, the first appointed Commandant of the Continental Marines. Nicholas's grandfather was also a member of the Tun Tavern Lodge of Free and Accepted Masons; it was this relationship among Mullan, Nicholas, and the tavern which led to the Tun Tavern's being enshrined in Marine hearts.

MARINE UNITS AND JOBS

Although every Marine is trained as a rifleman, and his sense of loyalty is primarily directed to the USMC as a whole, the Corps is divided into a number of units—some of them extremely specialized. Moreover, Marines must take up many specialized roles in addition to their basic one of rifleman. Here are some of the prominent ones.

Amphibious Assault. An Assault Amphibian Battalion's mission is to land surface assault elements of a landing force and their equipment during amphibious operations, and to conduct mechanized operations and related combat support in subsequent operations ashore.

Drill Instructor. He is the most hated and most loved man in the Marine Corps. He is also the first authority figure the recruit gets to know. The drill instructor (DI) is responsible for turning raw recruits into Marines. The USMC DI is considered the toughest and proudest drill instructor of all branches of the armed forces. His is one of the most demanding and exhausting jobs in the Corps. From his training will come the next generation of Marines who must uphold the honor of the Corps in war and peace.

But the position of the DI has changed considerably in the past thirty years. Those who know the position only from old movies or even personal memories will find that the DIs of today are forced to be quite different from their predecessors of a few decades back. They are strictly monitored now and may neither strike nor use "abusive language" toward a recruit. Whether these strictures will improve the next crop of Marines is, as yet, an open question.

What they share with DIs past is an exhausting workload. On the average, a DI tackles a one-hundred-hour week while training a platoon. In between platoons, he gets only a few days to rest up before the next crop arrives. If the training he gives is considered tough, the DI has been through worse. He is required to possess a diploma from DI School at Parris Island. This is a sort of boot camp for prospective DIs, and is one of the most demanding courses in the Corps—a body known for demanding courses.

As noted earlier, DIs wear campaign hats (see page 12). Senior drill instructors wear black leather belts; assistant DIs wear wide green webbed pistol belts. Until 1996, female DIs did not wear the "campaign hat" but rather a scarlet shoulder cord on their left shoulders.

What epitomizes the DI is the DI's Creed. Here it is, in honor of DIs past and present:

> These recruits are entrusted to my care. I will train them to the best of my ability. I will develop them into smartly disciplined, physically fit, basically trained Marines, thoroughly indoctrinated in love of Corps and Country. I will demand of them, and demonstrate by my own example, the highest standards of personal conduct, morality and professional skill.

Embassy Duty. By diplomatic convention, an embassy is a little bit of the country that owns it in the capital of a foreign power. Such installations are protected by treaty; the law of the host country stops at the embassy gate. From time to time throughout history, this protection has been violated. To prevent this from happening, it is standard practice throughout the world for various nations to man their embassies abroad (especially in unsettled areas) with small detachments of their own armed forces. At American embassies, this task falls to the Marines.

It was in 1835 that they first were posted to defend an American diplomatic mission. Over the next seventy years, scores of landings were made by Marines across the globe to provide protection to foreign service missions and American communities during various conflicts. Perhaps the most dramatic of these was the work of the Marines in defending the Legation Quarter in Beijing during the Boxer rebellion of 1900.

After World War II, increased intelligence activities by the Soviet KGB and allied intelligence services made it obvious to Congress that permanent protection of U.S. diplomatic missions abroad was required. The Foreign Service Act of 1946 declared that "The Secretary of the Navy is authorized, upon the request of the Secretary of State, to assign enlisted members of the Navy and the Marine Corps to serve as custodians under supervision of the Principal Officer at an Embassy, Legation or Consulate." Under this law, the Secretary of the Navy required the Marine Corps to provide enlisted Marines to guard Foreign Service posts throughout the world. Decolonization of the Third World by our European allies and the subsequent breakup of the Soviet Union both greatly expanded the number of American foreign missions abroad and created many more or less unstable regimes. Together with the growth of international terrorism, these developments have made embassy duty ever more important, challenging, and risky. In addition, as part of the public face of the United States in foreign countries, the role of Marine embassy guards will become increasingly important.

Marines assigned to the Marine Security Guard program are members of the Marine Security Guard Battalion headquarters at Quantico, Virginia, where the Marine Security Guard School is also located. Having finished their course, Marines are assigned to a foreign service post under the immediate command of a Marine Staff NCO (detachment commander), who is responsible to the ambassador or appointed delegates. Marine security guards, lance corporal through sergeant, provide security for more than 120 U.S. embassies and consulates around the world. Those on embassy duty are primarily responsible for interior security, normally the lobby or main entrance. Guards are trained to react to terrorist acts as well as a variety of such emergencies as fires, riots, demonstrations, and evacuations.

Gunnery Sergeant. A rank unique to the Marine Corps, Gunnery Sergeant was created in 1898, in accordance with the Corps's expansion for the war with Spain. Its badge was crossed rifles and a flaming bomb. Originally the rank meant a shipboard sergeant well trained with small arms, signaling, and naval gunnery. The rank's creation was a symbol of the Navy's internal struggle over the role of the Marines—was their primary mission to remain playing a part of naval gun crews, or were they to become primarily land based? By 1914 the question was decided, as only 5 percent of the Corps' strength remained aboard ship. In keeping with their signals tradition, some gunnery sergeants were trained in operating and maintaining radios; others specialized in telephone communications or the use of electrically controlled coast defense mines. The Gunnery Sergeant became the platoon sergeant rank, and has remained so to the present day. In time, a nickname for the rank (Gunny) was created. In 1935, the new superior rank of Master Gunnery Sergeant made its debut.

Heavy Weapons Platoon. The heavy weapons platoon in the weapons company comprises hardback Humvee-mounted heavy machine guns, automatic grenade launchers, and heavy anti-tank missiles. It also maintains shotguns and light machine guns for close-in defense. This platoon's primary mission is to attack and destroy the enemy's heavy and light armor. Due to its mobility, the Heavy Weapons Platoon occasionally combines with a light armored reconnaissance (LAR) platoon for specific missions, such as raids. In addition, the Heavy Weapons Platoon provides direct fire support to the rifle companies, using the long-range capabilities of heavy machine guns and heavy anti-tank missiles. The platoon can operate in its entirety, or else break down into smaller combined anti-armor teams (CAAT). These are led by corporals and consist of a heavy machine gun vehicle paired with a heavy anti-tank missile vehicle.

Horse Marines. As will have been seen in many of the entries in this book, the Marines have used an incredible variety of transports in their history: on sea, land, and air. But perhaps the least known and most unusual was—

the horse! The reason for this was the beefed-up Marine presence in China, following the Boxer Rebellion of 1900.

During the siege of the Legation Quarter by the rebels, the USMC had played a prominent part in the defense, alongside troops of a number of other countries. Still other Marines arrived with the multinational relief force, which marched inland from the coast to break the siege. In order to prevent such an occurrence from ever happening again, foreign troops were stationed in various parts of the country, especially on the major rivers, the larger ports, and, of course, the Legation Quarter itself—this in turn was heavily fortified, and the small national contingents of troops enormously expanded.

From 1900 until 1905 the legation guard was a company of the 9th U.S. Infantry. In the latter year, the soldiers were replaced by one hundred Marines. The American envoy, W. W. Rockhill, thought the Marines would provide a more prestigious guard. Their primary duty remained the defense of the Legation Quarter and scattered American missions and businesses in the city. Two years later, Marines guarding the Legation Quarter organized a small mounted detachment, which quickly bore the title of the "Horse Marines." Intended primarily for ceremonies, crowd control, and (in case of need) to warn Americans living away from the Quarter of trouble, they were initially mounted on Mongolian ponies discarded from the Beijing racetrack. In time, they became quite an elite unit, noted for their smart appearance and excellence in mounted drill. Entrance into the Horse Marines became quite competitive, not least because of various social privileges enjoyed by the troopers. It was for this reason that, during the interwar period, Marine officers were routinely sent for training to the U.S. Army Cavalry School at Ft. Riley, Kansas.

Despite the fact that a much larger number of Marines were attached to the ships of the Yangtze Patrol and the Asiatic Squadron (from whence, as the 1910s, '20s, and '30s progressed, and China suffered revolution, warlordism, and finally Japanese invasion, they were often disembarked at various river and coastal ports to safeguard American and European lives and property), "Horse Marine" became a term for all Marines on China duty. Alas, when the Marine contingent at the Legation Quarter was withdrawn to the Philippines prior to Pearl Harbor, they had to leave their ponies behind.

But the Corps and the horse were not quite done with one another. After Castro took control of Cuba, the role of the Marines in patrolling the U.S. Naval Base at Guantanamo became extremely important; the base was an obvious "trip wire" in the Cold War. Sixty-six horses at the NS Corral were used by the Marine guards for patrol duty; alas, when the Marines began using jeeps, Recreation acquired the corral and bought the horses. So passed quietly, and without fanfare, the last of the Horse Marines.

Lance Corporal. Another rank peculiar to the Marine Corps, Lance Corporal has (unlike Gunnery Sergeant, a USMC creation) foreign origins. The rank of Lance Corporal owes its origin to the French words *lance pesade*, or "broken lance," meaning an old soldier who had broken many lances in medieval combat) and "corporal." Originally, the rank was Lancepesade, but became Lancepesade-Corporal; the present title dates back to 1611. The Marine Corps has had Lance Corporals (and, for a time, Lance-Sergeants) since the 1830s. Originally, however, Lance Corporals were Privates who were filling Corporals slots without promotion (due to their experience), just as Lance Sergeants were Corporals likewise exercising the superior position without promotion. As the ranks structure became more rigid and the Corps expanded, the practice gradually passed out of use (although it is claimed that even as late as 1937, a private was acting as Lance Corporal). In 1958, however, the rank replaced "Private First Class."

Marine Aviators. Marine aviation has fought America's air battles in the South Pacific, Korea, Vietnam, and Afghanistan. Modern Marine aviation features a broad spectrum of aircraft and equipment and can build airfields as well as use them. Marine Air Wings conduct "air operations against enemy installations, facilities, and personnel in order to destroy, neutralize, interdict, or isolate enemy military forces and military resources."

The first USMC pilots, Alfred Cunningham and Roy Gieger, began in 1912 at the Naval Flying School at Annapolis. During World War I, Marine fliers were versatile: they flew anti-submarine patrols as well as front-line bombing missions. Despite this promising beginning, the interwar period was a difficult one, beset with tight budgets. Nevertheless, World War II saw an enormous expansion in Marine aviation. The 145 pilots in 1936 grew to over 10,000 by V-J day. Aces like the legendary Gregory "Pappy" Boyington (the subject of the 1970s TV series, *Baa, Baa, Blacksheep* in which Boyington was played by Robert Conrad) and Joe Foss deservedly won headlines and medals. Nevertheless, the dive bombers, torpedo bombers, and pilots flying ground attack displayed the same valor. In Korea and Vietnam, flying close support for Marines on the ground, more of the same bravery was shown in Panther jets, Douglas Skyraiders, and helicopters.

Marine Force Recon. The Marine Recon we know today dates back to World War II. Prior to 1944, the MR were mostly scout/snipers, but in April of 1944, a two-company amphibious reconnaissance battalion was formed. Operating with UDTs (underwater demolition teams), they conducted beach reconnaissance and hydrographic surveys. MR skills were put to the test successfully just before the landings at Iwo Jima in 1945. The Korean War saw the two groups in the same mode, raiding along the east coast of the country, destroying railroad tunnels and bridges. On occasion, the MR operated as far as two hundred miles behind enemy lines. They made the first helicopter assault in Marine Corps history in 1951. In Vietnam, the MR conducted deep and distant reconnaissance in seven-man teams—the "Stingray" operations. Since 1971, Marine Recon has taken part in the invasion of Grenada (1983), Operation "Just Cause," in Panama (1989), and both Gulf Wars.

Marine Rifleman. "Every Marine a rifleman" is not only a saying—it is the truth. From the age of sail, when Marines fired on enemy sailors from the rigging of warships, marksmanship has been at the core of their duties. In time, this was codified by an early commandant's order that every Marine would be a rifleman first, so that all Marines could support each other in

combat. Whatever their occupational specialty, rank, or sex, all Marines are trained in infantry combat.

Marine Aviation, Marine Armor, Marine Artillery, and all the supporting arms and units—down to the purely ceremonial ones—exist to support the rifleman. He must close with the enemy, in the last analysis, regardless of any advances in technology; this has been true in all of America's wars, down to the current conflicts in Afghanistan and Iraq.

Just before the attack by the Japanese on Pearl Harbor in 1941, Maj. Gen. William H. Rupertus, USMC, wrote the Rifleman's Creed. It has become part of the Corps' standard training, and must be memorized and put into practice by each Marine:

> THIS IS MY RIFLE. There are many like it but this one is mine. My rifle is my best friend. It is my life. I must master it as I master my life.

> My rifle, without me, is useless. Without my rifle, I am useless. I must fire my rifle true. I must shoot straighter than any enemy who is trying to kill me. I must shoot him before he shoots me. I will. . . .

> My rifle and myself know that what counts in this war is not the rounds we fire, the noise of our burst, nor the smoke we make. We know that it is the hits that count. We will hit . . .

> My rifle is human, even as I, because it is my life. Thus, I will learn it as a brother. I will learn its weakness, its strength, its parts, its

accessories, its sights and its barrel. I will keep my rifle clean and ready, even as I am clean and ready. We will become part of each other. We will . . .

Before God I swear this creed. My rifle and myself are the defenders of my country. We are the masters of our enemy. We are the saviors of my life.

So be it, until victory is America's and there is no enemy, but Peace.

Marine Sniper. If the Marine rifleman is the basic Marine, the Marine sniper is an incredibly souped-up version. Precision rifle fire is his specialty. Sniper platoons carry on the mission of being the rifle battalion's organic reconnaissance. Some Scout Sniper platoons are also trained as Maritime Special Purpose Force Recon and Surveillance platoons. These scout snipers develop urban R&S skills, long-range communications, airborne platform shooting and day/night precision fires in support of direct action missions. Their primary weapon is the M-40A1 sniper rifle. They are extremely well trained, combining good shooting with many other infantry and reconnaissance skills. Marine snipers must be independent thinkers, demonstrating great initiative. Operating in small teams well to the front of friendly forces, these snipers use camouflage and stealthy movement to either guide aviation or artillery fire to the enemy, or engage them themselves. It is a rigorous job, and snipers are required to combine intelligence gathering skills and woodcraft.

MEF—Marine Expeditionary Force. This is the principle Marine Corps tactical organization—especially for larger crises and contingencies. As such occurrences escalate, or if a major theater war should break out, smaller Marine air ground task forces (MAGTFs) and their supporting units would be deployed until the entire MEF is in place.

There are three Marine Expeditionary Forces: I MEF, based in southern California at Marine Corps Base Camp Pendleton; II MEF, located at bases in North and South Carolina; and III MEF, which is forward deployed on Okinawa, mainland Japan, and Hawaii. II MEF is under the control of the commander, Marine Forces, Atlantic; the other two answer to the commander, Marine Forces, Pacific. All three are located near major naval bases and excellent airports to ensure rapid deployment.

Usually commanded by a Lieutenant General, MEFs can include one or more divisions in its ground combat element, one or more aircraft wings in its air combat element, and one or more force service support groups in its combat service support element. Command element provides command and control necessary for operational planning and execution.

MEU—Marine Expeditionary Unit. While Marine Expeditionary Forces are intended for major operations on the scale of the Iraq intervention, MEUs are smaller, flexible units, consisting of over 2,100 Marines and sailors. They are intended to respond to attacks by terrorist organizations, or by smaller rogue states. Such threats often arise near sea lanes used by America and her allies, or in areas deemed essential to U.S. interests. Deployed from self-contained floating sea bases, the MEU is equipped and forward-deployed to respond to any threat, protect any American or ally, or neutralize any menace anywhere in the world, often within hours. With its complement of fully integrated air and ground forces, working closely with the Navy, the MEU is a powerful force that has proven itself time and again in recent years.

While the unit's command element remains permanently intact, subordinate air and ground combat units and their attendant combat service support elements are with the MEU for about a year on average. Then they are rotated elsewhere. These smaller units are referred to as major subordinate elements or MSEs. Among these will be the Battalion Landing Team (a reinforced infantry battalion with light armored vehicles, artillery, and amphibious assault vehicles); the Marine Medium Helicopter Squadron, a composite helicopter squadron (with air traffic control; crash, fire, and rescue units; and AV-8B Harriers); a MEU Service Support Group, the combat service support element providing logistical support; and, of course, the Command Element.

Commanded by a colonel, the MEU fulfills routine forward deployments with U.S. Naval fleets in the Mediterranean, the western Pacific, and, periodically, the Atlantic and Indian Oceans. It is deployed on three Naval amphibious ships and can operate in virtually any environment.

NCOs. The noncommissioned officers are those who really run the Corps. That is why Marines call them "The Backbone of the Corps." While their combat record is legendary, the NCOs in the Corps, as in any military organization, are the ones who see that orders are carried out, that discipline is maintained, and that Marine traditions survive. The "NCO's Creed" admirably sums up their ideals:

> I am an NCO dedicated to training new Marines and influencing the old. I am forever conscious of each Marine under my charge, and by example will inspire him to the highest standards possible. I will strive to be patient, understanding, just, and firm. I will commend the deserving and encourage the wayward.
>
> I will never forget that I am responsible to my Commanding Officer for the morale, discipline, and efficiency of my men. Their performance will reflect an image of me.

There is a lot more to a Marine NCO than the blood stripe and the sword. Every NCO must show an example to his men as well as order them about. The NCO must act as judge and jury regarding infractions of discipline; he must be ready to advise officers and enlisted alike, and then be ready to carry out the former's commands, regardless of his own opinions. Often more experienced than those above or beneath him, he must exhibit patience above all, as well as tenacity. It is a hard and often thankless role, and one which demands the most out of its holder.

Officers. As with officers in any military or naval establishment, those of the Marine Corps are expected to be a cut above. In addition to "taking care of their men" and proficiency in the art of war, officers must be honorable, chivalrous, and courteous, and they must reflect in their own characters the best traits of the Corps. This is, of course, a difficult task. Moreover, since their twin goals must be accomplishment of the mission and the welfare of their men, officers must avoid being either too remote or too close to their men. In this, as in so much else, General Lejeune wrote wisely:

> The relation between officers and men should in no sense be that of superior and inferior nor that of master and servant, but rather that of teacher and scholar. In fact, it should partake of the nature of the relationship between father and son to the extent that officers are responsible for the physical, mental and moral welfare as well as the discipline and military training of the young men under their command.

Regiment. Although the Regiment has historically (until after World War II) been the basic unit of most armies, its prominence in the USMC is relatively recent. The Corps as a whole has itself been the repository of tradition and object of love that the individual regiments were for the soldiers of the world's armies.

Before 1913, there were a number of temporary organizations in the Marine Corps created for specific purposes or tasks and designated as regiments, due purely to their size. When a particular unit was no longer needed—its particular purpose having been fulfilled—it was usually disbanded. The attached companies would then be returned to their original stations.

The expansion of the Marine Corps as a result of World War I, the tactical experience gained as a result of that conflict (and the forging of regimental tradition by the 5th and 6th Regiments), and various other factors led to the creation of permanent Marine regiments as part of permanent Marine divisions. Today, such a regiment consists of a headquarters company and two or more infantry battalions (normally three infantry battalions). The infantry battalions are the basic tactical units with which the regiment accomplishes its mission.

Sea Duty. While the Corps still performs its traditional role of providing maritime security to a degree, this function has dwindled to a shadow of its former self. So small is this commitment now that the Sea School at San Diego was disbanded in December of 1987. In recent years ship duties for Marines have been taken over mostly by sailors themselves.

Back when every major warship had a Marine detachment, however, its duties and responsibilities were extremely varied. The Marines aboard would mount the Guard of the Day, which meant manning designated posts and providing roving security patrols.

When the ship was docked in a foreign port, the detachment would provide perimeter defense. The detachment would man the designated gun mount for "rapid response" fire missions; as required it furnished armed landing parties, augmented shore patrols, participated in riot control, and provided rifle cover for flight and boat operations.

The Marines were also required to provide internal security aboard ship, a role that dated back to the days when sailors aboard warship were often undisciplined and unwilling—escaped prisoners, impressed civilians, and the like. Maintaining order among such folks was one of the reasons Charles II had founded the Royal Marines in the first place. As a relic of this period,

Marines were employed until recent decades as brig turnkeys and escorts, payroll guards, and as orderlies to Admirals, COs, and XOs. Incidental duties included providing color guards, drill teams, and honor formations. They kept their designated areas of the ship spick-and-span, and of course trained and trained.

Sea duty in this sense may be a thing of the past (although MEFs and MEUs still spend a great deal of time at sea, albeit with a more specialized function), but its memory lives on in many Marine traditions—the ship's bells, the use of naval terms, and the continuing of Navy service support personnel (corpsmen, chaplains, and the like). Above all, sea duty still survives in the proud history of countless engagements and the fond memories of many veterans.

MARINE LINGO

So specialized a world as the USMC naturally develops a language all its own. Like any other living tongue, this jargon is constantly changing. Every conflict the Corps is involved in leaves its mark—some phrases pass out of use, as new ones come in. Here are some of the most enduring ones.

4 B's. . . . Beans, Bullets, Band Aids, and Bad Guys. This acronym is used to remember logistics, administration, and POWs. Beans refer to chow (see below); bullets symbolize all weaponry. Band Aids reminds us of the need for medical supplies, and the bad guys are any captured prisoners who also will require food, medical attention—and weapons for their guards.

Bug Juice. Name for Marine juice/punch. Not necessarily alcoholic.

The Bumba. Working in the field, generally in some discomfort.

Chow. An almost universal word for food. It is found is such phrases as "chow hall."

Gee Dunk. Marine nickname for junk food, a not uncommon form of sustenance—especially today.

Gee Dunk Machine. Name for the ever-present machine that dispenses Gee Dunk.

Grape. An affectionate name for a recruit's sunburned head, generally a result of the initial (quite short) haircut. It's quite comical-looking to the unkind.

Grunt. Another name for Marines. This one has actually made it into *Webster's New Collegiate Dictionary*, which offers as one definition of grunt: "A Marine foot soldier, especially from the Vietnam War."

Jarhead. Another name for a Marine, which is probably derived from the "high-and-tight" haircut. To the undiscerning, it makes the average head look a bit like a jar.

Jireen. Another word for Marine. A contraction of "G(overnment). I(ssue). Marine."

Old Corps. In one sense, the "Old Corps" refers to the generation of Marines who were old when the speaker came in. For modern Marines, "Old Corps" might refer to Vietnam-era personnel, who came in before the restrictions on physical and mental action by DIs. For Marines of that vintage, the World War II and Korea Marines might qualify. Of course, if one stays in for over fifteen years, he will no doubt be thought of (and begin to think of himself as) "Old Corps."

But it is probably the interwar period that would best qualify. Despite their small numbers—around twenty thousand—Marines of that era were called upon to carry out tasks far beyond their proportionate size. In addition to sea duty, they defended a network of islands in the Pacific, as well as China. It was the day of Smedley Butler and of continuing interventions in the Caribbean. Then, with the attack on Pearl Harbor, they were forced to expand enormously and to fight and conquer in unprecedented circumstances. It was a challenge they met well. Another name for that generation is "Brown Shoe" Marines, referring to the former color of leather before the Korean War.

Pogey Bait. Another name for junk food.

Rack. A Marine's name for his bed, rarely posturepedic.

Sea-Going Marine. Old term for Marines on board Navy vessels. As sea duty has declined, so has the phrase.

SMEAC. An acronym for situation, mission, execution, admin and logistics, communication, the factors to be taken into account when planning an action.

WMs. Women Marines, often renowned for their strength and ferocity.

HISTORIC MARINE BATTLES

The business of the United States Marine Corps is fighting—a fact that both Marine traditions and Marine practices remind us of, and often. At the end of the day, it is not their spit and polish, nor their esprit de corps that give the Corps its value, but rather the effectiveness in combat these things foster. Here are some of the battles in which the ethos of the Corps has proved its effectiveness.

THE REVOLUTIONARY WAR

As is well known, November 10, 1775, is celebrated as the birthday of the U.S. Marines. The decade preceding this date had seen an escalating series of political disputes between the leading elements of the Thirteen Colonies and the home government in London. As the year 1775 progressed, the elected colonial governments were superseded by provincial congresses, which in turn were bonded together by the Continental Congress. Once the political struggle became military in April, the various royal governors were deposed one by one, and the Congress assumed the role of a government. A committee of the Congress drafted a resolution to create a new military unit, called the "Continental Marines," to fulfill for the rebels the same role accomplished by the Royal Marines for the Crown. Drafted in a popular Philadelphia inn named Tun Tavern, this resolution was later approved by the entire legislative body. The owner of the tavern, Robert Mullan, was named a Marine Captain; the owner of another, Samuel Nicholas, was appointed Commandant of the Continental Marines.

Two months after their founding, the new unit celebrated the new year by sailing toward Nassau, on the island of New Providence in the Bahamas. Arriving in March off the island, the fleet rendezvoused three leagues north of their target. A short time before noon on March 3, the fleet's Marines and a number of seamen under Marine Captain Nicholas came ashore (in what was the Corps' first amphibious assault) about two miles east of Fort Montagu, one of the island's two forts. This they captured in a battle as "bemused as it was bloodless." Overnighting in the captured fort, the invasion force completed the job the next morning by taking Fort Nassau, securing the town, and arresting the British governor at Government House, his residence. By March 16, the island's military stores (eighty-eight guns, 16,535 shells, and other supplies) were, with the exception of the gunpowder, loaded and secured. The Marines and sailors then embarked, taking the governor and two of the island's key officials as prisoners. The following morning the Marines weighed anchor. Returning from the raid, the fleet encountered a British ship; Marines engaged the ship with muskets and assisted in manning the broadside cannon.

The nature of the war altered irrevocably in July of 1776, when the

Congress declared the Colonies to be independent states. At first the war went very badly for the rebels; New York fell, three times (due to the incompetence of the British commander, Lord Howe), and the Continental Army barely escaped destruction. Not only was New York City and its environs lost, but the Americans were forced to withdraw almost entirely from New Jersey. If the rebel cause were to survive, a victory was needed. It came at the second Battle of Trenton, when Nicholas's Marines assisted Washington's Army (the first recorded joint Army–Marine engagement). Later that spring, Washington incorporated some of the Marines into artillery units of his reorganized Army.

But work awaited the Corps elsewhere. On January 10, 1778, Navy Captain James Willing left Fort Pitt (modern-day Pittsburgh) with a small company of Marines aboard the armed barge *Rattletrap*. As it proceeded down the Mississippi the Marine formation raided or looted the posts and homes of British sympathizers along the way. The Marine unit arrived at New Orleans in March, reporting to the American commercial agent. The unit operated around New Orleans until 1779, returning north up the Mississippi under the command of Lt. Robert George. He reported to Gen. George Rogers Clark, bringing his Marines to participate in Clark's campaign against hostile Indians.

Meanwhile, a force of twenty-six Marines and sailors under the command of Marine Capt. John Trevett landed at New Providence once more. Again the two forts were captured. With the town in rebel hands, the newly adopted Stars and Stripes (authorized by Congress on June 14, 1777) was raised over a foreign fortification for the first time. In two days of occupation,

Captain Trevett's Marines and seamen took five vessels, liberated a group of American prisoners, spiked the guns of a major British garrison, and acquired valuable ordnance.

Annoying as this second raid on the Bahamas was to the Crown, yet a more stinging gesture was in the offing. In April of 1778, a Marine detachment under the command of John Paul Jones made two raids on Great Britain soil (the first successful such incursion since William of Orange's landing in 1688). The reason for this attack was that Continental vessels found it more and more difficult to capture British ships from American ports. The vigilance of the Royal Navy forced the Yankees to shift part of their depredations to European waters. Raiding around the British Isles themselves, however, depended on French protection and supplies—not always reliable. This hesitation on the part of the French vanished with the news of the American victory at Saratoga. Since the negotiations for an alliance with the Americans were about to be completed, the French government in early 1778 gave American ships almost unrestricted access to its Atlantic ports.

In April 1778, John Paul Jones sailed in the twenty-gun sloop *Ranger* from Brest in France to the Irish Sea. Jones's intention was to descend upon an English port, destroy its merchant shipping, and carry away a person of distinction to hold as a hostage for the release of American prisoners. Of the numerous seaports that dotted the inlets and coves, Jones settled on the port of Whitehaven, where he had trained as a merchant seaman. On April 18, he attempted a descent on the town, but was foiled by contrary winds. At midnight on the twenty-second, Jones ordered two boats lowered. He sent thirty volunteer Marines and seamen over the side. The captain took command of one, while Marine Lieutenant Samuel Wallingford officered the other. His call for volunteers met with poor response, but eventually Jones set out to attack the fleet of two hundred collier vessels docked at Whitehaven. Owing to the defection of one of his crew, who alerted the town, he was forced to retreat, having created very little damage. The landing party did manage to burn a few colliers and fishing vessels, pillage the local fort, and (the following morning in a raid on St. Mary's Isle), confiscate Lord Selkirk's silver plate.

Although the raid on Whitehaven had been bloodless and the affair at St. Mary's Isle rather an amusement, the battle with HMS sloop *Drake* the next day tested the *Ranger*'s crew. But within one hour of the first broadside, the *Drake* was beaten at a cost of three lives, among them Marine Lt. Wallingford. With the *Drake* under a prize crew, Jones returned to France. Shortly thereafter, the *Ranger* sailed for America while Jones remained in France to find another command.

The Bahamas were treated to repeat performances by the Marines in 1778 and in 1782. This last time, they brought the French and the Spanish with them. Spain attempted to hold Nassau following the latter invasion, but they were fooled into abandoning the town the following year. Andrew Deveaux, a South Carolina loyalist, came to Nassau with just two hundred of his countrymen to recapture it for the Crown. He and his men sailed from their ships to the shore in longboats, to a landing point out of sight of Nassau. There they then lay down in the boats, returned to the ships, and stood up to sail back to the shore. They did this a number of times until the

Spanish were convinced that there was a massive army assembling. The occupiers decamped to Cuba. As a result, the Treaty of Paris returned the Bahamas to Britain, and they became another refuge for Loyalists.

In January of 1783, Marines boarded and seized the British ship *Baille* in the West Indies. This was their swan song, because after the war ended, the new country's warships were all sold; in June of 1785, the Continental Marines were abolished. They would remain so until called back to life by President John Adams on July 11, 1795.

BARBARY WARS

TRIPOLI

The Barbary states of North Africa—Morocco, Algiers, Tunis, and Tripoli— had given refuge to pirates for centuries. Not only did the pirates seize European ships in the Mediterranean, but they also ranged as far as Ireland and Iceland in search of slaves, sometimes taking whole villages captive. The Battle of Lepanto in 1571 had destroyed them as a strategic threat to Europe, but they continued their raiding and piracy. Where the Knights of Malta continued their centuries-long naval war against the Barbary pirates (many of their members would later use their skills in the service of other countries, such as the French Admiral Suffren), the British, French, and other naval powers either tried to buy them off or overawe them.

American merchantmen in the Med had been protected by the Royal Navy. But in 1783, with the Crown's recognition of American independence,

Yankee shipping was on its own. In 1798, Napoleon Bonaparte seized Malta and ejected the Knights, thus eliminating a major factor in keeping the pirates at bay. So annoying did their depredations on American shipping become that the next year the United States agreed to pay $18,000 a year in return for a promise that corsairs based in Tripoli would not attack American ships. They made similar agreements with the rulers of Morocco, Algiers, and Tunis.

By the time that Thomas Jefferson was elected in 1801, things had changed. The undeclared naval war between the French revolutionary regime and the United States had ended, and the Americans were feeling rather more confident at sea. The USS *George Washington*, which was charged with bringing the yearly tribute to Algiers, was instead ordered to sail to Constantinople to deliver the money directly to the Ottoman Sultan, to whom the Dey of Algiers, the Pasha of Tripoli, and the Bey of Tunis were all nominally tributary. By this time the American government, although having paid over $2 million in tribute and ransom to the Barbary States, reneged on paying the rest of the expected four-fifths of tribute.

In reprisal for the insults and delayed and undersized payments by the Americans, the Barbary States demanded more. At last, on May 14, 1801, the Pasha of Tripolitania, Yusuf Karamanli, ordered the flag staff (flying the American flag) standing in front of the U.S. consulate to be cut down. This was a declaration of war against America.

Jefferson's response was swift. A squadron of four ships commanded by Commodore Richard Dale sailed to the Mediterranean, under the slogan of "Millions for defense, but not one cent for tribute!" On July 17, 1801, a blockade was slapped on Tripoli harbor. Despite a few successes against the pirates, the squadron was too weak to win the conflict decisively. The U.S. envoy to Tripoli, James Cathcart, offered a compromise to the Pasha on the amount of tribute now being demanded—a one-time payment of $250,000, followed by an annual tribute of $20,000.

In 1803, another, enlarged squadron was sent to the Mediterranean under the command of Commodore Edward Preble (of the forty-four-gun frigate *Constitution*). On October 31, 1803, one of Preble's ships, the frigate *Philadelphia*, ran aground on a reef near the harbor. Captured by enemy gunboats, the frigate floated free and was taken into port. Capt. William Bainbridge and the ship's 307-man crew were imprisoned.

Lt. Stephen Decatur on February 16, 1804, led a raid on the harbor in a previously captured ketch, renamed *Intrepid*. Decatur was unsuccessful in recapturing the frigate, having to settle with burning the *Philadelphia* to the water line. The raiding party did, however, escape before an alarm was sounded. The British naval hero, Lord Nelson, described the raid as "the most daring act of the age." Unfortunately, the crew of the *Philadelphia* remained in prison; the Pasha demanded $200,000 for their release.

Commodore Preble decided on a show of force. Two ineffectual bombardments and a highly successful one on Tripoli were undertaken in August 1804. On September 4, Preble once again used the *Intrepid*, this time sacrificing it as a fire ship in the hope of destroying the Pasha's fleet. Unfortunately for the Commodore, the ship was spotted by enemy gunners—it was blown up at the entrance to the harbor, and was lost with all hands. Although the attack was a failure, the harbor was blocked and the Pasha's fleet severely restricted.

While Preble was bombarding Tripoli, the American Consul to Tunis, William Eaton, was planning a more subtle stroke. He proposed to President Jefferson that the United States should back Hamet Karamanli, the elder brother of the current Pasha and the rightful heir, in a military coup. Eaton returned to the Mediterranean with the title of "Navy Agent to the Barbary States" and permission to carry out his plans. Naval support was to be provided by Commodore Barron, who gave Eaton the use of the *Hero* commanded by Capt. Isaac Hull, and a detachment of seven Marines led by Lt. Presley Neville O'Bannon. Three ships, the *Argus, Nautilus*, and *Hornet*, would be made available to ferry provisions and provide offshore bombardment as needed.

Eaton negotiated with Hamet after finding him in Egypt. Despite the Prince's family being held hostage by the Pasha in Tripoli, he agreed to the plan. Eaton and Hull, based in Alexandria, recruited about four hundred mercenaries, including Europeans (mainly Greeks), Arab cavalry, Turks, and a caravan of camels. They were promised supplies and money on arrival at their first target, the Tripolitan port of Derna. Eaton led his little army on a fifty-day trek across five hundred miles of desert. On April 25th they received limited supplies and funds at a rendezvous with the ships just down the coast from Derna. Two days later, April 27, they attacked the port.

Derna has a revered spot in the memory of the United States Marine Corps. The trek across the desert is commemorated in the first verse of the Marines' Hymn: "to the shores of Tripoli."

Hamet and Muslim mercenaries attacked the castle at Derna; meanwhile, Lieutenant O'Bannon and his Marines assaulted the harbor fortress. At 2:45 P.M., backed up by a large number of European mercenaries, and following an offshore bombardment, O'Bannon bravely rushed the fortress walls. The defenders fled—leaving cannon loaded and ready to fire. After raising the "Stars and Stripes," O'Bannon turned the guns toward the town. By 4:00 P.M. the entire town had fallen. Hamet was so impressed by O'Bannon's bravery that he presented him with his own sword (an honor commemorated by presentation of a Mameluke sword, engraved with the motto "The Shores of Tripoli," to every U.S. Marine officer on graduation or direct commission).

Back in Tripoli, Yusuf Karamanli was not idle. Aware that Derna was to be attacked, he sent out reinforcements, which arrived a day after the city's fall. The Pasha's soldiers prepared to retake the town. On May 13, shelled by both the naval guns and the captured cannon, the Tripolitan army attacked the town. Only just beaten back, they were heavily bombarded by the *Argus* during their retreat. Several more unsuccessful attempts followed during the next month. Eaton prepared to mount an attack on Tripoli itself.

All in vain, however. While the fighting was going on at Derna, Col. Tobias Lear, Consul General to the Regency of Algiers, signed a treaty with Yusuf on June 4, 1805. By this pact, the Pasha received $60,000 for the release of Captain Bainbridge and the crew of the *Philadelphia*, although there would be neither treaty payment nor any further tributes. Lear prevailed on Yusuf to agree to Hamet's evacuation, with the promise that Hamet's family would be sent out to join him—a promise neither kept nor enforced.

The next day, the U.S. frigate *Constellation* was dispatched with instructions, reaching Derna on June 11. Eaton was ordered to remove his troops from the area and to take Hamet back to Egypt. Not having received any money to pay the mercenaries, Eaton left, taking as many of the European mercenaries as he could. The rest (including all the Muslim mercenaries), were left behind. With no funds, there was little they could expect from Yusuf.

Continuing friction prevailed with the Barbary pirates until 1830, when France began the conquest of Algeria. But the continued use of the Mameluke sword by USMC officers is an enduring tribute to the bravery of that little band of seven Marines, who marched and fought "on the shores of Tripoli."

THE WAR OF 1812

BLADENSBURG

One of the most tragic events in American history was the burning of Washington, D.C., by the British in 1814, in reprisal for the United States' burning of Toronto the previous year. The War of 1812 had gone badly for the United States, and in August of 1814, the British sailed into Chesapeake Bay. One wing of their invasion force headed to Baltimore, where they were successfully held off by the defenders of Fort McHenry (an event that inspired Francis Scott Key to write "The Star Spangled Banner"). The other wing, with more success, landed on the western shore of Maryland to attack Washington.

A force of 5,000 militia, 103 Marines, and 400 sailors was sent to block the 4,000 disciplined British troops under the command of Admiral

Cockburn and General Ross, who were advancing on the Capital. When the militia saw the organized British regulars, they fled. Even so, the Marines stopped three headlong charges before being outflanked and driven back. The invaders then proceeded along Bladensburg Road to Washington; there they burned a number of buildings, including the White House and the Capitol, before returning to their ships in the Chesapeake.

The home of the Commandant of the Marine Corps was one of the few buildings the British did not burn when they took the city. Cockburn and Ross were so impressed by the Marines' performance at Bladensburg that they ordered the house spared. As a result, it is the oldest, continuously occupied public building in Washington, D.C.

U.S.-MEXICAN WAR

CHAPULTEPEC

On March 9, 1847, Marines under the command of Captain Edson assisted the Army in the capture of Vera Cruz, Mexico. Later, another group of Marines, led by Brevet Lt. Col. Samuel E. Watson, were attached to the Army's 4th Division. This was commanded by Brig. Gen. John A. Quitman; it played an essential part in the capture of Mexico City. During the assault on Chapultepec and Mexico City, many Marines showed extraordinary heroism. The advance of General Quitman's troops having been halted by heavy enemy fire, Marine Capt. George H. Terrett, of Company C (which formed the right flank of the support), without orders advanced, cut his way past enemy batteries, pursued the fleeing artillerymen, and foiled a counterattack being by led Mexican lancers.

With the fall of the Castle at Chapultepec and another day of fierce fighting by Marines and soldiers, Mexico City fell to General Scott's forces on September 14, 1847. The city secured, it fell to Marine Lt. Augustus S. Nicholson to cut down the Mexican colors and run up the Stars and Stripes. To recognize the Marines' valor in the Mexican War, the citizens of Washington, D.C., presented Commandant Henderson with a blue and gold standard bearing the motto, "From Tripoli to the Halls of the Montezumas."

But there are, of course, two sides to every conflict. Today, a monument consisting of a semicircle of six freestanding columns at the entrance to Mexico City's Chapultepec Park honors six teenage cadets. They jumped to their deaths from the heights of Chapultepec Castle rather than surrender to the Marines.

KOREA

SALEE RIVER FORTS

The Korean War marked the second time that the Marines had entered Korea; ironically, their first arrival was only a few miles from the scene of the dramatic Inchon landing. The first time was in 1871; but it was a very different Korea from the one that faced the 1st Marine Division in 1950.

Since 1392, Korea had lived under the rule of the Yi dynasty. Although popular with their people, the Yi kings were suspicious of their neighbors, the Chinese and the Japanese (Korea having suffered a great deal in the past at the hands of both nations). It was the policy of the Korean monarchy to seal off their land from as much outside contact as possible, earning for them the nickname of "Hermit Kingdom." Europeans shipwrecked on the Korean coast, although well treated, were rarely allowed to leave.

Over the course of the nineteenth century, however, more and more Europeans and Americans began arriving in the Far East. In 1854, the United States forcibly opened Japan up to the world; six years later the British and French seized Beijing in the first Opium War, and Russia took the Ussuri River valley from the Chinese. This brought a European power to the very border of Korea.

Catholicism had arrived in Korea in 1780, when a Korean nobleman, having read the writings of Matteo Ricci at the Imperial Library in Beijing, accepted that religion. He brought it back to Korea, and by the time the first priest arrived in the country about four decades later, five thousand Koreans asked for baptism. Numbers of both missionaries and converts increased despite bouts of heavy persecution. In 1866, the King of Korea ordered the execution of nine priests and ten thousand laymen. When escaping missionaries brought word of this action to the French authorities in China, they resolved to send a gunboat to demand satisfaction. The French Foreign Minister asked the American Consul in Beijing if the United States would join the police action. Having just finished their own civil war, however, the Americans were reluctant to get involved. French action was delayed when a revolt in Indo-China required the presence of the French fleet there. But in August of 1866, the American merchant schooner *General*

Sherman lay at anchor in the Ping-Yang River. The Koreans boarded the vessel on the night of September 5 and slaughtered the entire crew. In November, the French finally attacked Korea, but were defeated. Emboldened by two victories, the Koreans considered themselves invincible.

Meanwhile, the Americans had tried unsuccessfully to determine the fate of the *General Sherman*. In May of 1871, the State Department had ordered its envoy in China, Frederick F. Low, to Korea. He was to negotiate the safe treatment of shipwrecked sailors, establish a trade treaty with the Hermit Kingdom, as well as investigate the loss of the *General Sherman*. Rear Adm. John Rodgers, commander of the Asiatic fleet based in Japan, was given the task of supporting the diplomatic mission. Admiral Rodgers assembled the five ships of his fleet and a force of 1,230 men. On May 29, they arrived at the entrance to the Han River.

After a cordial meeting with Korean officials, Admiral Rodgers presumed that he had permission to chart the Kanghwa Strait (also known as the Salee River), flowing between Kanghwa Island and the Korean mainland. He dispatched a small survey crew to take soundings and map the straights. They were attacked by the guns of a fort on Kanghwa Island, the Kwangsungbo Fortress (called the Citadel by the Americans). During the opening volley, two American ships, the USS *Palos* and the USS *Monocacy*, steamed rapidly up the strait and around the bend and raked the Kwangsungbo Fortress with their guns before withdrawing.

After conferring with Low, Admiral Rodgers gave the Korean government ten days to make an official apology, stipulating that if no apology were offered, the fortifications on Kanghwa Island would be assaulted and destroyed. Since the Koreans did not comply, at ten o'clock on Saturday morning, June 10, 1871, the *Palos* and *Monocacy* left the squadron's anchorage near Boise'e Island, bound again for the Kanghwa Strait. This time the *Palos* towed a long line of twenty-two smaller boats, each loaded with U.S. Marines and Navy Bluejackets. An apology from the Korean government had not been forthcoming, so Admiral Rodgers had assembled a force to teach them a lesson.

Commander Homer C. Blake of the USS *Alaska* directed the expedition from the *Palos*. His adjutant general was Lt. Commander W. Scott Schley, who decades later became a leading figure in the Spanish–American War. Ground forces were led under Commander Lewis A. Kimberly of the *Benicia*, while the landing force was led by Capt. McLane Tilton. With four junior officers, Tilton led the one-hundred-man Marine detachment ashore. Lt. Commander Silas Casey had assembled a Bluejacket battalion of 542 sailors from every ship. There was also an artillery detachment with seven twelve-pound guns under the command of Silas Casey.

Since the *Monocacy*'s armament had been enhanced by two nine-inch guns from the *Colorado*, the picture looked bright. Ordinary Seaman John Andrews of the launch from the *Benicia* led the way, dropping his lead-weighted line into the water and calling out soundings to guide the force around shallow shoals, deadly rocks, and into deeper water. Cannon fire from the *Monocacy* was replied to with fire from the Choji Fortress, but Andrews ignored the danger and stayed at his post. Andrews was the first of fifteen Americans to earn the Medal of Honor during this action. His citation states: "Stationed at the lead in passing the forts, Andrews stood on the gunwale of the *Benicia*'s launch, lashed to the ridgerope. He remained unflinching in this dangerous position and gave his soundings with coolness and accuracy under a heavy fire." The *Monocacy*'s guns drove the Koreans back, and the Choji Fortress fell silent.

Led by Tilton, the Marines and Bluejackets struggled ashore, men and cannon sinking in the tidal mud. Fortunately for them, the Koreans did not attack, save for an occasional artillery round. When the landing party approached the Choji Fortress, they found it wrecked by the *Monocacy*'s guns and abandoned by its garrison. It was late afternoon before the entire party arrived. The Korean weaponry found at the fort was destroyed, and the Marines renamed it the "Marine redoubt." The Bluejackets having arrived, the Marines moved off in advance of the main body of the force to bivouac, accompanied by a howitzer. Sentries guarded against night-time surprises.

At midnight, the Koreans fired a few shots into the American camp; this was stopped by rounds from American howitzers. After reveille sounded at 4:00 a.m., the tired Marines ate their breakfast and watched the earthen walls of the Dukjin Fortress up the Salee River about a mile from their redoubt. This was their next objective. Joined by the Bluejackets, the Marines advanced, leaving the newly arrived Bluejackets to finish dismantling the Choji Fortress. That task completed, the sailors moved up the river behind the Marines.

The *Palos* had run aground, leaving the *Monocacy* to provide heavy fire on the enemy positions. The Marines continued their trek north while the ship made its way through the shallow waters. The small side-wheel gunboat then opened fire on the Dukjin Fortress, turning the fortress walls into rubble. Nearing Dukjin from behind, the Marines formed a skirmish line while awaiting arrival of the naval personnel. After the sailors came up, a third of the Marines were sent forward to reconnoiter the fortress, the remainder being held in reserve. There was no fire from the deserted position, and the full force entered the deserted fortress. The Marines and sailors began dismantling it as well. In tribute to the warship's role in its capture, Dukjin Fortress was renamed Fort Monocacy by the Americans.

From Fort Monocacy the Americans set out to capture Kwangsungbo, the "Citadel," a prominent horseshoe-shaped fortress defended by three thousand Koreans under General Uh Je-yeon. The 650 Americans marched toward it over very difficult terrain, bringing their howitzers close behind them.

At last they arrived at the base of the Citadel. The artillery was set up to cover their flanks while six companies prepared for the assault on Kwangsungbo. The *Monocacy* shelled the Citadel, and at 11:00 a.m., the main force reached the Marine position opposite the fort. Navy Lt. Hugh McKee had the honor to lead the advance as the commander of D Company. The Americans began to fire on the fortress from the ridge as the *Monocacy* shelled the earthen walls of the Citadel; the warship's guns were joined by two howitzers that were brought forward. The Americans prepared to assault the Citadel, while the Koreans' poorly aimed bullets killed a single Marine, PFC Dennis Hanrahan.

The Marines and Blujackets were given the order to attack and swiftly advanced up the hill. The Koreans fired a volley, but so swift was the American assault that they did not have time to reload. Lieutenant McKee was the first over the walls of the fort, receiving what turned out to be a mortal wound. But the rest of the party followed him, swarming over the defenses and engaging in an extremely bloody hand-to-hand melee; the defenders used spears and swords. In moments, the Star Spangled Banner was flying over the fort but the defenders fought on for about twenty more minutes. Those who were not killed or wounded leaped over the walls or fell on their swords in suicidal determination not to surrender.

When the Sunday sun set on Kanghwa Island, there was little left of the Citadel, except rubble and Korean bodies. The American dead were Lieutenant McKee, Landsman Seth Allen, and Marine Private Denis Hanrahan. Ten Bluejackets and Marines had been wounded. The Marines renamed the fortress Fort McKee.

The following morning, the Marines and Bluejackets reembarked on the transports that had brought them to the island. The now-freed *Palos* and the *Monocacy* towed them out to the open sea and the waiting big ships. Admiral Rodgers decided not to attempt an expedition up the Han River to Seoul. On July 3, the American squadron sailed out of Korean waters.

Despite their victory, the Admiral realized that he did not have the resources to carry out a full-scale attack on the country. But fifteen Medals of Honor were awarded, including one to PFC John Coleman, USMC, who had saved the life of Boatswain's Mate Alexander Mackenzie. This was the first of at least three times in history when the medal was given to a man who saved the life of another recipient.

BOXER REBELLION

CHINA

As with Japan and Korea, China's encounter with the West during the nineteenth century shook its traditional culture to its foundations. By 1898, Great Britain, France, and Russia had sheared off portions of Chinese territory, and they had carved the country up into spheres of influence. Most galling of all, upstart Japan, under Emperor Meiji, had, after an initial decline of its own at the hands of the Europeans, embraced sufficient amounts of their technology and methods to become a great power in her own right. Not only did she detach the Ryukyus from Chinese influence, but two years previously she had defeated China outright, snatching Taiwan from the empire and eliminating China's traditional hegemony over Korea. Now the Japanese, along with the Germans, the Italians, and the Austrians, was looking for a share of the spoils. Even little Belgium had joined the game.

China's humiliation was enormous; the question facing the country's intellectuals was this: Could the country be saved from being gobbled up by the Powers? If so, could it be regenerated through the ruling dynasty, as

Japan had been? Under the leadership of philosopher K'ang Yu-wei, just such a reform movement grew. He argued that China should imitate Japan in its program. Like Meiji Japan, China should adopt a constitutional monarchy; thus, it would maintain its traditional strengths while harnessing the power of the modern world.

Desperate for solutions, the Kuang-hsü Emperor who had come to the throne as an infant in 1875, under the regency of the Empress Dowager, called upon K'ang. Coming of age in 1898, he asked K'ang to take over the government in June of that year. Immediately, K'ang launched "The One Hundred Days of Reform." Edicts poured out of the imperial court with the express purpose of changing China into a modern, constitutional state. These edicts included Western studies in all Chinese education, adoption of a public school system, establishment of popularly elected local assemblies, eventual creation of a national parliamentary government, Westernization of the Chinese bureaucracy, development of official ministries to promote commerce, industry, and banking, and, most crucially, reform of the army.

Certainly, it was an ambitious project. The last reform met with bitter opposition since the military was largely in the hands of a few Governor-Generals, but these reforms dramatically threatened entrenched interests in all levels of society—to say nothing of the foreign powers intent on partitioning the country. The edicts were implemented in only one of fifteen provinces; the rest of China resisted them. After three months in power, a coup d'etat returned authority to the Empress Dowager and a conservative administration came to power. The Emperor was imprisoned by the Empress Dowager for the remaining decade of his life and K'ang and a few disciples fled the country.

So passed the last chance China had to resist the outside on her own terms: subsequent reformers would look to purely foreign inspiration, whether Western or (later) Communist. In the meantime, however, the foreign problem remained. The Empress Dowager was as disturbed by it as her imperial prisoner had been, although not really understanding the problem. The imperial court responded to the foreign threat by giving aid to various secret societies. Such secret societies traditionally had been formed in opposition to imperial government; as such, they were actually a threat to the Ch'ing government itself. But antiforeign sentiment had risen so greatly in China that the Empress Dowager genuinely believed that the secret societies could be the vanguard in a military expulsion of Europeans. This policy reached its climax in 1900 with the Boxer Rebellion.

The Boxers, or "the Righteous and Harmonious Fists," were a religious society that originally rebelled against the imperial government in Shantung in 1898. They practiced rituals and spells that they believed made them impervious to bullets and pain. They further held that the expulsion of foreign devils would magically renew Chinese society and begin a new golden age.

Actually, the Boxer Rebellion was neither a rebellion nor a war against the Europeans. China was largely under the control of regional Governors-General; these ignored the Empress Dowager's instructions, putting forth every effort to prevent disorder or harm coming to foreigners. The Boxer Rebellion, then, was only limited to a few places, especially Beijing.

The first sign of trouble occurred in 1900, when more than 20,000 Boxers marched through the gates of Beijing. Unopposed by Chinese Imperial forces, they laid siege to Legation Quarter. FC Dan Daly and a force of forty-eight Marines and three sailors commanded by Capt. John T. Myers arrived in the capital on May 31, 1900. Shortly afterward the city was surrounded by the Boxers. Another detachment of Marines and sailors under Capt. Newt Hall, USMC, was assigned to defend the Methodist mission located at some distance from the legation.

Fighting to defend the legation wall, Marines fought alongside German troops, repelling Chinese hand-to-hand attacks under artillery fire. At the insistence of Captain Myers, the Americans and Germans deserted the wall and moved back into the legation, probably avoiding defeat and massacre of the inhabitants of the legations. The Boxers next raked the defenders with concentrated fire. The combined national forces held Legation Quarter under Myers's leadership. Eventually, Captain Hall, unable to hold his position at the Methodist church, organized his band of Marines into a surprise attack on the tower on the night of July 2. Hall took the Chinese tower in a demoralizing defeat for the Boxer forces.

Private Daly's Congressional Medal of Honor citation states that he distinguished himself for meritorious conduct for acts of heroism on August 14, 1900. The most famous of Daly's now-legendary exploits throughout the July–August defense of Legation Quarter was during the afternoon of July 13 when German soldiers had been driven back from their position on the east end of the wall. Daly volunteered to take up point and provide cover fire while repairs were made to the fortification. Daly held his position, alone, throughout the course of the night, withstanding repeated Boxer assaults. Relieved at dawn, Daly was found to have accounted for more than two hundred Boxer dead, subsequently allowing the Marines to reclaim the position the German forces had lost.

Boxer assaults continued at other portions of the legation wall, but no further attempts were made at the position held by the Germans and Americans along the west wall.

As the Marines and others were defending the legations, a multinational force of 2,000 (including a detachment of 112 American sailors and Marines under Navy Captain B. H. McCalla) was assembled from among ships of the foreign fleets off the coast. Among the Marines was Smedley Butler. They landed at the Taku forts and were embattled immediately, forcing them to pull back. When Butler realized that a wounded man was left behind, he and five others fought their way back to him and carried him to safety. They then carried this man eighteen miles through hostile territory to a hospital. The four enlisted men in this group received the Medal of Honor. Smedley and the other officer got breveted to Captain (officers were not eligible for the MOH in those days).

After this, Butler led a company of Marines in an attack on the walled city of Tientsin—now Tianjin—again carrying a wounded man to safety. He himself had been shot in the leg doing this, but refused aid until other wounded men were taken care of; even then he only submitted to a bandage, rejoining his men in the attack. Despite his leg wound, a fever, and an abscessed tooth, Butler exposed himself to enemy fire and dragged a British soldier back to safety. He was even struck by a bullet that glanced off one of his tunic buttons. The British army wanted to give him a medal but he had to refuse it, given regulations forbidding a U.S. soldier from getting medals from a foreign service. Butler was shipped back to the States with typhoid fever in 1900; he was a Captain and Medal of Honor winner—and nineteen years old.

Captain McCalla, meanwhile, was wounded three times at Tientsin, later being reinforced by 142 Marines led by Maj. W. T. Waller, USMC. After the heavy fighting in Tientsin, these later relieved the Legation Guard in Peking.

As might be expected, these events simply intensified the onrush of foreign control over China. The United States and the other powers signed the Boxer Protocol of 1901. This provided that the foreign powers would have extraterritorial status in Beijing, sharing responsibility for keeping communications open from the coast to the capital, with military forces if necessary. But the U.S. Department of State had already sent its allies the "Open Door" notes of 1899 and 1900. These announced that the "United States supported the territorial integrity of China as a sovereign state and asked the other nations to accept the principle of equal trading and personal rights throughout China, even within their established spheres of interest. Although the Chinese government should honor all its earlier treaty concessions to foreign governments and businesses, it could assume some diplomatic assistance from the United States, whose policy would be to seek a solution which may bring about permanent safety and peace to China, preserve China's territorial and administrative entity, protect all rights granted to friendly powers by treaty and international law, and safeguard for the world the principle of equal and impartial trade with all parts of the Chinese Empire."

The Boxer Protocol retained its validity despite the overthrow of the monarchy in 1911, the breakup of the country into warlord-run territories, the creation of the Nationalist government, and (until its declaring war on its Protocol partners the United States and Great Britain in 1941) Japan's invasion of China. For almost thirty years, an Army infantry regiment, the Asiatic Fleet, and Marine units gave the United States a share of control in China.

The American military presence in China from 1905 to 1941 manifested in three areas. In north China, in accordance with the Boxer Protocol, the United States maintained a legation guard at Peking. From 1900 until 1905 the legation guard was a company of the 9th Infantry, but in 1905 the soldiers were replaced by one hundred Marines. In 1912, a battalion of the 15th Infantry arrived in Tientsin with the dual mission of guarding the international settlement and keeping the railroad open to Peking. From 1923 until its departure in 1938, the entire 15th Infantry became the main American contribution to the Tientsin defense force.

The second American military concentration was primarily naval. After the war with Spain, the U.S. Navy maintained a flotilla of shallow-draft gunboats along central China's Yangtze River and its tributaries. Marines from the Asiatic Fleet could and did sail with the Yangtze gunboats as well as their cruisers.

Other vessels of the Asiatic Fleet sailed the China coast, able to provide additional warships and Marines from the Philippines and Guam to the Peking and Tientsin garrisons and the Yangtze patrol. Moreover, they could dispatch shore parties into any Chinese coastal city threatened with urban violence.

Increasing and decreasing with the various emergencies engendered by the Chinese Revolution and local civil wars, the Legation Guard grew from two officers and one hundred men to a small battalion of more than five hundred men by the early 1920s. The legation guard specialized in hiking, marksmanship, and dress parades, and it remained one of the social adornments of the international community. For the officers and men of the Legation Guard, life was most comfortable. The Marine Corps' mess had at least three servants for each officer, and the enlisted men hired coolie labor to do laundry, clean the barracks, and cook for them. For the Legation Guard, military duty narrowed to the interesting essentials: field training, shooting, dress parades, and athletic contests against the other foreign detachments. One American minister declared of them: "It was a delight to see the fine-looking companies of American marines, who among all the troops at Peking are noted for their well-groomed, smart, and soldierly appearance."

The early days of the Chinese Revolution spared the Peking guard, leaving military action to the ship's guards of the Asiatic Fleet. On three occasions from 1911 to 1913, they went ashore in or near Shanghai for a few days to guard American property and symbolize the State Department's dedication to international rights in China. In addition, Navy gunboats steamed up the Yangtze with Marine detachments embarked to cope with riots in Wuchang, Hanyang, and Hankow. Marine battalions shuttled from the Philippines to underline U.S. commitment to the defense of foreign property.

The increase in fighting during the early 1920s between various warlords and the expanding government of Chiang Kai-Shek filled the American diplomats with alarm. In 1922, faced with Chiang's arrival in the Beijing area, the legation requested and received additional Marines. One ship's detachment went there while a small Asiatic fleet battalion occupied

Tientsin in support of the 15th Infantry (and for any needed attempt to rescue the legation, if necessary). The Marines peacefully guarded American business installations and missions there.

Through 1924 and 1925, the scene of fighting shifted to the Yangtze River valley. Small detachments of Marines were, with depressing regularity, disembarked at Shanghai or elsewhere as a show of force; fortunately, none of these incidents resulted in bloodshed. In 1926, the United States increased its naval presence on the river, adding two destroyers to the gunboat flotilla of seven. Things worsened the following year when the British concession in Hankow was forced to surrender to the Nationalists. This led to further disorders in central China, causing many Americans to flee to Shanghai. Much of the Asiatic Fleet was deployed to Chinese waters.

From December 1926 to January 1927, consular officials and military commanders in Shanghai's International Settlement decided that reinforcements were in order. The British agreed to send a full division but President Coolidge announced that the United States would not send troops, as it had no concessions to defend. Accepting, however, the advice both of the State Department and the admiral commanding in Asia, Coolidge approved the assembly of the 4th Marine Regiment at San Diego on January 25. Three days later, the regiment was ordered to sail for China. The Chinese, despite assurances by the State Department, interpreted the act as hostile military intervention. Eventually, the 4th Marines became a permanent fixture in Shanghai; Gen. Smedley Butler was sent to command the Marines in China, including the 4th, the Legation Guard, and the temporarily greatly expanded Marine presence in Tientsin (the 3rd Brigade). The continued fighting in China did not again menace the international settlements until 1931.

As Japanese slowly gained control in North China, the position of the Marine Guard at Beijing became ever more tenuous. In 1938, the Army finally received State Department permission to withdraw the 15th Infantry; a detachment of two hundred Marines from Beijing took up their place in Tientsin. In 1941 both detachments surrendered in the early days of the war with Japan.

The 4th Marines in Shanghai had their hands full trying to maintain order during the Japanese attack against China in 1932. They managed successfully amid the fighting to keep the international settlement both safe and neutral, despite several dangerous incidents. But in the interior of China, the struggle between Chiang, the Communists, and Japan continued.

When war broke out again between China and Japan in 1937, the settlement was again menaced and the 4th Marines went on alert. Although they once again safeguarded the place during the fighting, after the Chinese were swept from the area, the State Department ordered the Marines to begin the evacuation of all American citizens who wished to leave. The 4th's position was untenable. By the end of 1940, the Commander of the Asiatic Fleet was urging the regiment's withdrawal, and the Yangtze Patrol itself began to abandon the river. Marine dependents were sent home and the regiment prepared desperate breakout plans. Finally, as diplomatic relations with Japan worsened in 1941, the State Department consented to the 4th Marines' departure. At the end of November 1941, the regiment left—for Corregidor.

BANANA WARS

The breakup of the Spanish Empire in the New World, while welcomed by most Americans as an imitation of their own revolution, nevertheless provoked two different reactions in the United States. Many felt that the country should intervene directly in affairs to the south. But President James Monroe and his Secretary of State, John Quincy Adams, were not willing to risk war for nations that might not survive. Given the recent lackluster performance of American forces (for the most part) in the War of 1812, the prospect of another conflict was not pleasing to them. As far as they were concerned, if the other European powers did not get involved, they were quite content to let Spain fight it out with the Latin American rebels.

In 1823, the French invited Spain to restore her control; some spoke of France and Spain fighting the new republics with the help of Russia, Prussia, and Austria. In response, British Foreign Minister, George Canning, proposed that the United States and Great Britain join together to prevent such intervention. Both Jefferson and Madison urged Monroe to accept the offer, but John Quincy Adams was more suspicious. At the Cabinet meeting of November 7, 1823, Adams argued against Canning's offer and declared: "It would be more candid, as well as more dignified, to avow our principles explicitly to Russia and France, than to come in as a cockboat in the wake of the British man-of-war." He was successful in winning over the Cabinet to an independent policy. In Monroe's message to Congress on December 2, 1823, he delivered what is known as the Monroe Doctrine, although in truth it should have been called the Adams Doctrine. The United States informed the Old World that the American continents were no longer open to European colonization. Any effort to extend European political influence into the New World would be considered by the United States "as dangerous to our peace and safety." The United States would not interfere in European wars or internal affairs, and, conversely, expected Europe to stay out of American affairs. This policy succeeded mainly because it met British interests as well as American, and for the next one hundred years was secured by the backing of the British fleet.

During the remainder of the nineteenth century, from time to time American forces (primarily Marines and Bluejackets) would intervene in Latin American conflicts to safeguard threatened lives and property. Diplomatically and financially, the United States would sometimes aid anticlerical forces in their bids to take over various countries; private citizens (most notably the filibusterer William Walker) would mount private efforts to seize various Latin American countries or parts thereof, and of course half of Mexico was annexed after the 1845–1848 Mexican-American War. Once the American Civil War ended, the U.S. government armed the forces of Benito Juarez in order to eject the French and end Emperor Maximilian's abortive reign in Mexico. But it was the defeat of Spain by the United States in 1898, together with her annexation of Puerto Rico and reduction of Cuba into a protectorate, that established the American government as the arbiter of Latin American, and particularly Caribbean, destiny. The desire of President Theodore Roosevelt to obtain a canal in Panama (with or without the consent of Colombia, of which country Panama was then a part) focused the country's foreign policy; a focus reinforced by the large American corporations that went to work exploiting Central American agricultural and mineral resources.

At the turn of the twentieth century, European governments began to use force to pressure several Latin American countries to repay their debts. British, German, and Italian gunboats blockaded Venezuela's ports in 1902 when the Venezuelan government defaulted on its debts to foreign bondholders. Many Americans worried that European intervention in Latin America would undermine the dominance of the United States in the region. As part of his annual address to Congress on December 6, 1904, President Theodore Roosevelt stated that in keeping with the Monroe Doctrine, the United States was justified in exercising "international police power" to put an end to chronic unrest or wrongdoing in the Western Hemisphere:

> It is not true that the United States feels any land hunger or entertains any projects as regards the other nations of the Western Hemisphere save such as are for their welfare. All that this country desires is to see the neighboring countries stable, orderly, and prosperous. Any country whose people conduct themselves well can count upon our hearty friendship. If a nation shows that it knows how to act with reasonable efficiency and decency in social and political matters, if it keeps order and pays its obligations, it need fear no interference from the United States. Chronic wrongdoing, or an impotence which results in a general loosening of the ties of civilized society, may in America, as elsewhere, ultimately require intervention by some civilized nation, and in the Western Hemisphere the adherence of the United States to the Monroe

Doctrine may force the United States, however reluctantly, in flagrant cases of such wrongdoing or impotence, to the exercise of an international police power. If every country washed by the Caribbean Sea would show the progress in stable and just civilization which with the aid of the Platt Amendment Cuba has shown since our troops left the island, and which so many of the republics in both Americas are constantly and brilliantly showing, all question of interference by this Nation with their affairs would be at an end. Our interests and those of our southern neighbors are in reality identical. They have great natural riches, and if within their borders the reign of law and justice obtains, prosperity is sure to come to them. While they thus obey the primary laws of civilized society they may rest assured that they will be treated by us in a spirit of cordial and helpful sympathy. We would interfere with them only in the last resort, and then only if it became evident that their inability or unwillingness to do justice at home and abroad had violated the rights of the United States or had invited foreign aggression to the detriment of the entire body of American nations. It is a mere truism to say that every nation, whether in America or anywhere else, which desires to maintain its freedom, its independence, must ultimately realize that the right of such independence can not be separated from the responsibility of making good use of it.

In asserting the Monroe Doctrine, in taking such steps as we have taken in regard to Cuba, Venezuela, and Panama, and in endeavoring to circumscribe the theater of war in the Far East, and to secure the open door in China, we have acted in our own interest as well as in the interest of humanity at large. There are, however, cases in which, while our own interests are not greatly involved, strong appeal is made to our sympathies. Ordinarily it is very much wiser and more useful for us to concern ourselves with striving for our own moral and material betterment here at home than to concern ourselves with trying to better the condition of things in other nations. We have plenty of sins of our own to war against, and under ordinary circumstances we can do more for the general uplifting of humanity by striving with heart and soul to put a stop to civic corruption, to brutal lawlessness and violent race prejudices here at home than by passing resolutions and wrongdoing elsewhere. Nevertheless there are occasional crimes committed on so vast a scale and of such peculiar horror as to make us doubt whether it is not our manifest duty to endeavor at least to show our disapproval of the deed and our sympathy with those who have suffered by it. The cases must be extreme in which such a course is justifiable. There must be no effort made to remove the mote from our brother's eye if we refuse to remove the beam from our own. But in extreme cases action may be justifiable and proper. What form the action shall take must depend upon the circumstances of the case; that is, upon the degree of the atrocity and upon our power to remedy it. The cases in which we could interfere by force of arms as we interfered to put a stop to intolerable conditions in Cuba are necessarily very few. Yet it is not to be expected that a people like ours, which in spite of certain very obvious shortcomings, nevertheless as a whole shows by its consistent practice its belief in the principles of civil and religious liberty and of orderly freedom, a people among whom even the worst crime, like the crime of lynching, is never more than sporadic, so that individuals and not classes are molested in their fundamental rights—it is inevitable that such a nation should desire eagerly to give expression to its horror on an occasion like that of the massacre of the Jews in Kishenef, or when it witnesses such systematic and long-extended cruelty and oppression as the cruelty and oppression of which the Armenians have been the victims, and which have won for them the indignant pity of the civilized world.

This Roosevelt corollary to the Monroe Doctrine paved the way for far more extensive interventions in Latin American nations than had ever yet been seen; these were primarily carried out using the United States Marines. As the unstable nations of Central America were often called "Banana Republics" (because of their largest crop), these intermittent conflicts were dubbed by the Marines the "Banana Wars." While the government's motivations behind these actions may be debated, what cannot be are the many stirring episodes of Marine valor which took place during their prosecution.

HAITI

The United States intervened in Haiti in 1915 to restore order and to forestall possible intervention by any European power—a great fear in that second year of World War I. After the brutal murder of President Vilbrun Guillaume Sam, a reign of terror enveloped the Haitian capital of Port-au-Prince. President Woodrow Wilson sent in the Marines to protect the lives and property of Americans and other foreigners, and to prevent the extension of German, British, or French hegemony over Haiti. Strategically located in the Caribbean, Haiti covers the Windward Passage and is scarcely more than six hundred miles from the Panama Canal. At 5:50 P.M. on July 28, two companies of Marines and three sailors landed in Haiti. The Marines and sailors under Admiral Caperton rapidly reestablished order and set up an interim government. Police, customs, schools, and hospitals were all placed under the purview of the Marines and naval personnel assigned to the occupation. Roads were built or improved, cities and towns were refurbished. It was an early example of "nation building."

To ensure internal security, the Marines established a law enforcing constabulary, *Gendarmerie d'Haiti*. Officered by Marine NCOs, the seconded personnel were granted Haitian commissions as officers and leaders of native troops. The Gendarmerie was tasked with enforcing all laws of the country and providing a quasi-military force. They were further backed by the Krag-Jorgensen rifles of the 1st Marine Brigade with eighty-eight officers and 1,941 men garrisoning ten towns.

Despite these benefits of American occupation, a group of rebels called the *Cacos* emerged. Although the south and center of Haiti were largely pacified, in the north, skirmishing continued in the villages, jungles, and mountains. While on patrol against the Cacos, a detachment of thirty-five Marines, among whom was Gunnery Sgt. Dan Daly (a Congressional Medal of Honor winner during the Boxer Rebellion in China). The Marines were pushing the Cacos into the old French Fort Liberte in order to consolidate and destroy the remaining rebels.

While the Marines were fording a river, four hundred rebels opened fire from ambush. The Marines made it to the bank safely; however, the horse carrying the machine gun was killed in midriver, along with many others. During the night, the embattled Marines were again attacked; the patrol leader called for the machine gun. Daly immediately volunteered to return to the river and retrieve the weapon.

Making his way back to the river through enemy patrols, Daly found the dead horse and cut the gun from it. Strapping the gun to his back, Daly returned to the Marine position. This action earned him his second Navy issue of the Medal of Honor. Daly's citation reads: "Serving with the Fifteenth Company of Marines on 22 October 1915, Gunnery Sergeant Daly was one of the company to leave Fort Liberte, Haiti, for a six-day reconnaissance. After dark on the evening of 24 October, while crossing the river in a deep ravine, the detachment was suddenly fired upon from three sides by about 400 Cacos concealed in bushes about 100 yards from the fort. The Marine detachment fought its way forward to a good position, which it maintained during the night, although subjected to a continuous fire from the Cacos. At daybreak, the Marines in three squads, advanced in three directions, surprising and scattering the Cacos in all directions. Gunnery Sergeant Daly fought with exceptional gallantry against heavy odds throughout this action."

Less than a month later, Col. Smedley Butler, who had also won the

Medal of Honor during the Boxer Rebellion, likewise garnered a second one. By night, on November 17, 1915, Butler led a strong force of Marines and sailors and surrounded the last stronghold of the Cacos—Fort Riviere, perched on a mountain to the south of Grand Riviere du Nord. At 7:30 a.m., Butler gave a signal on a whistle—the Marines attacked. The surprise was total and the Cacos were taken in confusion. Crawling through a tunnel, Butler and his men were involved in bloody hand-to-hand fighting. In fifteen minutes, more than fifty Cacos were killed. The citation for Butler's second Medal of Honor reads: "As Commanding Officer of detachments from the Fifth, Thirteenth, Twenty-third Companies and Marine and Sailor detachment from USS *Connecticut*, Major Butler led an attack on Fort Riviere, Haiti 17 November 1915. Following a concentrated drive, several different detachments of Marines gradually closed in on the old French bastion fort in an effort to cut off all avenues of retreat for the Cacos bandits. Reaching the fort on the southern side where there was a small opening in the wall, Major Butler gave the signal to attack and Marines from the 15th Company poured through the breach, engaged the Cacos in hand-to-hand combat, took the bastion and crushed Caco resistance. Throughout this perilous action, Major Butler was conspicuous for his bravery and forceful leadership."

Eventually, in 1916, an agreement was reached between the United States and Haiti. Similar to the Platt Amendment, the treaty turned Haiti into a virtual protectorate of the United States. To ensure repayment of Haiti's debts, America took over collection of customs duties. Americans also arbitrated disputes, distributed food and medicine, censored the press, and ran military courts. In addition, the United States helped build about a thousand miles of unpaved roads, as well as a number of agricultural and vocational schools, and trained the Haitian army and police. In addition, the United States helped replace a government led by blacks with a government headed by mulattoes, and forced the Haitians to adopt a new constitution that gave American businessmen the right to own land in Haiti. While campaigning for Vice President in 1920, Franklin D. Roosevelt, who had served as Assistant Secretary of the Navy in the Wilson administration, later boasted, "I wrote Haiti's Constitution myself, and if I do say it, it was a pretty good little Constitution."

Nevertheless, many Haitians resisted the American occupation. In the fall of 1918, Charlemagne Peralte, a former Haitian army officer, launched a guerrilla war against the U.S. Marines. The initial cause was a system of forced labor imposed by the United States to build roads in Haiti. In 1919, Peralte was captured and killed by U.S. Marines. His body was photographed against a door with a crucifix and a Haitian flag, in warning to others. During the first five years of the occupation, American forces killed about 2,250 Haitians. In December 1929, U.S. Marines fired on a crowd of protesters armed with rocks and machetes, killing twelve and wounding twenty-three. The Marines left Haiti at the behest of President Franklin Roosevelt on August 1934, after a stay of almost two decades. All that they had built was given to the Haitians for free and remains a testament to their ingenuity.

DOMINICAN REPUBLIC

Haiti's neighbor on the island of Hispaniola, the Dominican Republic, suffered from a similar round of instability and a presidential assassination. To quell the unrest, President William H. Taft sent a commission to Santo

Domingo on September 24, 1912, to mediate among the warring factions, accompanied by 750 Marines. The Marine presence convinced the Dominicans to appoint an interim president and settle their differences for the moment.

Honored more in its breach than observance, the agreement broke down completely two years later. President Woodrow Wilson delivered an ultimatum: elect a president or the United States will impose one. For another couple of years presidents succeeded each other, and at last on May 13, 1916, Rear Adm. William Caperton, Military Administrator of Haiti, ordered interim President Arias to leave Santo Domingo or face bombardment. The first Marines landed three days later. In two months the Marines occupied the entire country, and in November a military government was proclaimed. Most Dominican laws and institutions were retained; military governor Rear Adm. Harry S. Knapp dealt with the reluctance of the locals to serve in his cabinet by filling a number of the seats with U.S. naval officers.

Except for the eastern region, the Marines restored order throughout most of the country. The country enjoyed a balanced budget, diminished debt, and economic growth; new roads linked all regions for the first time in the country's history; a professional military organization—the Dominican Constabulary Guard—replaced the partisan forces that had produced the country's unending instability.

Opposition to the occupation nevertheless flared in the eastern provinces of El Seibo and San Pedro de Macorís. From 1917 to 1921, the Marines fought a guerrilla movement in that area known as the gavilleros. Profiting from their considerable support among the population and a superior knowledge of the terrain, the movement managed to survive the capture and execution of its leader, Vicente Evangelista. Initially, the gavilleros fought some fierce encounters with the Marines. Eventually, though, they yielded to the Americans' superior firepower, air power (a squadron of six Curtis Jennies), and determined methods.

After World War I, the now-anti-interventionist public in the United States turned against the occupation. Warren G. Harding, who succeeded Wilson in March 1921, fought his election campaign against the occupations of both Haiti and the Dominican Republic. In June 1921, the Harding Plan, calling for Dominican ratification of all acts of the military government, approval of a loan of U.S. $2.5 million for public works and other expenses, the acceptance of United States officers for the constabulary—now known as the National Guard (Guardia Nacional)—and the holding of elections under United States supervision, was unveiled. With the inauguration of Horacio Vásquez Lajara on July 13, 1924, control of the republic returned to Dominican hands and the Marines withdrew.

CUBA

The Marines figured largely in the conquest of Cuba from Spain in 1898. Not surprisingly, then Lt. Smedley Butler was present, as was Sgt. Dan Daly and two future commandants of the USMC, Capt. George F. Elliott and Lt. Wendell C. Neville. The Marines landed at Guantanamo Bay on June 10, 1898. On June 14 they fought a decisive battle at Cuzco Well, during which Sgt. John Quick earned the Congressional Medal of Honor. To direct the support fire of the USS *Dolphin*, Quick climbed to the top of a hill in full view of the enemy. Amid a hail of hostile fire, Sergeant Quick semaphored instructions to the ship. The Marines have been at Guantanamo ever since.

The Platt Amendment to the Cuban Constitution gave the United States the right to intervene in Cuba whenever the American government felt it necessary. The first time this was invoked was in 1906. Six years later, the Negro Rebellion forced the United States to intervene once more, this time in Oriente province. To protect U.S. lives and property, the First Provisional Brigade was organized under Col. Lincoln Karmany and stationed at Guantanamo Bay. From there small detachments were dispatched to occupy and defend strategic points in the interior. Beginning with the occupation of several towns near Santiago on May 30, troops from the brigade were sent to Guantanamo City, Soledad, Los Canos, San Antonio, and other places. The Marines thus providing security, the Cuban army was freed to track down the rebels. By July the evacuation of Marines had begun.

Though Guantanamo provided essential logistical and strategic support for Marine interventions throughout the Caribbean, it continued to allow the United States to watch Cuba as well. So, in March of 1917, the "Sugar Intervention" began, brought about through infighting among local factions. Oriente province was again the focal point for Marine activities. To protect the vital water supply for the station and to safeguard American property, detachments from the Naval Station and the 7th Marines were ordered first to Guantanamo City and later to other threatened points inland; as trouble spread to Camaguey province, ships' detachments were landed at various points in that province.

Invoking the specter of the Russian Revolution, President Wilson ordered the Marinesto to occupy Cuba again from 1917 to 1923. They put down strikes and protected U.S. property. An American governor managed the finances of the Cuban government and representatives of U.S. sugar interests were leading political figures. But once again, President Harding and the general isolationist thrust of public opinion brought the Marines back.

NICARAGUA

In 1893, the Liberals under José Santos Zelaya overthrew the Conservatives who had ruled Nicaragua between 1863 and 1893. A brutal dictator, Zelaya wanted to rule Central America. Mexico and the United States created the Central American Court in 1908 to rein him in. Zelaya was also hostile to U.S. private capital in Nicaragua; he wanted to cancel the U.S.–Nicaragua concession—mining property owned by U.S. Steel.

In October of 1909 , there was a Conservative rebellion in Bluefields on the Moskito Coast. The rebels enjoyed the support of U.S. Steel. When the Zelaya forces caught and executed two American citizens (professional dynamiters who worked for the company) for being in the rebellion, Taft broke relations with Zelaya and sent Marines to Bluefields. Zelaya was forced out and, in August 1910, Governor Estrada of Bluefields became the provisional president.

Financial chaos resulted, however, and Adolfo Díaz, a former company employee, came to power through yet another revolt. Placing the country under American protection, on June 6 he signed the Knox-Castrillo

Convention of 1911. This gave the United States the right to intervene in Nicaragua to maintain order and protect American interests; gave loans of $15 million to Nicaragua to refinance the national debt through American private banks; and gave the American government control of the customs house to insure payments. The U.S. Senate rejected the Knox-Castrillo Convention, however. Nicaraguan Liberals then revolted and the Marines were sent in to protect American interests. The Marines would remain on and off until 1933.

In 1925, upon repayment of the national debt to American banks, the United States withdrew the Marines. Predictably, the Liberals rose once more in revolt. The Americans restored Conservative Adolfo Díaz; Liberals, however, declared Juan B. Sacasa as president—he enjoyed the backing of the revolutionary government in Mexico. Díaz's and Sacasa's forces fought until, in 1927, American warships brought some two thousand Marines and material. Angry at American interference in Nicaraguan affairs, Augusto Sandino joined the war, engaging in guerrilla actions against the American troops.

President Calvin Coolidge then sent his personal representative, Henry L. Stimson, to settle the conflict. Stimson induced the rival leaders, Díaz and Moncada, to disarm and allow American supervision of forthcoming elections. The United States had the army abolished and replaced by the *Guardia Nacional* led by U.S.-educated and -trained Anastatio Somoza. The liberal Moncada was elected president of Nicaragua in a fair election on November 4, 1928, but Sandino refused to accept this and continued his guerrilla attacks on Marine detachments. In response, U.S. warplanes bombed the guerrillas' mountain strongholds; fleeing to Mexico, Sandino vowed not to lay down his arms until the removal of the Marines from Nicaragua. In 1932, Sacasa was elected president and attempted to reach an accord with Sandino, who capitulated after the Marines withdrew in 1933. In Managua in 1934, Sandino was assassinated by national guardsmen angry over the amnesty given to him by the government. Thus began the Somocista/Sandinista conflict that ended with the Revolution in 1976.

WORLD WAR I

BELLEAU WOOD

The Americans entered World War I in 1917, three years after it had begun. By this time both Allies and Germans were exhausted. But the fall of Russia to Communism took that country out of the war, freeing many German divisions for service in France. Augmented by these reinforcements, on May 27, 1918, German General Ludendorff launched his Chemin des Dames offensive with forty divisions. The northern front was smashed in two; the Germans poured through a four-kilometer gap left by the wreckage of the French 43rd Division. The 4th Brigade was sent in to stop the German drive on Paris. A French colonel drove up and advised Col. Wendell Neville to retreat. "Whispering Buck" Neville was supposed to have roared in reply, "Retreat, Hell! We just got here"; although this was actually said by Capt. Lloyd Williams.

On June 1, 1918, the U.S. Second Division formed a line astride the

Paris-Metz road; the 23rd Infantry was on the left flank, the 6th and 5th Marines in the center, and the 9th Infantry on the right. At dawn on the second, the German 28th Division attacked along the axis of the road, hitting the Marine center. The German offensive was blocked by rifle fire that began to kill at eight hundred yards. They attacked again on the fourth and fifth of June; halted again, they dug in. Belleau Wood, a square mile of woods and tumbled boulders, made a perfect defensive position.

Ensconced in the wood were two battalions of the 461st Imperial German Infantry, equipped with a large number of Maxim (heavy) machine guns. The Marines were ordered to attack on the morning of June 6. They marched forward in orderly formation, until the German machine guns laid down a grazing fire. The Marines hit the dirt. To rally his men, Gunnery Sgt. Dan Daly yelled at them, "Come on, you sons of bitches. Do you want to live forever?" Hearing his words, the men jumped up, advanced, and took

the village of Bouresches. Lacking mortars or grenades, the Marines either shot the German machine gunners or crawled up and bayoneted them. On June 23, the Marines had secured the woods. The German troops, shocked at being defeated, called the Marines, *Teufelhunden*—or "Devil Dogs."

To commemorate the bravery of the Marines, the French Army commander changed the name of the forest to *Bois de la Brigade de Marine*, or "Wood of the Marine Brigade," and awarded the 4th Brigade the Croix de Guerre.

WORLD WAR II

WAKE ISLAND

One of the key American outposts in the central Pacific, Wake Island was, along with Guam, a vital part of the supply line between Hawaii and the Philippines. It was, for example, on the path of Pan Am's famed "Philippine Clipper" air service from San Francisco to Manila. A small atoll 2,300 miles west by southwest of Hawaii, Wake was early targeted by the Japanese high command. Located just outside the Japanese Mandate Islands—including Truk, the Marianas and Marshall islands, and Palau—Wake was thus within range of Japanese bombers based on Kwajalein to the south. Flat, possessing few natural defenses, the island provided great temptation for invasion.

On December 7, 1941, a few hours after the last Japanese fighter had left a now-devastated Pearl Harbor, thirty-four Japanese bombers attacked Wake Island, specifically targeting the airfield, fuel storage tanks, and other facilities on the atoll. On three small islands (Peale, Wilkes, and the main island of Wake) 450 Marines and sailors were garrisoned. There were also 1,500 civilians, some of whom worked for Pan Am. The company maintained a hotel and seaplane station as part of the aforementioned Philippine Clipper service.

The Japanese enjoyed nearly complete surprise, thanks to the foggy weather. The dead numbered fifty-two, including eighteen Marines. Seven of the Grumman F4F Wildcat fighters delivered to the island just a week before were destroyed. After the attack, the wounded and a few others embarked on a Martin 130 flying boat moored at the island and headed for Hawaii. The remaining garrison island readied themselves for the next attack, and for the arrival of an enemy cruiser and destroyer force that a Clipper pilot had spotted over the horizon.

Japanese bombers based about seven hundred miles south of Wake at Roi, in the Kwajalein atoll, attacked over the following three days, reducing the Marine fighter squadron to four usable planes and wearing down the defenders. Nevertheless, the remaining planes, as well as six five-inch and twelve three-inch anti-aircraft guns met the Japanese landing force upon its arrival early on December 11.

This invasion force, made up of three light cruisers, six destroyers, and two transports carrying an Imperial Marine detachment, was under the command of Rear Adm. Sadamichi Kajioka. The cruisers and destroyers bombarded the atoll at 5:22 a.m. About forty minutes later, having approached within 2,500 yards of Wake, the transports moved in, escorted by the destroyers. During the Japanese bombardment, the Marine gunners held back; but at 6:10 they opened up on the enemy.

Over on the southern tip of Wake, Peacock Point, a battery commanded by Lt. Clarence Barninger opened up on Kajioka's flagship, the cruiser *Yubari*. In minutes they had made four direct hits. Meanwhile, on Peale Island, Sgt. Henry Bedell's gunners ripped into the destroyer *Hayate*; the hapless ship exploded, broke in two, and sank. Cheering and laughing, the crew stopped firing, but Bedell's outraged roar quickly put them back to work. Then, resuming their fire, they and other gunners on Peale scored hits on the three remaining destroyers. One of the Japanese transports caught fire as well. With the invasion force now in disarray, the four Grumman fighters joined in the fun. One of them, as it strafed the destroyer

Kisaragi, managed to detonate the depth charges on the destroyer's aft deck, thus mortally wounding the ship. Admiral Kajioka called off the assault and left aboard his flagship. So it was that the 450 Marines on Wake thus earned the noble distinction of being the only force in the entire war to defeat an amphibious assault.

After that assault on Wake was repelled, Admiral Kimmel's staff at Pearl Harbor planned to relieve the island. A major difficulty was presented by the fact that the remaining U.S. naval forces were widely scattered. President Roosevelt had ordered the carriers out to sea prior to December 7, thus they had been preserved from the ruin that befell Battleship Row. But the *Lexington* and Task Force 11 were far to the southwest of Wake, and *Saratoga* and Task Force 16 were approaching Hawaii from the west coast. Only *Enterprise*'s Task Force 8 was anywhere near Hawaii. Admiral Kimmel ordered the seaplane tender *Tangier* to Wake, manned by the 4th Marine Defense Battalion.

Tangier and its attendant oiler were to be escorted by Task Force 16. But due to the delay in *Saratoga*'s arrival, *Tangier* departed Pearl Harbor alone on December 15. A day later, *Saratoga* followed, accompanied by her escorts. In the meantime, Japanese land-based bombers and flying boats continued to bomb Wake twice daily. Marine and civilian mechanics kept two to four Wildcats in good working order and ruined aircraft were used as decoys on the landing strip. Against all odds, Wake's pilots and gunners took a steady toll on the Japanese attackers.

On December 17, Adm. W. S. Pye, former commander of the Battle Force, relieved Kimmel of his command. Pye ordered the *Lexington* force to cancel a planned raid against a Japanese-held island in the Gilberts and to sail northeast to support *Saratoga* and the Wake relief force. Meanwhile, the *Tangier* and its accompanying oiler slowly advanced toward Wake. By December 21, they were still six hundred miles from the island. The Japanese fleet was much closer and stronger. The previous day, Admiral Kajioka left Kwajalein with a second assault force, now reinforced with four heavy cruisers. In the north, the carriers *Soryu* and *Hiryu* were detached from the Pearl Harbor strike force; their planes attacked Wake on December 21. Wake's last two Marine Wildcats took off, downing a Zero before being forced down in turn. Wake was now defenseless against aerial attack. *Saratoga* was still hundreds of miles away.

Hearing of the latest raid, Admiral Pye feared that *Saratoga* and *Lexington* were sailing into a trap. For caution's sake, he ordered the two task forces to approach no nearer than two hundred miles to Wake. *Tangier*, rather than landing reinforcements and supplies on Wake, was ordered to evacuate the atoll. The admiral also lifted restrictions on *Lexington*'s and *Enterprise*'s operating areas, in hopes that they could more effectively support *Tangier*.

Alas, the Japanese were swifter. By night, Admiral Kajioka's force approached quite close to Wake; before daybreak on December 23, they landed the one-thousand-man Maizuru 2nd Special Naval Landing Force. Seventy Marines on Wilkes island, armed with only old 1903 Springfield bolt-action rifles and hand grenades, set a transport on fire and trapped the Japanese on the beach. While that landing was defeated, on Wake Island, a mere two hundred Marines faced hundreds of Imperial Marines. The

Marine commander, Maj. James Devereux, radioed his superiors in Hawaii: "Enemy on Island: Issue in Doubt."

Saratoga was still a day away. *Tangier*, the relief ship, was even farther. Given the situation, a half hour after receiving word from Pearl, Devereux surrendered Wake. Admiral Pye ordered the relief forces to turn back.

Despite the eventual surrender, the resistance of the Marines on Wake against overwhelming odds gave the Japanese a taste of what they could expect from the USMC.

GUADALCANAL

Guadalcanal is one of the largest of the Solomon Islands. Initially discovered by the Spanish in the sixteenth century, they were lost until their rediscovery in 1767 by the British Capt. Philip Carteret. It was not however, until 1893 that Queen's government declared the central part of the group to be a British protectorate. This was done to counter German advances in New Guinea, where the Kaiser's men were quickly turning the northwest part of the island into a colony. But the British government was also reacting to appeals from Protestant missionaries. The Solomons had become a dangerous place; islanders, angry at the raids by slave traders known as "blackbirders" (who would kidnap the natives for labor on the sugar plantations in Queensland, Australia), would cook and eat outsiders, including missionaries and ship-wrecked sailors, in response. In 1898 and 1899, more outlying islands were added to the protectorate; in 1900, the remainder of the Solomons, formerly under German rule, was transferred to British administration. Under the protectorate, missionaries settled in the islands and converted most of the population to Christianity.

In the early twentieth century, a number of British and Australian companies began coconut planting in the Solomons. Economic growth was slow, however, and the islanders benefited little. At the outbreak of World War II, most planters and traders evacuated to Australia, and most cultivation ceased. In April 1942, the Japanese took the Shortland Islands and then moved to Tulagi; the seizure of the islands was part of their drive toward Australia. When they began to build an airfield on Guadalcanal, the Allies knew that the time had come for action.

Beginning with the Battle of the Coral Sea in May of 1942, until December 1943, the Solomons were almost constantly a scene of combat. U.S. forces landed almost without opposition on Guadalcanal in August 1942, but they were soon engaged in a bloody fight for control of the islands' airstrip; the Marines called it Henderson Field. One of the most furious sea battles ever fought took place off Savo Island, near Guadalcanal, also in August 1942.

On Guadalcanal itself, after the Marines landed on August 7, the Japanese beefed up their defenses. The 1st Raider Battalion and 1st Parachute Battalion were brought back from Tulagi and Gavutu, being placed in reserve near Henderson Field. This airstrip, called an "unsinkable aircraft carrier," became the target of Japanese attacks. As long as Allied airplanes used the airfield, they could both protect their own convoys and attack Japanese reinforcements.

The Raiders mounted two raids to protect the airfield. The first, on Savo

Island, met no Japanese resistance. The second raid hit the crucial enemy supply base at Tasimboko. Both Raiders and parachutists participated, and a number of Japanese artillery pieces and a lot of supplies were destroyed. Further, captured documents revealed the size of the Japanese force destined for Henderson Field.

This information convinced Marine Col. Merritt Edson that the Japanese would attack Henderson from the lightly defended southern direction. Edson shifted his men (including the attached 1st Parachute Battalion) to a broken grassy north-south ridge about a mile from the airfield. Long spurs extended on each side of this formation. The Marines dug in, stringing what barbed wire they had along the ridge. The ridge's spine provided a rough dividing line, with paratroopers dug in on the east side and Raiders on the west.

At sunset on September 12, 1942, two thousand Japanese under Maj. Gen. Kiyotaki Kawaguchi were in place in front of some 840 paratroopers and Raiders. If they broke through they would surely capture Henderson. This inevitably would lead to the loss of Guadalcanal, both damaging the Allied war effort and once again possibly endangering Australia. As Kawaguchi prepared for the assault, he realized that only one of his battalions was at its assigned jump-off point. He tried to delay the attack but was unable to communicate his new orders in time. After Japanese cruisers and destroyers bombarded the Marine positions, Japanese foot soldiers assaulted them in piecemeal fashion. Several Raider platoons stationed near the lagoon side of the ridge were isolated and forced to withdraw. By sunrise, the Japanese broke off the attack. Kawaguchi regrouped his men in the jungles around the grassy hogback.

Colonel Edson in turn pulled his troops back along the ridge; the Japanese were forced to cross open ground. The Japanese attacked forward again with more men at nightfall, hitting the right flank of B Company near the lagoon. At 10:00 P.M., the Japanese advanced all along the ridge, breaking the center of the Marines' line. Some sixty B Company Raiders, cut off and exposed on both flanks, still held steady. Edson ordered his men to retreat to the last defensive position before Henderson Field, a small knoll. There, the remaining Marines (about three hundred in all) formed a horseshoe-shaped line around the knoll for their final stand. When a few men started retreating farther to the rear, their officers shouted, "Nobody moves, just die in your holes!"

In an attempt to envelop the ridge's left flank, the Japanese continued their advance. Two companies of parachutists then counterattacked, fighting them to a standstill. The Marine artillery pummeled the attackers, while cases of grenades were tossed at the Japanese. At 4:00 a.m. on September 14, Kawaguchi launched two more unsuccessful attacks on the ridge; despite their defeat, a small party of Japanese soldiers reached the western fringe of the airfield (Henderson's Fighter One). There they encountered the 1st Engineer Battalion and Headquarters Company, which turned them back. The dawn made visible the corpses of seven hundred Japanese and scores of Marines, leading the defenders to dub the place "Bloody Ridge." Henderson Field remained in American hands.

During their month and a half of fighting on Guadalcanal, more than half of the 1st Parachute Battalion was wounded or killed in action. Shortly after the battle for Bloody Ridge, the surviving parachutists left for much-needed rest and an infusion of replacement troops. The Raiders, too, had suffered heavy losses on the ridge (163 men in all), but remained to fight for another month.

Wanting to go on the offensive, General Vandegrift, the overall commander of the Marines on Guadalcanal, attempted to push the enemy off the west side of the Matanikau River (several miles west of Henderson) where more Japanese were arriving. There had been some fighting there in August. Three Marine battalions then commenced the Second Battle of the Matanikau with an attack on the Japanese in the last week of September. Joining the exhausted Raiders were the 2nd Battalion, 5th Marines. They would push at the Japanese near the mouth of the Matanikau; at the same time, most of the 1st Battalion, 7th Marines launched an amphibious assault to the west at Point Cruz. This last effort was intended to cut off any possible Japanese withdrawal. The attack, however, failed when the Raiders and the 2nd Battalion, 5th Marines encountered heavy resistance from enemy positions near the river and they were forced to withdraw. Although the 1st Battalion, 7th Marines was surrounded, nearly being annihilated after making its amphibious assault, most of the Marines managed a safe evacuation. This would be the only defeat the Marines underwent during the Guadalcanal campaign.

Intelligence suggested that the enemy was preparing for another offensive. On October 7, the 5th and 7th Marine Regiments (each lacking a battalion) and the debilitated 1st Raiders were sent to attend to this development. The result was the Third Battle of the Matanikau, in which the Marines devastated a Japanese infantry regiment, disrupting their offensive and capturing assembly as well as artillery positions on the east bank of the Matanikau.

On October 13, the Raiders left for New Caledonia to rest up and be reinforced. The Guadalcanal campaign had taken a very heavy toll on the 1st Raider Battalion. Out of the battalion's original strength of around nine hundred, only five hundred remained for the trip to New Caledonia.

Rested and recouped, the 2nd Raider Battalion was sent to Guadalcanal on November 4, arriving at Aola Bay, forty miles east of Henderson Field. Col. Evans Carlson, the battalion's commander, was dispatched to pursue a Japanese force of about three thousand troops. Commanded by a Colonel Shoji, the Japanese had withdrawn to the eastern part of the island after their failed offensive on Henderson back in late October. Marines from Henderson Field were already in pursuit of Shoji's regiment; Carlson's men were to harass it from the rear. This operation was dubbed the "Long Patrol," and the Raiders doggedly pursued Shoji for a month through the rain forest, while they chipped away at his unit. The battle casualty figures were 488 Japanese soldiers killed, compared to 16 Raiders killed and 17 wounded. An additional 225 Raiders were plagued with malaria, dysentery, dengue fever, and other maladies, however.

As 1943 approached, the role of the Marines began to diminish. Early December saw the departure of the 1st Marine Division and its replacement by the U.S. Army. The 2nd Raider Battalion left as well on December 15, bound for Espíritu Santo in the New Hebrides. Impressed by the record of the Raiders on Guadalcanal, the Marine Corps formed two new Raider battalions, the 3rd and the 4th; eventually, these four battalions condensed into two Raider regiments.

Guadalcanal was America's first toehold in the Pacific, one that was achieved at great cost in human lives. By the time Japanese completely withdrew from Guadalcanal in February 1943, more than seven thousand Americans and twenty-one thousand Japanese had died. At last, in December of that year, the Allies were in command of the entire Solomon chain.

TARAWA

Today, Tarawa atoll is the capital of the Republic of Kiribati (formerly the Gilbert Islands) and as crowded a place as Hong Kong. But it was not always so; seeing it now, it is hard to believe that one of the proudest moments in Marine history occurred there. The Gilberts were first discovered in 1606 when Spanish explorer Pedro Fernandez de Quiros sighted the atoll of Butaritari. British naval captains John Marshall and Thomas Gilbert (for whom the Gilberts would be named) visited several of the other islands while sailing from Australia to China in 1788. Through the 1820s and 1860s, American and British whalers operated in the surrounding waters, leaving some deserters behind. These went on to deal coconut oil and then copra with European, Australian, and American trading ships.

An American Protestant missionary, Hiram Bingham, arrived in 1857. He began to spread Christianity through the northern Gilbert Islands, assisted by Hawaiian pastors. In 1870, the London Missionary Society placed Samoan pastors on several of the southern Gilbert Islands. Catholic missionaries arrived from Tahiti in 1888. Over the following decades, Catholicism became the dominant religion of the northern Gilbert Islands (despite being illegal until 1954), while some of the southern Gilberts remained Protestant.

In 1892, to install orderly government in the islands, British Capt. E.H.M. Davis declared as British protectorates sixteen of the Gilbert Islands and, to the South, nine of the Polynesian-inhabited Ellice Islands (now Tuvalu). The British took Ocean Island (now Banaba) under their wing in 1900 after phosphates were discovered there. In 1916, Britain annexed the area outright as the Gilbert and Ellice Islands Colony (GEIC). Subsequent years saw several of the present-day Line Islands added to the colony; in 1937, the present-day Phoenix Islands were joined to the GEIC. Two years later, the British agreed that Kanton and Enderbury—two Phoenix islands strategically important to the United States—would be administered jointly by the United States and Britain.

These arrangements flew out the window when the Japanese occupied the Gilbert Islands in 1942. Most of the European residents evacuated the islands, while the colonial administration established temporary headquarters in Sydney, Australia; later it moved to Fongafale (now in Tuvalu).

Strategically, the Gilberts were very important to the Allies. Tarawa would be the scene of a major amphibious assault, one of the proudest testaments to their valor in U.S. Marine Corps history.

Before the assault, Japan's Rear Adm. Shibasaki Meichi was quoted as saying that it would take the American forces "a million men and a hundred years" to capture the atoll. The Japanese had heavily fortified the island of Betio in the southwestern corner of the atoll, garrisoning it with an elite force of almost five thousand men. After capturing the islands three days following Pearl Harbor, the Japanese employed the next two years positioning coastal defense guns, anti-aircraft guns, anti-boat guns, light and heavy machine guns, as well as an airstrip they could use to strike at allied troops stationed in the area. The atoll was vital to both sides.

Serious problems could be expected with any attack on Tarawa. Big coastal guns would keep the U.S. Navy either under constant fire or at bay. Worse still, the Japanese had used sunken ships and other metal scrap in the creation of obstacles to block the sea approaches. Invading craft would be slowed down, forcing them into ambush sites. There, they would be the targets of deadly, concentrated fire from fortified positions. Presuming that that threat was overcome, the next line of defense included a double apron of barbed wire, log barriers, and concrete obstacles surrounding the island. Should they get past that, the Marines would still be faced with the beach itself, where the Japanese had fortified heavy machine guns, creating a series of interlocking fields of fire. There were also anti-personnel mines and anti-vehicle mines in the fringing reefs where the boats would have to land. With anti-aircraft guns and planes of their own, the defenders were well prepared.

But Tarawa had to be taken. On November 19, 1943, the assault began. Facing near-impossible odds, fired at from all sides, the Marines made it to the beach. By the last day of battle the Japanese were forced into the east end of the three-mile-long island. They fell back on a series of fortified positions in their retreat, defending each almost to the last man. The Marines advanced over those three miles yard by bloody yard. At last, organized Japanese resistance on Tarawa had ceased by 1:30 P.M. on the third day.

The Battle of Tarawa took seventy-six hours and the lives of 1,020 Marines. The wounded list came to 2,296. The cost was much higher for the Japanese. Of 4,386 elite troops on Betio, only 146 survived the battle.

Four Marines received the Medal of Honor for their heroism, three of them posthumously. The fourth, Col. David M. Shoup, Commanding Officer of the 2nd Marines and Betio Island Assault forces, later became the Commandant of the Marine Corps.

The Europeans returned, and colonial officials set up a new headquarters on Tarawa. The Japanese continued to hold Banaba atoll until 1945. During their occupation, they deported most of Banaba's residents to Tarawa, the island of Nauru, the Millennium Islands, and the Marshall Islands. The Japanese massacred nearly all remaining Banabans before surrendering the island. After the war, the British resettled deported Banabans on the Fijian island of Rabi.

Iwo Jima

The Volcano Islands comprise three islands, of which the most important is Iwo Jima. Japanese fishermen and sulfur miners arrived in 1887 (Iwo Jima means "Sulfur Island") and Japan annexed the islands in 1891. The topography of Iwo Jima made it a natural site for airfields during World War II. Eventually, the Allies would have to take the island, an eventuality for which the Japanese were ready. They had garrisoned it with twenty-two thousand soldiers, and fortified Iwo Jima with a network of underground bunkers. Moreover, each defender was expected to die in defense of the homeland, taking ten enemy soldiers with him.

The Allies wanted Iwo Jima not merely to eliminate threats to their warplanes and shipping, but also to use the island's airfields for fighter escort and emergency bomber landings. On February 16, 1945, they began a fierce three-day air and gun assault on the island, which nevertheless had little effect on the entrenched garrison. At last, on February 19, 1945, about thirty thousand United States Marines of the 3rd, 4th, and 5th Marine Divisions, under V Amphibious Corps, landed on Iwo Jima. Called "Operation Detachment," this landing began one of the most remarkable battles in an unprecedented war.

At 2:00 a.m. on the morning of February 19, battleships guns opened up on the island, signaling the commencement of D-day. More than 450 ships massed off Iwo as the H-hour bombardment pounded the island. One hundred bombers attacked the island, swiftly followed by another volley from the naval guns. At 8:30, Marines of the 4th and 5th Divisions hit beaches code-named "Green," "Red," "Yellow," and "Blue," initially facing little Japanese resistance. Coarse volcanic sand hampered the movement of men and machines up the beach. As gunfire subsided to allow the Marines to advance, enemy troops emerged from fortified underground positions to begin heavy fire against the invaders. Next, the 4th Marine Division pushed on against heavy opposition to take the Quarry, a Japanese strong point. The 5th Marine Division's 28th Marines had the mission of isolating Mount Suribachi, a major objective due to its commanding position on the southern part of the island. Both tasks were performed by day's end.

Heavy fire rained down on the Marines from the mountain. Terrain was inhospitable, made up of rough volcanic ash that allowed neither secure footing nor the digging of foxholes. Still, when night fell, the mountain had been surrounded and thirty thousand Marines had landed. About forty thousand more would follow. The day after the landing, the 28th Marines secured the southern end of Iwo, and moved to take the summit of Suribachi. By day's end, one-third of the island and Motoyama Airfield No. 1 was controlled by the Marines. Suribachi was fought for yard by yard. Although gunfire did little against the enemy, flame throwers and grenades cleared the bunkers. By February 23, the 28th Marines would reach the top of Mount Suribachi and raise the U.S. flag.

There were, in fact, two flag raisings on Mt. Suribachi. At 8:00 a.m. on February 23, a patrol of forty men from 3rd Platoon, E Company, 2nd Battalion, 28th Marines, under the command of 1st Lt. Harold G. Schrier, assembled at Mount Suribachi's base. Their mission: take the crater of Suribachi's peak and raise the U.S. flag atop it.

Slowly climbing steep trails to the summit, they encountered no enemy fire. Reaching the top, the platoon positioned itself around the crater, on the lookout for Japanese resistance. Meanwhile, some of them looked for something on which to raise the flag. Finding a steel pipe, the flag was raised above the island by Schrier, Sgt. Ernest I. Thomas, platoon sergeant, Corp. Charles W. Lindberg, and PFC James R. Nicel at 10:20 a.m. Marine Corps photographer Sgt. Lou Lowery captured this first flag raising on film. At that moment, a Japanese grenade was tossed in his direction. Lowery threw his body over the edge of the crater, tumbling fifty feet. He and his film were safe, though his camera lens was broken.

Three hours later, another patrol was dispatched to raise another, larger, flag. This second raising was captured on film by Associated Press photographer Joe Rosenthal. His photo, seen around the world as a symbol of

American values, would earn him many awards including the 1945 Pulitzer Prize. The flag raisers, as seen in the photo, were PFC Ira H. Hayes, PFC Franklin R. Sousley, Sgt. Michael Strank, Pharmacist's Mate 2nd Class John Bradley, PFC Rene A. Gagnon, and Cpl. Harlon Block.

Meanwhile, the 3rd Marine Division joined the fighting on the fifth day of the battle. They immediately began securing the center sector of the island. Each division was forced to fight hard to gain ground against determined Japanese troops. With the fall of Suribachi and the capture of the airfields, the Japanese knew they could not halt the Marine advance on the island. But they would make the Marines pay for every inch of land.

The Japanese commander, Lt. Gen. Tadamishi Kuribayashi, concentrated his troops in the island's central and northern sections. Here miles of interlocking caves, concrete blockhouses, and pillboxes were among the most indomitable defenses encountered by the Marines in the Pacific.

The northern section of the island comprised three notable points: these were the highest point on that portion of the island, Hill 382; an elevation nicknamed "Turkey Knob," reinforced with concrete and home to a large Japanese communications center; and the "Amphitheater," a southeastern extension of Hill 382. The Marines fought hard to drive the enemy from this high ground. It came, fittingly, to be known as the "Meat Grinder." In their drive on Airfield No. 2, the 3rd Marine Division would encounter the most heavily fortified portion of the island. They used frontal assault to gain every inch of ground. By nightfall on March 9, the 3rd Division had reached the island's northeastern beach, cutting the enemy defenses in two.

To the left of the 3rd Marine Division, the 5th Marine Division advanced along the west coast of Iwo Jima from the central airfield to the island's northern tip. Moving to seize and hold the eastern portion of the island, the 4th Marine Division encountered a small *banzai* attack from the few remaining Japanese sailors on Iwo. This attack resulted in the death of nearly seven hundred of the enemy; it also ended the centralized resistance of Japanese forces in the 4th division's sector. On March 10 the 4th Division joined forces with the 3rd and 5th at the coast. Operations entered the final phase the next day, as enemy resistance was no longer centrally directed. Individual pockets of resistance were taken one by one. As commanded, the Japanese had defended the homeland to the death. Of over twenty thousand defenders, only one thousand were taken prisoner.

After a March 26 *banzai* attack against troops and Air Corps personnel near the beaches, the island was declared secure. The U.S. Army's 147th Infantry Regiment assumed ground control of the island on April 4, relieving the largest body of Marines committed in combat in one operation during World War II. The thirty-six-day assault had resulted in more than 26,000 American casualties, including 6,800 dead. The Marines' efforts provided a vital link in the U.S. chain of bomber bases. By war's end, 2,400 B-29 bombers carrying 27,000 crewmen made unscheduled landings on the island. Twenty-seven Medals of Honor were awarded to Marines and sailors, many posthumously—more than were awarded for any other single operation during the war.

The comment of Adm. Chester W. Nimitz, who commanded the Navy at Iwo Jima, is fitting: "By their victory, the 3rd, 4th and 5th Marine Divisions and other units of the Fifth Amphibious Corps have made an accounting to their country which only history will be able to value fully. Among the American who served on Iwo Island, uncommon valor was a common virtue." But for the Japanese leadership, the capture of Iwo Jima meant the battle for Okinawa, and the invasion of Japan itself, was not far off.

Okinawa

As the center of the Ryukyu chain, Okinawa was considered to be—by the Japanese—one of their home islands. Certainly it was seen as a staging ground for any direct assault on Japan; after the fall of Iwo Jima to the Americans, it was the obvious next step.

Prior to 1872, Okinawa had supported a nominally independent kingdom, centered at Shuri Castle at the capital of Naha. Tributary to both the Chinese and the Japanese empires, Okinawa served as a means whereby Chinese goods could enter Japan, sealed off from the outside world since the seventeenth century. The Ryukyus had their own language and culture, and although very poor, they were very proud.

The opening of Japan to the outside world by Admiral Perry in 1854, and the eventual consolidation of feudal Japan into a modern centralized state by Emperor Meiji, doomed Okinawan independence. In 1872, the Japanese prevailed upon the ever-weaker Chinese court to cede their rights over the islands; seven years later, they abolished the Okinawan Monarchy and annexed the Ryukyus outright. From that time on, the Imperial authorities ordered the royal family to live in Tokyo, demanded the sole use of Japanese in schools, and in every way possible merged the complete cultural assimilation of the islands into Japan. Although they were treated as second-class citizens, in World War II the Okinawans were nevertheless expected to contribute fully—in manpower and money—to the war effort. All the while, the Americans came ever closer.

By April of 1945, although German resistance in Europe was in near collapse, Japan continued its defiant resistance to American advances across the Pacific. If the Allies took control of Okinawa, it would enable them to cut off Japan from its essential raw materials in the south. Were it necessary after all to invade Japan itself, Okinawa's harbors, anchorages, and airfields would be perfect to stage the ships, troops, aircraft, and supplies necessary for the amphibious assault. In addition, the island had several Japanese air bases and the only two substantial harbors between Formosa and Kyushu.

From the first days of World War II in the Pacific, Okinawa had been fortified as the location of air bases and as the front line in the defense of mainland Japan. Land and farms were forcibly expropriated throughout Okinawa and the Imperial Japanese Army began the construction of air bases.

The invasion began at last on April 1, 1945. Over sixty thousand troops (two Marine and two Army divisions) landed with little opposition. That day saw the heaviest concentration of naval gunfire ever expended in support of an amphibious landing. At 8:30 a.m. that day, the 7th and 96th Infantry Divisions of the XXIV Corps and the 1st and 6th Marine Divisions of the III Amphibious Corps crossed the Hagushi beaches, with sixteen thousand troops landing unopposed in the first hour. By nightfall, more than sixty thousand were ashore.

As yet, there was no sight of the one hundred thousand troops of the Japanese garrison. General Ushijima, commander of the Japanese 32nd Army, chose not to defend the beaches. This was part of Ushijima's strategy to avoid casualties in a senseless defense of the beach against overwhelming Allied firepower. Instead, his men manned a system of defense in depth, particularly in the southern portion of the island. This permitted the Japanese to fight a protracted battle that would heavily damage, if not annihilate, the attacking amphibious forces and the fleet alike. The Japanese dug into caves and tunnels on the high ground away from the beaches in an attempt to cancel out the Allies' superior sea and air power.

The battle proceeded in four phases: first, the advance to the eastern coast (April 1 to 4); second, the clearing of the northern part of the island (April 5 to 18); third, the occupation of the outlying islands (April 10 to June 26); and fourth, the main battle against the dug-in elements of the 32nd Army that began on April 6 and did not end until June 21. The first three phases encountered slight opposition, but the final phase proved extremely difficult because the Japanese were well entrenched and, as Ushijima had planned, American naval gunfire support was ineffective.

By April 19, Marines and soldiers of the U.S. 10th Army under Army Lieutenant General Simon B. Buckner were fighting fiercely along the fortified outer ring of the Shuri Line. The Shuri defenses were formidable. Deeply dug into the limestone cliffs, they boasted mutually supporting positions as well as a wealth of artillery of various calibers. As the action dragged on, American casualties mounted. This delay in occupying the island annoyed the American naval commanders greatly since the fleet of almost sixteen hundred ships was exposed to heavy enemy air attacks. The most damage from the Japanese attacks came from the kamikazes.

Assaulting points on the Shuri Line such as Sugar Loaf, Chocolate Drop, Conical Hill, Strawberry Hill, and Sugar Hill, casualties among both soldiers and Marines mounted. By the end of May, the monsoon rains arrived. These turned the slopes and roads where the battle raged into a morass. The attackers were mired in mud, while the evacuation of the wounded was slowed down by the flooding of roads. Troops lived in fields sodden by rain, while unburied Japanese corpses decayed into a disgusting mix of mud and flesh.

Nevertheless, the unrelenting pressure on the Shuri Line forced General Ushijima into a withdrawal southward to his final defensive positions on the Kiyamu Peninsula. The Japanese departed on the night of May 23 but left rear guards behind to slow the American advance. Those wounded Japanese who were unable to travel were given lethal injections of morphine or left behind to die. By the first week of June, the Americans had captured only 465 enemy troops—they had killed 62,548. Two more weeks of hard fighting (during which time Lt. Gen. Buckner was killed by artillery fire on June 18), and an additional two weeks of "mopping up" action (featuring the use of explosives and flamethrowers against pockets of resistance) would have to be undertaken before the battle would finally end. This last period between June 23 and 29 brought an additional 9,000 enemy dead and 3,800 captured. Refusing to surrender, many Japanese held grenades against their stomachs. General Ushijima himself committed hara-kiri on June 16, convinced that he done his duty in service to the emperor.

At last, the document that ended the Battle of Okinawa was signed at the present-day Kadena Air Base on September 7, 1945. Long before that, army engineers and construction battalions began transforming the island into a major base for the projected invasion of the Japanese home islands.

Okinawa was the largest amphibious invasion of the Pacific campaign and the last major campaign of the Pacific War. More ships were used, more troops put ashore, more supplies transported, more bombs dropped, more naval guns fired against shore targets than any other operation in the Pacific. More people died during the Battle of Okinawa than all those killed during the atomic bombings of Hiroshima and Nagasaki. Casualties totaled more than 38,000 Americans wounded and 12,000 killed or missing, more than 107,000 Japanese and Okinawan conscripts killed, and perhaps 100,000 Okinawan civilians who perished in the battle. Total American casualties in the operation numbered over 12,000 killed [including nearly 5,000 Navy dead and almost 8,000 Marine and Army dead] and 36,000 wounded. Somewhere between one-tenth and one-fourth of the civilian population perished, although some estimate that the battle of Okinawa killed almost a third of the civilian population.

KOREAN WAR

INCHON

On June 25, 1950, the North Koreans invaded the South. Striking in overwhelming force, without warning, they crushed the unprepared Republic of

Korea (ROK) army. The NK were only halted by the entry of the United States into the conflict, who were quickly supported by the United Nations.

At first, the outcome was uncertain. Although the NK had virtually annihilated the ROK forces, the southerners had resisted desperately. As a result, the NK suffered tremendous losses in men and materiel. When the NK first fought American troops, they paused for a few weeks to regroup. This gave the United States and the UN time to build up their forces. They halted the North Koreans completely in the battle of the Pusan Perimeter.

On September 15, 1950, Joint Task Force Seven (comprising more than 320 warships including four aircraft carriers) carried the nearly 70,000-man strong force of X Corps into Inchon harbor. Preceded by heavy naval bombardment and air support, elements of the 1st Marine Division led by the 5th Marines were landed one hundred miles behind the North Korean lines. These Marines led the Inchon invasion with a dawn assault on Green Beach, at Wolmi-do Island, killing over 200 enemy troops and capturing 136 more. The Americans suffered only 17 casualties themselves. In the afternoon, after the tides had gone out and in, the rest of the 5th Marines took Red Beach. The enemy was now fully alert, and the 5th lost 8 killed and 28 wounded in besting the NK. At the same time, the 1st Marine Regiment assaulted Blue Beach, suffering few casualties. Spearheading the assault were LCVPs, carrying 22 men apiece. These swarmed up the sea walls over assault ladders. But between the morning and afternoon landings, with the tides out, the Marines on Wolmi-do were surrounded by a sea of mud.

By evening of September 18, the Marines had arrived at Kimpo air field, six miles from Inchon. They captured the 6,000-foot runway the next day.

While displaying great valor, the Marines had fewer than 300 casualties and less than 30 killed in action. In all, the assault seized a major seaport, eliminated hundreds of enemy soldiers, destroyed 12 of their T34 tanks, and captured a major airport. The 1st Marine Division was positioned to cut off the retreat of 70,000 North Koreans in the south. They had taken Seoul by September 25. The invasion had suddenly positioned the Marines across the main NK lines of supply, and retreat, far to the rear of their attacking armies. Within two weeks, the bulk of the North Korean army was largely destroyed. The way to the Yalu and the reunification of Korea seemed inevitable.

CHOSIN RESERVOIR

The Korean War had initially gone very badly for the United States and their allies. But after holding the North Koreans at bay at the Pusan Perimeter, reinforced United Nations troops got through to push them back. A real breakthrough came when X Corps landed behind the North Korean lines at Inchon on September 15, 1950; within two weeks, the North Korean army was decimated. The way to the Yalu, and total destruction of North Korea's military power, seemed assured. Given the incredible atrocities practiced by North Korean troops on South Korean civilians and troops, as well as on UN prisoners, revenge was sweet. There was even talk of carrying the war into China, and ending the year-old Communist control of the country. The United States, after all, had supported Chang Kai-shek's Nationalists in the Chinese civil war.

Fearful of this possibility, and keen on keeping North Korea as a buffer between her and the West, Red China warned that if UN forces crossed the thirty-eighth parallel, China would enter the war. As UN forces separated from one another in pursuit of the dissolving North Korean army (the Eighth Army attacked in the north and west, and X Corps in the east), the Red Chinese shifted men, weapons, and supplies into the central mountains, behind the advancing UN troops.

The Chinese Communist Forces began their attack on October 25, demolishing the ROK 6th Division in an action lasting ten days. They then drove back the American 1st Cavalry Division with the ROK units. In the east, the 7th Marines managed to relieve the battered ROK units at the Sudong Gorge, thirty miles below Chosin. The 7th killed around fifteen hundred Chinese and destroyed the fighting capability of the CCF 124th division in a brutal three-day battle. Gen. O.P. Smith, commanding the 1st Marine Division, knew that despite the success against the 124th, it was only one division in the CCF 42nd Army. General Smith wondered very much where the other two divisions might be.

On November 27, the 8th Army was ordered to move toward the Yalu River, in hopes of "ending the war by Christmas." Heedlessly, they pressed forward, extending their supply lines and ignoring their flanks. Meanwhile, in the east, X Corps had about 100,000 men: the 1st Marine Division (22,000), and the Army's 7th Division, along with the under-strength 3rd Infantry Division in reserve at Wonsan; and the ROK I Corps, consisting of the 3rd and Capital Divisions, operating along the east coast.

On the night of November 25-26, the CCF struck against the overextended 8th Army. They hit the ROK II Corps, and by morning had torn an eighty-mile hole in the UN lines. The entire 8th Army right flank was exposed, particularly the 2nd Division. The Turkish Brigade was thrown in the gap, only to be destroyed. By the evening of November 27, the reserves of the 1st Cavalry and the British Brigade were thrown in to cover the withdrawal of the 8th Army.

On November 29, the 8th Army began the longest retreat in U.S. military history. Within six weeks, they had fallen back 275 miles, abandoning huge amounts of materiel and suffering almost ten thousand casualties on the way. The 8th Army retreated across the Chongchon River, then below the 38th parallel, paused momentarily at the frozen Imjin, and at last abandoned Seoul. The Chinese advance finally halted forty-five miles south of Seoul at Pyontaek.

Meanwhile, isolated in the east, the 1st Marine Division and the 31st Regimental Combat Team were battling tremendous odds. One of the spots the Marines had occupied was the small town of Yudam-ni. This place sat in a long, narrow north-south valley, bisected by the main supply road (MSR). The valley of Yudam-ni flows into five smaller valleys separated each from the next by a high, hilly ridge complex. North-northeast lies the Reservoir; to the south is Toktong pass, a bottleneck reached by a steep, narrow section of the one-lane MSR.

On the catastrophic day of November 27, four Marine rifle battalions and the three artillery battalions, about seven thousand men in all, were positioned at Yudam-ni. While preparing to link up with the 8th Army, most of the 5th and 7th Marine regiments had come together. There were also elements of divisional headquarters fourteen miles back at Hagaru-ri. Thus, all the main fighting elements of the 1st Marine Division were within thirty-five miles of each other along the lonely, single track MSR. In addition, General Smith had ordered the building of an airfield at Hagaru-ri, as well as ammunition and supply dumps.

The 5th and 7th Marines were unaware of the disaster that had overtaken the 8th Army. Their orders were to occupy the ridges surrounding Yu Dam Ni and then attack toward Kanggye in the heart of north central Korea. This would permit them to link up with the 8th Army—had the 8th been where it was supposed to be.

Instead, the disaster that befell the 8th Army had the effect of leaving the two Marine regiments surrounded (unknown to them) by three CCF divisions (about thirty thousand men). Worse still, seven more CCF divisions were moving behind them; the entire CCF 9th Army Group was moving to cut the MSR in sections and to cut the 1st Marine Division in two.

By the next day, all twenty-five miles of MSR between Yudam-ni, Hagaru-ri, and Koto-ri had been enfiladed by the CCF. The Marines in the towns were facing continuous attacks by overwhelming numbers of enemy troops. Having been left high and dry by the 8th Army's retreat, they were none too happy. The 1st Marines were holding Koto-ri to keep the road open back to the coast. A reporter with the regiment asked its commanding officer, then Col. Lewis B. (Chesty) Puller: "Colonel, you've got Chinese to your front, to your rear, to your left and to your right. What are you going to do now?" Puller's reported reply was: "The bastards aren't going to get away this time!" Actually, that reply was made up by the reporter to protect the colonel. Chesty's actual reply was: "Damn sight better than the U.S. Army. At least I know they'll be there in the morning!"

On November 30, X Corps ordered the Marines to withdraw. So began a breakout and thirteen-day fighting retreat by about twenty thousand troops, spread out as they were over a narrow, mountainous, one-lane supply road. The Marines had to cover about seventy-eight miles to the Sea of Japan and Hungnam. From Yudam-ni to the Army's 3rd Infantry Division positions at Chinhung-ni, a distance of about thirty-five miles, the Marines battled continuously with ten Red Chinese divisions.

Although the 1st Marine Division benefited from artillery and air support, the Marines battled the Red Chinese hand to hand while cut off from the rear and with transportation at a dead stop. Despite the bitter cold and the round-the-clock assault, the Marines successfully defended against every attack. When the CCF cut the MSR, the Marines would counterattack—again, always successfully. With them, the Marines brought out their wounded, as well as most of their dead and equipment.

So battered were the Red Chinese that they were unable to follow the retreating Marines or harass the retreat from Hamhung-Hungnam. When the division finally got to Hungnam, the Navy was waiting. In all, 105,000 troops and 91,000 civilians were evacuated successfully. As a result of his skill and bravery during the operation, Chesty Puller earned an unprecedented fifth Navy Cross.

Chosin was a major defeat for the United States. The Marines were driven off the battlefield. Of the 25,000 Marines who faced the 120,000 Chinese at Chosin, 6,000 were killed, wounded, or captured; at least 6,000 others suffered frostbite. During their thirteen-day walking battle back, 1st Marine Division suffered 718 dead, 192 missing, and 3,508 wounded, plus their frostbitten casualties. But the Red Chinese paid a terrible price for their victory. They suffered 72,500 casualties—sixty percent of their 120,000-man army—to defeat 25,000 Marines.

VIETNAM CONFLICT

KHE SANH

During the buildup of the American presence in Vietnam following the Gulf of Tonkin incident in 1964, it soon became apparent that the arrival of men and supplies from North Vietnam in support of the Viet Cong was being made along the Ho Chi Minh Trail in eastern Laos. The Marine Corps had been assigned to interdict this route and so were sent to northernmost South Vietnam, alongside the DMZ, to do so. One particularly strategic point was the hamlet of Khe Sanh. In 1966, the 26th Marine Regiment was sent there to hold the spot, threaten the HCM Trail, and train the locals to defend themselves. The NVA and VC forces began to probe around Khe Sanh, engaging the Marines in firefights through the latter part of 1967. As 1968 commenced, the Marine Corps command in Vietnam (III MAF) strung out the 3rd Marine division along the eastern DMZ in stationary positions: this was the so-called McNamara Line. The North Vietnamese for their part were not idle. As they pressed the 3rd Marine Division in eastern Quang Tri Province, they isolated the 26th Marines. Cutting Route 9, the main east-west land artery, the NVA forced the Marines to rely entirely upon airborne supplies. It was a situation eerily (and unpleasantly) reminiscent of Dienbienphu, the battle in northern Vietnam where the French had likewise, in 1953–1954, been under siege and dependent on air supplies. The loss of that battle had convinced the French to withdraw from the country.

At first, General Westmoreland had planned to mount deep penetration operations into enemy base areas in the Do Xa and A Shau areas in I Corps. Abandoning this idea, he decided upon reinforcing Marine forces in the north with the 1st Air Cavalry and 101st Airborne Divisions. Westmoreland believed that the enemy's major attack would come either across the DMZ or at Khe Sanh; he supposed that the NVA would mount diversionary attacks throughout South Vietnam.

III MAF shifted Marine forces around in the north in mid-January, sending another battalion to reinforce the garrison at Khe Sanh among other moves.

Six thousand U.S. Marines and ARVN (Army of the Republic of Vietnam) forces were now holed up at Khe Sanh, surrounded by an estimated 40,000 NVA troops. On January 21, 1968, the Communists began shelling Khe Sanh. At the same time, they launched the Tet Offensive, which saw attacks on cities and roads throughout South Vietnam—even striking within Saigon. But Khe Sanh remained besieged until early April.

The NVA probed the Khe Sanh perimeter, among other things overrunning the Special Forces at Lang Vei; this was coupled with maintaining large military units around the base. But they never launched a full-fledged ground assault against Khe Sanh. All the while the Tet Offensive raged, however, the

Communists kept up the pressure on the embattled outpost. The NVA were defeated in the end throughout Vietnam, most spectacularly at Hue, but the siege wore on in the North. As the enemy offensive ended, MACV planned a breakout from Khe Sanh. Although the North Vietnamese troops did not follow up on their Lang Vei attack, they kept probing the hill outposts and perimeter. Marine and Air Force transport and helicopter pilots kept the base supplied using extremely innovative tactics. At last, on April 14, the 1st Cavalry Division, reinforced by a Marine regiment, relieved the base: the seventy-seven-day siege of Khe Sanh was over. About 37 percent of the North Vietnamese Regulars were dead, and the Marines had suffered a staggering casualty rate of nearly 50 percent. Neither side could claim victory at Khe Sanh, really. Though the Americans had held their ground, they abandoned the base a few months later, calling it "strategically unimportant." When the U.S. forces finally pulled out of Khe Sanh, everything that could be used by the Viet Cong was blown up, bombed from the air, or buried. Rumor has it that the Vietnamese are planning to rebuild Khe Sanh combat base as a tourist attraction.

Nevertheless, if as many claim, the action at Khe Sanh was a pointless act in a pointless war, the fact remains that once again the USMC proved its determination to get the job done regardless of the circumstances. Whatever the failures or otherwise on the part of MACV and on that of the political leadership at home, once again the individual Marine, whether on the ground or in the air, had proven his grit and resourcefulness. So it proved with the Marines throughout the Vietnam War. This is why the Corps continues to take pride in its record during that conflict. At the Vietnam War

Memorial (the Wall) in Washington, D.C., there is a flag pole; at its base are the seals of all the services: Army, Navy, Marines, Air Force, and Coast Guard. Every day, throughout the year, a detachment from Marine Barracks, Eighth & I, marches to the flag and polishes the Marine Corps emblem. The other services have never touched theirs. There is, perhaps, a lesson here.

THE SIX-DAY WAR

USS *LIBERTY*

The summer of 1967 saw the Six-Day War, an event that momentarily distracted the attention of the population of the United States from Vietnam and San Francisco's "Summer of Love." In the Eastern Mediterranean, the USS *Liberty*, a small U.S. Navy surveillance ship, was plying the waters and tracking Soviet and Arab radio transmissions. Aboard were three Marine translators—two spoke Arabic, while the third, Staff Sgt. Bryce Lockwood, was a Russian speaker. In the tension-filled atmosphere of the conflict taking place on land, the Israeli government was extremely sensitive. On June 8, the Israeli Navy undertook more than six hours of intense low-level surveillance, carefully tracking the ship.

For reasons that remain a mystery, the Israelis attacked the ship, using both aircraft and motor launches. One Israeli pilot, when he realized the nationality of the ship, disobeyed orders and returned to base, where he was arrested on his arrival. The action lasted over two hours; the attackers jammed the ship's distress signals, and it was only when a mayday message made it through and was acknowledged by the carrier USS *Saratoga* that the Israeli attack ceased.

Two of the Marines aboard were killed during the initial attack. Sgt. Lockwood, who was in the hold when the attack commenced, found himself swimming in the water rushing through the holes created by the explosion of a torpedo within the ship. About twenty-five nearby sailors were killed but Lockwood survived. Feeling flesh and movement underfoot, he ducked underwater to find a sailor trapped by a piece of what had been the third deck. He freed the man, pushed him toward the hatch, and then started searching for other survivors. Lockwood rescued a number of men before being forced out of the hold himself. He had had a nasty scare when the manhole cover was closed on him for a time, but managed to attract attention by yelling and a couple of sailors kept the hatch open while he looked for survivors. Satisfied that there weren't any more, he left the hold.

In the meantime, the Israelis dispatched four attack helicopters, fully loaded with Israeli combat troops armed with automatic weapons. But when the USS *Saratoga* finally heard and acknowledged the *Liberty*'s mayday distress signal, the helicopters were recalled, as were the planes and motor torpedo boats.

When the 6th Fleet received the *Liberty*'s call at last, four Phantom F-4 fighters were scrambled to come to the ship's rescue and blast the attackers. As is standard practice, the Pentagon was immediately informed. In response, over a high-command Pentagon circuit manned by a Navy warrant officer, Secretary of Defense Robert S. McNamara himself ordered: "Tell Sixth Fleet to get those aircraft back immediately, and give me a status report." Minutes later, the Chief of Naval operations, Adm. David L. McDonald, was patched through to the Sixth Fleet flagship. He ordered: "You get those f—ing airplanes back on deck, and you get them back now!" The four were duly recalled.

Liberty was left to lick her wounds. Her losses were grievous: 34 Americans killed and 171 wounded; when the smoke cleared there were over 821 rocket, cannon, and machine-gun holes in the ship. But while much about the affair remains mysterious, what is clear is the gallantry of the ship's company. The commanding officer, Capt. William Loren McGonagle, received the Congressional Medal of Honor "for conspicuous gallantry and intrepidity at the risk of his life above and beyond the call of duty during the attack," although, to avoid embarrassing the attackers, Captain McGonagle's Medal of Honor was presented in a quiet ceremony at the Washington Navy Yard instead of in the White House by the President.

Among other decorations quietly awarded, Sgt. Lockwood received the Silver Star. His citation reads, in part: ". . . despite severe burns, the rapid rise of water, heavy smoke and complete darkness, was instrumental in the rescue of personnel from the flooded compartments, thus averting even further loss of life. Without regard for his personal safety or his injuries, he assisted in the rescue until ordered to leave. His calm, rational thinking and actions evidenced a high degree of professional competence and moral fibre." Certainly, Bryce Lockwood was a good example of the USMC ideal of every Marine, regardless of how technical or specialized his job might be, being capable of acting as a combat rifleman at a moment's notice.

PERSIAN GULF WAR

OPERATION DESERT SHIELD AND DESERT STORM

Saddam Hussein had been considered something of an American ally during his decade-long war with Iran. As a result, his invasion of Kuwait came as a surprise to the first Bush administration. On July 25, 1990, Hussein summoned the American ambassador to Baghdad, April Glaspie, to his office. This would be the last high-level contact between the two governments prior to the Iraqi invasion of Kuwait. At that time, in response to Hussein's complaints about Kuwait, Ambassador Glaspie replied: "I think I understand this. I have lived here for years. I admire your extraordinary efforts to rebuild your country. I know you need funds. We understand that and our opinion is that you should have the opportunity to rebuild your country. But we have no opinion on the Arab-Arab conflicts, like your border disagreement with Kuwait." Shortly after making this comment, the ambassador went on vacation. Reinforcing Saddam's notion that the United States was not concerned about any intention he might have toward Kuwait, was the testimony given six days later by John Kelly, Assistant Secretary of State for Near Eastern affairs. Just two days before the invasion, he testified to Congress that the "United States has no commitment to defend Kuwait and the U.S. has no intention of defending Kuwait if it is attacked by Iraq."

Thinking he had a green light, on August 2, 1990, Hussein launched an invasion of Kuwait with two armored divisions, one division of mechanized infantry and a special forces division, spearheaded by the elite Republican

Guard. The special forces division utilized helicopters and boats to attack Kuwait City itself.

The initial response of CENTCOM—which was code-named "Desert Shield"—was to send the XVIII Airborne Corps to Saudi Arabia to support Saudi forces, should Iraqi troops advance into the oil field region along the Saudi east coast (the first units deployed were the 3/502 Infantry, 2nd Brigade, 101st Airborne Division, and 4/325 Infantry, 2nd Brigade, 82nd Airborne Division). In time, the entire XVIII Airborne Corps would be deployed, comprising the 101st Airborne Division, the 82nd Airborne Division, the 24th Mechanized Infantry Division, the 1st Armored Cavalry Division, and the 3rd Armored Cavalry Regiment. Along with these American units, the British sent their 7th Armoured Brigade from Germany, while the French deployed their heavily reinforced 6th Light Armored Division. These forces were joined by Kuwaiti and Saudi units, and eventually by troops from several other nations, most notably Egypt and Syria.

The 7th Marine Expeditionary Brigade (MEB), commanded by Maj. Gen. John I. Hopkins, began flying into Saudi Arabia on August 14. At the same time, three ships of Maritime Preposition Squadron (MPS) 2 sailed toward the Gulf with the unit's heavy weapons, vehicles, and supplies. Within two weeks, 15,248 Marines deployed in the desert north of the Saudi port of Al Jubayl and began their education in 110-degree heat and fine sand that covered their bodies and fouled their weapons and equipment. According to Lt. Gen. Walter E. Boomer, commanding general of the First Marine Expeditionary Force (MEF), who would lead most of the U.S. Marines in the Gulf War, "The quick arrival of the 7th MEB and the MPS squadron must have put Saddam Hussein on notice that our president was serious about defending Saudi Arabia."

More and more Marines arrived from their bases in California, Hawaii, and Okinawa, and Hopkins's brigade was integrated into Gen. Myatt's First Division. This marked the first time a full Marine division would deploy overseas since Vietnam. At the same time, helicopter, fighter, and attack squadrons of the 3rd Marine Aircraft Wing, under Maj. Gen. Royal Moore, flew from air stations in California and Arizona to occupy airfields prepared by Marine engineers and Navy Seabees.

Myatt organized his division into five task forces with different capabilities and goals. The first of these was Task Force Shepherd, using its nimble eight-wheeled light armored vehicles (LAVs) for screening and scouting. Myatt then formed two assault units, Task Force Ripper, commanded by Col. Carlton W. Fulford, and Task Force Papa Bear, led by Col. Richard W. Hodory. Expecting a fast-moving battle in the desert, these units were equipped more like Army-mechanized brigades than the usual Marine light infantry regiments. Each assault force was made up of two infantry battalions plus combat engineer and reconnaissance units. For the mobility essential in desert warfare, each had two companies of thinly armored, tracked assault amphibious vehicles. Ripper also had two companies of M-60 main battle tanks, and Papa Bear had one. Task Forces Taro and Grizzly were more typical Marine units, with two battalions of infantry but no tanks or armored vehicles. As the Marines of the 1st MEF were moving into defensive positions in the desert, fifteen thousand of their comrades were sailing for the Gulf aboard ships.

The allies began shifting their focus from the defense of Saudi Arabia to attacking the Iraqi army in Kuwait. General Boomer recalls that he and his commanders "began to think and talk among ourselves about offensive ops as early as October." By November, President George H.W. Bush was doing the same with his advisers. He ordered Gen. Norman Schwarzkopf, Commander-in-Chief, Central Command (CENTCOM), to begin planning for an offensive to liberate Kuwait. At Schwarzkopf's request, Bush authorized additional deployments that nearly doubled the U.S. troops in the Gulf. Boomer's 1st MEF was strengthened by the 2nd Marine Division and the 2nd Marine Aircraft Wing from bases in North and South Carolina.

General Schwarzkopf developed a plan to use the XVIII Airborne Corps to attack Kuwait, consisting of a frontal assault by Army and Marine forces, with a flanking maneuver by the 1st Armored Cavalry Division along the Wadi Al-Batin. To carry out this plan, several more Army divisions were deployed.

Prior to launching any ground assault on Iraqi forces, an air campaign to weaken Iraqi forces in the field and to destroy command and control capabilities was tailored for the situation by Air Force planners. This was Operation Instant Thunder. Though it would not have the effect of neutralizing the Iraqis completely, as the Air Force hoped, it was instrumental in severely weakening Saddam's forces.

Hussein hoped that any American attack would be delayed by his border fortifications long enough for the American public to demand peace. But as Instant Thunder progressed, Hussein became fearful that the Army would not attack, and that the Allies would simply bomb his forces into submission. He thereupon ordered an attack by his own army. Fearful of the American air superiority, however, most of Saddam's generals refused. Only the Iraqi III corps, commanded by Lt. Gen. Salah Abud Mahmud, obeyed, launching an attack on the Saudi coastal city of Ras al-Khafji (already evacuated of civilians). This attack consisted of a direct assault down the coast road, supported by an amphibious assault to cut the coast road south of Khafji, and another assault inland to cover the right flank of the frontal assault. Another diversionary attack was made farther inland.

The diversionary attack was stopped by U.S. Marines, while the inland flanking attack was stopped by the only Qatari unit in the war, a tank battalion; the amphibious assault ran into the attack helicopters of the British Royal Navy and never made it to shore. The frontal assault brushed a small Saudi border detachment aside and entered the undefended Khafji.

So swift was this last attack, however, that the enemy was unaware of two Marine Corps artillery spotting teams remaining in Khafji after the Iraqi occupation. On January 29, 1991, three Iraqi battalions crossed the border with tanks and troops on armored personnel carriers, headed for the evacuated town. The Iraqis used the 5th Mechanized Infantry Division, one of their better and larger regular divisions holding the Kuwait-Saudi border. Three brigade-sized columns moved on a sixty-mile front between the coast and the "elbow," the bend in the border. The plan called for the two columns to the west to penetrate the border and push east, toward the coast, where it would link up with the third column at Khafji. Further brigades that were assigned to support the attack started twelve to twenty-four hours late. They never participated in the fighting.

The westernmost tank brigade ran into the light armored infantry battalion of the 1st Marine Division fifty to sixty miles from the coast. There was a running gun battle at the border, with Marine and Air Force planes hitting the tanks. The Marine vehicles, not designed to fight tanks, found that their night sights made it possible for them to outrange and destroy the Iraqis that survived the air strikes. It was during this fighting near Umm Hujul that an A-10 destroyed one of the LAVs with a Maverick missile, mistaking them for Iraqis. Seven Marines were killed. A second LAV was destroyed by an Iraqi tank, killing another four. The center brigade tried to cross near the Wafra oilfield. As luck would have it, it engaged the 2nd Marine Division's light armored infantry battalion. Stalled by the Marines, it retreated.

The third brigade attacked Khafji itself, which was held by the Saudis and Qataris with the Marines in support. Lead elements consisting of five T-55s with 150 infantry accompanying them moved in, the tanks positioning themselves on the outskirts while the infantry occupied the buildings. A twelve-man Marine reconnaissance force in the town, led by Corp. Jeff Brown, was cut off. At one point, Iraqi soldiers searched the main floor of a building where Brown and his team were hiding on the floor above. The Iraqis then used a ruse to bring their tanks within close range of the Coalition units. Shortly before noon on Tuesday, the Saudis saw a line of tanks approaching, as many as eighty vehicles, with their turrets facing to the rear, the signal they were surrendering. Accompanying infantry had their hands in the air and were not visibly armed. As the Saudis and Qataris held their fire, the Iraqis came closer, then swung their barrels around and opened up on them, the infantry pulling hidden guns from their boots. The Marines were displeased. "They have engaged the Saudis in combat," declared Marine Maj. Craig Huddleston over the radio net, "and we're going to kill them." The American howitzers opened up, followed by fire from multiple rocket launchers and supporting Cobra helicopters flying overhead.

The allied response to the thrust was quite effective. Saudi and Qatari troops counterattacked the following day, backed by U.S. Marine artillery, Harrier jets, and Cobra helicopter gunships. "The Saudi tripwire alerted the Marines who, with their allies, took on the task of containing and destroying the invaders," Col. David Hackworth wrote. "Gunships and Harrier jets backed up by rapid-firing Marine artillery rolled in and did their job, enabling the Saudis and Qataris to move in for the final mop-up." Corporal Brown and his team, stuck inside the town, called in continuous air and artillery strikes.

The counterattack began on January 31. Saudi and Qatari armor pushed into the town. A Marine observer who watched the battle called the exchange of fire "hellacious." The Qataris and the 7th and 8th Battalions of the Saudi Arabian National Guard 8th Brigade, brought the Iraqis under fire from M-60 tanks, the 90-mm guns of their Cadillac-Gage V-150s, 84-mm Carl Gustav recoilless guns, and anti-tank-guided missiles. The town was declared secure at 6:30 P.M. on February 1.

In one incident, a Marine unit was attacked by two allied planes that dropped cluster bombs within a few hundred yards of its position but caused no injuries. All twelve Marines of the two patrols that were in the town when it was attacked survived. Two soldiers were missing near Khafji—one male, one female. Baghdad said they were POWs.

A few days later, a Marine artillery battalion, three Saudi MLRS battalions, and the battleship USS *Missouri* pounded a concentration of Iraqi tanks and artillery for three hours, then moved back out of range. Forty-five minutes later, a few Iraqi rounds were fired in response, the nearest landing about a mile away from the allied troops. The U.S. Marines soon realized that the Iraqis were uncoordinated and vulnerable to tactical air attack. The Marines completely redesigned their attack plan after this action, changing from two divisions leap-frogging each other, to two divisions abreast, on the assumption that they would penetrate the fortified border quicker than previously expected.

The assault on Kuwait found Marine and Arab units on the right flank, tasked with frontally assaulting the Iraqi fortifications along the Saudi-Kuwaiti border. Their twofold object was to (1) entice the Republican Guard forces forward and into the path of VII Corps, and (2) to penetrate the fortifications and move on Kuwait City. For political reasons, the Marines were not to enter the city until Kuwaiti units preceded them. The Marines were supported by the 1st ("Tiger") Brigade, 2nd Armored Division, from the U.S. Army, since the Marine Corps Sherman tanks could not take on the Iraqi T-72 tanks evenly, whereas the Army M1-A1 Abrams tanks could.

Finally, the Marine expeditionary forces that were afloat would act as a decoy, pinning down large Iraqi forces on the Kuwaiti coast, in anticipation of an amphibious assault. In fact, there was never any real consideration of an amphibious assault on the heavily defended urban coastline, which would expose the Marines to heavy casualties without good reason. However, the option of an amphibious assault on Basra, up the Shat al-Arab, was kept open until well after ground fighting began. Such an assault would have put a major force deep in the Iraqi rear area, but proved ultimately to be unnecessary.

As it turned out, the invasion moved much faster than planned. The Marine and Arab forces were supposed to be hung up in the Iraqi fortifications for eighteen to twenty-four hours and maybe longer. This would entice the Republican Guard out into the open, giving VII Corps a straight shot at them. But the Marines blew through the Iraqi fortifications and accomplished in a few hours what was expected to take days. Instead of being lured into the range of VII Corps, Iraqi units fled backward.

As twilight approached on February 23, 1991, U.S. Marine Col. James A. Fulks was getting desperate. Although the ground campaign of Operation Desert Storm would not begin for more than twelve hours, Fulks had nearly twenty-seven hundred U.S. Marines a dozen miles inside of Iraqi-occupied Kuwait, with orders to move that night through the first of the two thick minefields the Iraqi army had planted just to the north. After days of searching, however, his scouts still had not found a path through the mines. Now

Fulks was preparing a rapid and potentially dangerous effort to clear a way through the deadly obstacle belt.

Ten miles to the east, Corp. Michael Eroshevich hunkered down in a small, hastily dug hole on the edge of that same minefield, trying to stay unseen until night fell. The twenty-one-year-old marine was tired, cramped, cold, and rather nervous about his unit's exposed position.

Fulks's Marines, designated Task Force Grizzly, and Eroshevich's unit, Task Force Taro, commanded by Col. John H. Admire, marched into Kuwait two days earlier. Without tanks and with few heavy weapons, the 5,300 Marines were vulnerable to an attack by any of the five heavily armed Iraqi divisions waiting on the other side of the mines. Admire recalled that "We were essentially up there alone."

He and Fulks had orders from the First Marine Division commander, Maj. Gen. James M. "Mike" Myatt, to infiltrate through the first minefield before the start of the ground war. They would then march farther into Kuwait, shielding the breach of mines by Myatt's two powerful mechanized regiments the next morning. In the midst of the most technologically advanced conflict in history—the so-called Nintendo War—most of the Marines in the two task forces marched the twenty miles from the Saudi border to their blocking positions, carrying their gear on their backs or pulling it in crude handcarts.

According to Fulks, this infiltration "was part of our strategy in the division to be very aggressive." The idea was to mentally overwhelm the Iraqis, who had shown little ability to respond rapidly to changing conditions. The Task Force Grizzly commander, having conceived the infiltration plan months earlier while he was the division's ops officer, conceded that initially "it was not a very popular idea." But it was typical of the boldness that enabled two Marine divisions to punch through the Iraqi minefields on "G-day," February 24, starting the allied ground assault that ended with victory in one hundred hours. That attack was the culmination of the largest deployment of U.S. Marines in history.

Khafji had a major impact on the planning for the ground war. The Iraqis' poor coordination and lack of aggressiveness persuaded the Marine leadership that the attack into Kuwait would not be as difficult as they had feared. "At that particular point, there was a significant psychological change in all of us," Task Force Taro Commander Admire recalled. "We realized that if we hit the Iraqis hard and fast, they would back down. There was no fight in them." According to Admire, the successful counterattack by the previously untested Arab troops also emboldened their commanders to offer to make their own attack up the coast highway during the ground war, instead of following the Marine assault. That allowed Boomer to move the focus of his attack about eighty miles to the west, into the area of Kuwait known as the "elbow," and to alter his battle plan.

At first, Boomer planned to have Myatt's division clear paths through the minefields, followed by General Keys's more powerful 2nd Division to pass through their lines and lead the attack. But neither Boomer nor his commanders liked this. "Any passing of lines under combat conditions is a horribly complicated evolution. And the thought of a division-size passage—with troops and vehicles strung out for miles, vulnerable to artillery—really made me uneasy," the 1st MEF commander recalled. With more mine-clearing equipment provided by Israel and the Tiger Brigade available, Boomer accepted Keys's proposal for his division to make its own breach of the Iraqi barriers. Schwarzkopf, who had allowed Boomer great freedom in planning his attack, also approved the new plan.

The two Marine division commanders had devised different plans for breaching the minefields, albeit with similar goals. The 1st Division would use Task Forces Grizzly and Taro to protect the main assault forces—Ripper and Papa Bear—which would conduct their own breaches. The 2nd Division would rely on artillery and air cover to defend against counterattacks and assigned only one regiment—the 6th Marines—to make their breaches. Each of the regiment's three battalions would cut a single lane. The desire in both cases was to move through the minefields quickly. "We were concerned about speed, and building momentum going north, to get through those two obstacle belts, because the worst thing that could happen was to get trapped between them," Myatt said.

As they moved closer to the Kuwaiti border, most of the Marines left behind their tents and sleeping bags; the unexpectedly wet and frigid nights caused them to shudder terribly. The ground war was set to start on February 22, but Boomer asked for a delay in the hope of getting better weather to allow full use of Marine air support. The weather did not improve, and Schwarzkopf decided to attack despite the poor conditions. "We fought the ground campaign over the worst four flying days of the whole war," Moore, the Marine air commander, later complained. "General Schwarzkopf and every weather guy in Southwest Asia promised seventy-two hours of good weather, but we probably didn't get seventy-two minutes."

Corp. David Jackson, a radio operator with Grizzly, recalled that the task force's Marines felt "a lot of excitement and some confusion" but "not a lot of fear" about their mission: "People asked me if I was afraid. The honest answer was 'no.' Our battalion had trained so hard. . . . By the time we got to the Gulf, we really were family."

Meanwhile, Corporal Eroshevich remembered a more fatalistic reaction among the Marines of Task Force Taro. "We all looked at each other and said, 'Well, it was nice knowing you,' " he recalled. "This was pretty much a Nintendo war. But we were going to walk thirty miles and go through a minefield on hands and knees." And Taro's commander, Admire, knew his unit faced a daunting task: "It would be clandestine, with no armor, no tractors, or artillery. We were literally going to walk across that minefield."

The 1st Division began its move into Kuwait on February 18. Myatt sent reconnaissance teams across the border to look for paths through the first minefield for Taro and Grizzly. Locating a clear route in Taro's sector, the Scouts could not find one for Grizzly. Nevertheless, Fulks marched Grizzly into Kuwait shortly after midnight on the twenty-second, stopping most of the regiment just south of the mines. There they could see the minefield but not be observed by anyone on the other side of the barriers. The Marines dug two-man fighting holes and used slight depressions in the desert and camouflage nets to mask their vehicles. Meanwhile, Fulks's scouts resumed the search for an opening through the mines.

After daylight, the Iraqis fired poorly aimed artillery at the Marines.

Return fire from their 155-mm howitzers, however, quickly silenced the enemy guns. Iraqi tanks then approached Grizzly's position, and Fulks had to withdraw, covering his movement with artillery and air attacks.

Taro began its long walk into enemy-held territory that evening. Both task forces had a number of vehicles loaded with radios or carrying TOW (tube launched, optically tracked, wire guided) missiles or other heavy weapons. Some of the Marines pulled four-wheel handcarts loaded with equipment. Most of them marched into Kuwait, carrying heavy loads of their personal gear and extra ammunition.

Eroshevich called the trek "the most grueling physical experience of my life. Each of us carried over one hundred pounds of equipment and our ammo for thirty kilometers." The fire team leader's load consisted of his own gear, including a chemical protective suit and gas mask, his M-16 rifle, and three bandoliers of ammunition. In addition, Eroshevich carried a vest with ten 40-mm grenades for his M-203 gunner, a two-hundred-round magazine for his team's M-249 squad automatic weapon (SAW), and two 60-mm mortar rounds. Some men also carried night vision goggles, telephones, and extra barrels for the machine guns. "The guys I really felt sorry for were the Dragon [anti-tank rocket] gunners and the machine gunners," Eroshevich said. (Each Dragon weighed fifty pounds, while an SAW weighed fifteen and an M-60 light machine gun twenty-six.) When the Marines started to march from the border, Eroshevich recalled that "we had to help each other stand up. I thought: 'There's no way in hell I'm going to make this.' "

The unusually cold, damp weather may have prevented the heavily burdened Marines from overheating during the strenuous march. But when they stopped, the cold cut through their sweaty clothes and chilled them. The only casualty of the potentially dangerous movement was a young Marine killed by an accidental hand-grenade blast. By midnight, Taro had reached the edge of the minefield and then hurried to get into defensive cover before daylight. Most of the Marines then dug fighting holes into which they squeezed, their knees against their chests. They remained in the tight foxholes all day.

Preparing for the next night, Admire had his combat engineers and some infantrymen begin marking the task force's path through the minefield. Having no mine-detection equipment, they advanced on their knees, probing into the sand with bayonets and listening for the clink of metal on metal. Mines would be marked with glowing chemical light sticks.

Task Force Grizzly, meanwhile, still sought a way through the mines. When allied aircraft started bombing Iraqi positions just across the barrier, Fulks withdrew his men to avoid the risk of friendly-fire casualties. With only hours left before the ground war was scheduled to start, Fulks was getting desperate about being able to complete his mission. As sporadic Iraqi artillery fire landed nearby, the colonel called his battalion commanders together to plan a rapid breach, using explosives to clear a path through the mines. Before he had to launch that effort, however, Fulks received a radio message that his scouts could see Iraqi defectors walking through the minefield with their hands over their heads. Thinking quickly, Fulks told the recon teams to run down and give the surrendering Iraqis chemical lights to mark the lane through the mines. Three Marines followed the defectors' path and attacked a bunker, killing three Iraqi soldiers and capturing others. At last, Grizzly had a way to get to its blocking position.

But then the two task forces' leaders received an unsettling radio call from Myatt, who relayed word from Boomer that President Bush wanted to give Soviet President Mikhail Gorbachev more time to attempt to persuade Saddam to withdraw his army from Kuwait. This meant Taro and Grizzly were not to push any farther into Kuwait until the deadline passed, about midnight. The two commanders protested that the delay would not give them time to reach their assigned positions before the division started its attack. Fulks, moreover, was reluctant to pull back the company of Marines he already had on the other side of the mines, guarding the lane. "Boss, you can't do this to me," he told Myatt. After a brief delay, Myatt called back to tell him that Boomer had given permission to put a reconnaissance team across, but not to do anything irreversible. Fulks said he quickly ordered an entire battalion through the mines, as "a recon in force." Given the same warning, Admire said he told Myatt: "I will do nothing irreversible. But I can't guarantee that the Iraqis won't."

Meanwhile, the two U.S. Marine divisions moved toward the border, reaching their assault positions on February 23. That night, Boomer sent a message telling his Marines that they would attack into Kuwait the next day, "not to conquer, but to drive out the invaders and to restore the country to its citizens. . . . We will succeed in our mission because we are well trained and well equipped; because we are U.S. Marines, sailors, soldiers and airmen, and because our cause is just. . . . May the spirit of your Marine forefathers ride with you and may God give you the strength to accomplish your mission. Semper Fi."

As night fell on the twenty-third, the Marines and navy corpsmen in Taro and Grizzly climbed out of their holes, pulled on chemical protective suits, and checked their gas masks and weapons. Suddenly an explosion stunned the Marines of Task Force Taro and destroyed their artillery fire-direction radar van, killing one Marine and wounding another. A U.S. HARM anti-radar missile had caused the explosion, another of the friendly-fire incidents that were to blame for nearly half of the Marines' casualties thus far.

Shortly before midnight, Corporal Eroshevich and the rest of Taro shouldered their heavy loads and started following what they hoped was a clear path through the minefield, a narrow route outlined by chemical lights. Having passed the obstacles, the Marines formed a wedge. Moving north, they reached their blocking position about six miles beyond the minefield, well before dawn. The cold, misty, rainy weather was miserable but "almost ideal for an infiltration," Admire said. Reducing visibility, it limited the chances that the Iraqis would spot them. The Taro commander hoped for better weather the next morning, when Marine air cover might be needed, should Iraqi tanks attack.

While Taro had reached its position without major incident, Task Force Grizzly's troubles continued. First, the march through the mines was delayed as the lead elements dealt with more Iraqi defectors. Corporal Jackson, driving a communications vehicle carrying two of his battalion's staff officers, had followed a barely visible light on the vehicle ahead of his. "My biggest worry was the guys off to the side on foot," he recalled of the slow advance. "I thought about them, hoped they didn't step on anything" (meaning mines).

Grizzly passed through the first minefield belt without incident. But about eight hundred yards farther, they ran into an unexpected belt of anti-personnel mines. As a team of engineers led by Staff Sgt. Charles Restifo crawled through the field probing for mines with bayonets, TOW gunners used their thermal sights to watch for any Iraqi movement. Restifo earned the Silver Star for his actions.

Grizzly was at its blocking position near the second minefield by dawn. The ground war officially began at 4:30 a.m., with the 2nd Division and the 1st Division's Task Forces Ripper and Papa Bear starting their penetrations at the first minefield. Rocket-propelled mine-clearing line charges, or "mick licks," were used to make the initial breaches. Each line charge consisted of a 110-yard-long cable along which explosives were attached. A rocket on the cable's end would carry the line across the minefield, and the subsequent detonation of the charges would set off any nearby mines. Finding little Iraqi resistance, the Marines pushed through the first minefield, reaching the second barrier by noon They were, however, plagued with more defective line charges, more damaged tanks, and increased Iraqi artillery fire.

The push through the two minefields left eleven tanks damaged and fourteen men wounded. There had been concern about massed artillery fire catching them bogged down among the mines. But, "None of our fears materialized," Boomer said. Despite low clouds, scattered rain, and dense smoke from burning wells in the sabotaged Kuwaiti oil fields, the Marine aviators did their best to support the ground forces. Cobra helicopters had to get under the clouds in order to attack Iraqi tanks or artillery firing on the Marines. "I had six or eight Cobras air taxiing down highways in Kuwait with their landing lights on to get into the First or Second Division areas to help them out," Moore later recalled.

The two heavy task forces ran into only scattered pockets of opposition from dug-in Iraqis, most of whom surrendered following being hit by long-range TOW missiles or tank fire. By late afternoon, Papa Bear had reached its first objective just behind the second minefield belt.

Due to premature darkness, Ripper had to postpone its move onto Al Jaber Airfield, about nine miles to the northwest. Still, the Marines' aggressiveness and light Iraqi resistance had put the advance hours ahead of schedule. This created a major problem for General Schwarzkopf. The Marines' rapid drive increased the exposure of their left flank; they might just push the Iraqi troops out of Kuwait before the main attack arrived. As a result, Schwarzkopf ordered VII Corps to begin its assault by 3 P.M., fifteen hours ahead of schedule.

After a relatively easy first day, both Marine divisions would face their toughest fights of the war on February 25, when Iraqi armored units staged strong counterattacks. For the 1st Division, the battle included a defense of Myatt's forward command post, featuring an aggressive attack by a company of Marine LAV-25s against a superior force of Iraqi tanks and armored vehicles. The 2nd Division fought off separate attacks from Iraqi mechanized and armored units in what was called the biggest tank battle in Marine history. In one fight, the "Reveille Engagement," Marines, including

Bravo Company, the reserve tank unit with its M1A1s, woke from their sleep to destroy thirty T-72s and four T-55s. Counterattacks and darkness, however, prevented both divisions from moving north.

The weather remained bad on February 26. Even so, Boomer ordered Myatt to move on Kuwait International Airport and had Keys sweep to the west of Kuwait City to cut off the highways out of the capital. With supporting shellfire from the battleships *Missouri*'s and *Wisconsin*'s sixteen-inch guns, the assault units broke through the defenses. Shortly after dawn on the twenty-seventh, marines raised the U.S. flag in front of the airport terminal.

To the south, Grizzly worked its way through the maze of bunkers and buildings at Al Jaber Airfield, without meeting any resistance. Meanwhile, the 2nd Division occupied a ridge northwest of Kuwait City, sealing off major roads and trapping hundreds of fleeing Iraqis. On February 28, Arab troops passed through the Marines' lines and entered Kuwait City, which erupted in a joyous celebration. Later that day, President Bush ordered a cease-fire and the Persian Gulf War ended for the Marines.

The Marines had driven about one hundred miles in one hundred hours, defeated seven Iraqi divisions, destroyed 1,040 tanks, 608 armored vehicles, and 432 artillery pieces, and taken 22,308 prisoners: at the cost of five killed and forty-eight wounded. At a February 27 press briefing in Riyadh, Schwarzkopf lauded the Marines: "It was a classic, absolutely classic, military breaching of a very, very tough minefield. . . . And I think it will be studied for many, many years to come as the way to do it."

AFGHANISTAN

OPERATION ENDURING FREEDOM

As all the world knows, at 8:45 a.m. on Tuesday, September 11, 2001, an airliner was crashed into the north tower of New York City's World Trade Center. Shortly after 9:00 a.m., a second plane hit the south tower. An hour later, another commercial plane hit the Pentagon, in Washington, D.C., and a fourth was downed in Somerset County, Pennsylvania, about eighty miles southeast of Pittsburgh. Shortly after that, the south tower collapsed; less than thirty minutes later, the north tower followed. Then, at 5:30 in the afternoon, Building No. 7, a third tower in the building, also collapsed. Wednesday evening, September 12, yet another building fell.

So began the ongoing war against global terror, at home and abroad. President George W. Bush immediately ordered the seizure of terrorists' financial assets, as well as decreeing steps to disrupt their fund-raising network. Fought on both domestic (for the first time since the Civil War) and foreign soil, this conflict required deployment of American troops to Southwest Asia and countries surrounding Afghanistan (whose Taliban government were sheltering the Al Qaeda network who had claimed responsibility for 9/11) in the days following the attacks.

The military response to 9/11 was given the name Operation Enduring Freedom, and began on October 7, 2001. Early combat operations included a mix of air strikes from land-based B-1, B-2, and B-52 bombers; carrier-based F-14 and F/A-18 fighters; and Tomahawk cruise missiles launched from both U.S. and British ships and submarines. As declared by President

Bush, the military objectives of Operation Enduring Freedom included the destruction of terrorist training camps and infrastructure within Afghanistan, the capture of al Qaeda leaders, and the cessation of terrorist activities in Afghanistan.

At the time hostilities began on October 7, Taliban forces controlled more than 80 percent of Afghanistan; the coalition of anti-Taliban forces were on the defensive. Al Qaeda was entrenched throughout the country. But, by October 20, U.S. and Coalition forces had destroyed virtually all Taliban air defenses and had conducted a highly successful direct action mission on the residence of Mullah Omar in the middle of the Taliban capital of Kandahar. During this period, Special Forces detachments linked up with anti-Taliban leaders and coordinated operational fires and logistics support on multiple fronts. Twenty days later, the provincial capital of Mazar-e Sharif fell. In rapid succession, Herat, Kabul, and Jalalabad followed.

The stage was set for the biggest single engagement by the Marines thus far in the Afghan Campaign. The 26th MEU deployed aboard the USS *Bataan*, the USS *Shreveport*, and the USS *Whidbey Island* on September 20, 2001. None of the Marines or sailors aboard ship knew their destination. "We started in the normal fashion," said Marine Col. Andrew Frick, commander of the 26th MEU. The unit went on to Spain, following which it participated in the Operation Bright Star exercises in Egypt. Frick said there was a lot of supposition that the 26th MEU would be going into Afghanistan, but it didn't become official until after the Marines exercised in Albania. "Then planning really went into high gear," he continued. The 26th arrived at the Arabian Sea, off the coast of Pakistan. Meeting it there was the

15th MEU from Camp Pendleton, California, aboard the Amphibious Assault Ship USS *Peleliu.*

It was to be the farthest strung amphibious landing in history. The Navy placed the Marines more than five hundred miles from their ships. Navy Capt. Martin Allard, commander of the Bataan, said training paid off. "I'd say the training we did was harder than the actual operation. It was an extremely successful deployment. We supported our Marines farther from shore than they've ever been. The ship set a flying-hour record for large deck amphibious ships—6,700. The landing craft air cushion vehicles set flying-hour records and records for cargo moved." Allard said it felt good to go on a combat deployment following the events of September 11, 2001. He said the group went halfway around the world and carried the war to the enemy. "They advertised a lot of Taliban resistance in southern Afghanistan, and that just didn't pan out. I think they were afraid of the combat power of the Marines ashore and combat power from the air."

The target allotted the Marines was the Taliban center of Kandahar. Founded by Alexander the Great (fourth century BC) as Alexandria Arachosia, Kandahar had been the object of many conquerors. India and Persia had long fought over the city, strategically located as it was on the trade routes of central Asia. It was conquered by Arabs in the seventh century, by the Turkic Ghaznavids in the tenth century, and by Genghis Khan in the twelfth century. After this event, it became a major city of the Karts until their defeat by Tamerlane in 1383. Babur, founder of the Mughal empire of India, took Kandahar in the sixteenth century. It was later contested by the

Persians and by the rulers of newly emerging Afghanistan, who made it their capital. The British occupied Kandahar during the First Afghan War (1839–1842) and from 1879 to 1881. Together with Peshawar, Pakistan, Kandahar is the principal city of the Pashtun people. During the Soviet military occupation of 1979 to 1989, it was the site of a Soviet command. A major prize, Kandahar changed hands several times until the fall of the Najibullah government in 1992. Now it would host the Americans.

As the Marines worked to establish a base south of Kandahar, U.S. warplanes launched the most intensive raids on the city in weeks, according to reports from the ground. About five hundred of the expected one-thousand-plus Marines landed south of the Taliban stronghold of Kandahar and established a post with an airstrip dubbed "Camp Rhino." They moved into action; the Pentagon confirmed reports the following day that U.S. helicopter gunships had attacked an armored column near the airstrip they controlled. Although heavy fighting continued around the city, it was not known who exactly was participating.

The Northern Alliance troops moved south from Herat toward Kandahar, while Pashtun tribesmen threatened to advance on the city themselves if Taliban leader Mohammed Omar did not withdraw.

Seven weeks of U.S.-led bombardment and Northern Alliance victories had left the Taliban with control of less than a third of the country. Nevertheless, as the Marines were positioning at Camp Rhino, Gen. Richard Myers, Chairman of the Joint Chiefs of Staff, warned that "a substantial amount of time" remained before U.S. forces could declare victory. He added that Kandahar was "the last bastion, we think, of Taliban resistance," adding that city would not fall easily. "We think they'll dig in and fight and fight, perhaps to the end."

By December 2, the Marines and Afghan opposition groups were preparing for a final assault on Kandahar; the number of U.S. attack and support helicopters on the ground nearly doubled overnight. Maj. James "Bo" Higgins, an intelligence officer with the 15th Marine Expeditionary Unit, told the press that the military campaign for Kandahar had reached "a culmination point. In every way, the Taliban is looking at a lot of pressure, kind of like a snake squeezing in on them. We hope to be able to get them out of there in the pretty near future."

What worried the American leadership was the presence in Kandahar, alongside the Taliban's Afghan fighters, of Arab, Pakistani, and Chechen volunteers who might well resist until death, being, according to Defense Secretary Donald Rumsfeld, "the most determined and the hardest fighters."

On Thursday, December 13, the Marines attacked the Kandahar airport, south of the city. Swiftly taking the field, they then went to work clearing and searching the area for mines and booby traps. Their intention was to rebuild the airport, twenty kilometers outside the city, and hand it back to civilian control.

A week after the Taliban surrendered Kandahar City, the Marines moved in. Some traveled by road convoy and cut off routes, while more were brought in by helicopters. Lt. Col. Jerome Lynes, commander of the 3rd Battalion, 6th Marines, said his riflemen did everything asked of them and then some. "They seized and secured Kandahar airport. They helped clear the area and made it safe. A group of artillerymen went up and opened and secured the U.S. Embassy in Kabul." A company in his battalion "went up to help special operations forces search the caves in Gardez," he continued. "They were supposed to be gone twelve hours; they came back nine days later."

Colonel Frick declared that the proudest moment he experienced in Afghanistan was when the Marines raised an American flag in Kandahar that had been given to them by New York firefighters. The flag had flown at Ground Zero.

Lynes lauded Marines under his command. Their actions on January 10, when Taliban fighters attacked the Kandahar airfield, were superb, he said. "No one was napping. There was not one chance that the Taliban were going to break through. I love these kids. The motivation and professionalism they displayed [were] awesome. Some parents did their jobs when they raised them. I guess I'm proudest of bringing them all back." By mid-March 2002, the Taliban had been removed from power and the al Qaeda network in Afghanistan had been destroyed.

IRAQ

OPERATION IRAQI FREEDOM

The Second Gulf War was, of course, in some ways the result of the First. Due to the fact that this conflict is still ongoing at press time, only the barest of outlines will have to satisfy the reader. On March 17, 2003, President

George W. Bush declared in an address to the nation that "The Iraqi regime has used diplomacy as a ploy to gain time and advantage. . . . All the decades of deceit and cruelty have now reached an end. Saddam Hussein and his sons must leave Iraq within forty-eight hours. Their refusal to do so will result in military conflict, commenced at a time of our choosing." The President's deadline passed without any reply from Hussein.

U.S. troops and Coalition forces were in place, as the culmination of months of buildup. In the early morning hours of March 20, a missile attack was launched on selected targets in Baghdad; Operation Iraqi Freedom had begun. The operation's stated goals were to liberate the Iraqi people, eliminate Iraq's weapons of mass destruction, and end Saddam Hussein's regime.

On the first day of the operation, Marine units from Camp Pendleton, California; Camp Lejeune, North Carolina, various Marine Corps air stations, and reserve Marines from throughout the United States were already staged in the Kuwaiti desert at camps like Ripper, Matilda, Commando, and Coyote. Many of the Marines spent some portion of the day in gas masks and mission-oriented protective posture gear due to nuclear, biological, and chemical alerts and the possibility of incoming Scud missiles launched by Iraq.

On March 22, 2003, the Iraqi 51st Mechanized Division at Basrah surrendered as U.S. Marines and the United Kingdom's 7th Armoured Brigade secured the area. Forces from the 15th Marine Expeditionary Unit and the 3rd Commando Brigade Royal Marines took part in taking the port of Umm Qasr. Two hours later, the 1st Marine Expeditionary Force secured the gas oil separation plants (GOSPs), crude oil export facilities, and oil wells in the Rumaylah Oil Fields. Although the oil infrastructure was confirmed to have been extensively booby-trapped, the installations were secured intact and U.S. and British troops began clearing the demolition charges. According to Lt. Gen. James Conway, Commander of the 1st Marine Expeditionary Force: "Over half of the Iraqi oil production, approximately 1.6 million barrels per day produced by 1,074 Rumaylah oil wells, has been secured for the Iraqi people." Two U.S. Marines were killed in action in southern Iraq.

On March 27, in An Nasiriyah, the 1st Marine Expeditionary Force defeated an attack by irregulars, supported by armored personnel carriers, rocket launchers, and anti-aircraft artillery systems. The fight lasted for about ninety minutes. The Marines in that battle suffered some wounded but remained fully effective. Over the next three days, the MEF continued its advance beyond Kulat Sukhayr.

Marines captured at Al Hillah two of the Al Samoud II missiles that contravened UN resolutions on April 1. An attack by U.S. Marines drove back the Baghdad division of the Republican Guard at Al Kut. The 1st Marine Expeditionary Force attacked the Baghdad division near the town of Al Kut and crossed the Tigris River. The Baghdad division was decimated. Over the next several days, the Marines isolated Al Kut, and continued their attacks west of An-Numaniyah. Seizing the road that runs along the northern side of the river gave the 1st MEF commander the ability to attack toward Baghdad up the main road on the northeast side of the Tigris. As they pushed toward the Iraqi capital, the Marines inflicted further damage on the Baghdad and Al Nida divisions of the Republican Guard near Al Kut and Baghdad. They then turned northwest along Highway 6 to the southeast corner of Baghdad. After attacking remnants of a regular army division and a Republican Guard infantry division, they destroyed those forces as they moved forth to establish an operating base on the southeast edge of Baghdad.

By April 5, the 1st MEF had formed, along with V Corps, part of the ever-tightening noose around Baghdad, denying reinforcements or any escape by Iraqi military forces. The Marines controlled the corridor from Samanpak to Baghdad. They conducted a raid that hit a training camp near Salman Pak. This raid occurred in response to information that had been gained by coalition forces from foreign fighters encountered from other countries, not Iraq, and this camp, it was claimed, had been used to train these foreign fighters in terror tactics. In reality, the camp near Salman Pak had been set up in the late 1980s as an anti-Iranian counter-terrorism training center. It was built with U.S. assistance during the Iran-Iraq war (when the U.S. supported Iraq), in the wake of the 1986 hijacking and crashing of an Iraqi airliner by pro-Iranian extremists. The camp's subsequent use remains unclear.

For the most part, however, the Marines' energies were focused on isolating Baghdad from the east along the Biala River. April 6 saw the 1st MEF enter the Baghdad city limits, as the Marines pushed into the city from the southeast, taking Rasheed airport, and consolidating their position to the east of the city. They encountered forces, including T-72 tanks, armored personnel carriers, other armored vehicles, surface-to-surface missiles, artillery pieces, and numerous technical vehicles. These forces were encountered and destroyed, and they proceeded on their attack to seize the Rashid

Airport. The Marines' aircraft wing flew more than 250 sorties in twenty-four hours.

On April 8 and 9, the 1st MEF encountered minimal resistance from regular Iraqi Army units near Al Amarah, and continued to push into southeast Baghdad. Near Al Amarah, the Marines there met minimal resistance from two of the divisions that had originally been deployed on the eastern flank. Those were the 10th and the 14th divisions. The divisions had already abandoned their weapons and departed the battlefield, after a period of air attacks and leaflet drops, and also following the liberation of Basra. Coalition forces at this point occupied the 10th Armored Division headquarters, and began to make the transition into humanitarian assistance and civil military operations in the Al Amarah area. The Marines continued their attacks across the Diyala River, into the southeast corner of Baghdad. They also proceeded along the west edge of the river into the northeast corner of Baghdad. After entering in the southeast corner, the Marines continued their attacks into the heart of Baghdad, near key government facilities.

By April 10, elements of the 1st MEF and the 3rd U.S. Division completed their cordon around Baghdad, and cut the major routes in and out of the city, eliminating the opportunity for large forces to move in and reinforce, and certainly complicating the problems of anyone trying to leave the city.

Through the next several days the Marines and their Army partners continued to occupy new areas of the city. On Friday, April 11, Marines searching a school in Baghdad discovered scores of suicide-bomber vests that were fitted with blocks of C4 plastic explosive laced with ball bearings. The black leather vests appeared to be professionally made, every one a near-replica of the others. Empty hangers indicated that some of the vests had already been taken. Reporting the discovery, CENTCOM spokesman, U.S. Army Brigadier General Vince Brooks, said, "There are individuals willing to carry out actions of violence and terrorism." Although the Battle for Baghdad had ended, the war was clearly not over.

After the fall of Baghdad, Marines remained on duty in southern Iraq and Kuwait. By July 2003, their numbers had dropped from 65,000 to 19,000 troops who were employed in the search for Saddam supporters and the dispersal of humanitarian aid. In September 2003, the remaining Marines were replaced with a multinational division made up of 9,000 troops from Poland, Spain, Ukraine and fourteen other nations.

As it turned out, the "peace" in Iraq was deadlier than the war, as diehard Baathists and other clandestine groups waged a bloody harassment campaign against Coalition troops. The ongoing need for a U.S. military presence prompted Washington to announce plans in early December 2003 for "Iraqi Freedom II," an operation that would replace units rotating out of Iraq in January 2004 with fresh troops—including 5,000 Marines. Once again, the Corps would be on the frontline of the nation's military endeavors.

ADDENDUM

The list of Marine interventions abroad will impress the reader with the fact that the Corps has had a worldwide reach from its beginning. As mentioned, while the political reasoning behind each action might be debated, the valor of the deployed Marines cannot be. Moreover, the enormous number of American lives preserved overseas by these interventions cannot be overestimated.

Source: Department of the Navy–Naval Historical Center
805 Kidder Breese, SE–Washington Navy Yard
Washington, DC 20374-5060

(*Note*: The following represents the views of the author and not necessarily the views of the Naval Historical Center.)

Taken from "Instances of Use of United States Forces Abroad, 1798–1993" by Ellen C. Collier, Specialist in U.S. Foreign Policy,
Foreign Affairs and National Defense Division
Washington, DC
Congressional Research Service
Library of Congress
October 7, 1993

1798–1800 Undeclared Naval War with France. This contest included land actions, such as that in the Dominican Republic, city of Puerto Plata, where marines captured a French privateer under the guns of the forts.

1801–1805 Tripoli. The First Barbary War included the USS *George Washington* and USS *Philadelphia* affairs and the Eaton expedition, during which a few marines landed with United States Agent William Eaton to raise a force against Tripoli in an effort to free the crew of the Philadelphia. Tripoli declared war but not the United States.

1806–1810 Gulf of Mexico. American gunboats operated from New Orleans against Spanish and French privateers off the Mississippi Delta, chiefly under Capt. John Shaw and Master Commandant David Porter.

1814–1825 Caribbean. Engagements between pirates and American ships or squadrons took place repeatedly especially ashore and offshore about Cuba, Puerto Rico, Santo Domingo, and Yucatan. Three thousand pirate attacks on merchantmen were reported between 1815 and 1823. In 1822 Commodore James Biddle employed a squadron of two frigates, four sloops of war, two brigs, four schooners, and two gunboats in the West Indies.

1815 Algiers. The second Barbary War was declared by the opponents but not by the United States. Congress authorized an expedition. A large fleet under Decatur attacked Algiers and obtained indemnities.

1815 Tripoli. After securing an agreement from Algiers, Decatur demonstrated with his squadron at Tunis and Tripoli, where he secured indemnities for offenses during the War of 1812.

1818 Oregon. The USS *Ontario* dispatched from Washington, D.C., landed at the Columbia River and in August took possession of Oregon territory. Britain had conceded sovereignty but Russia and Spain asserted claims to the area.

1824 Puerto Rico (Spanish territory). Commodore David Porter with a landing party attacked the town of Fajardo, which had sheltered pirates and insulted American naval officers. He landed with two hundred men in November and forced an apology. Commodore Porter was later court-martialed for overstepping his powers.

1825 Cuba. In March cooperating American and British forces landed at Sagua La Grande to capture pirates.

1827 Greece. In October and November landing parties hunted pirates on the islands of Argenteire, Miconi, and Androse.

1832 Sumatra, February 6 to 9. A naval force landed and stormed a fort to punish natives of the town of Quallah Battoo for plundering the American ship *Friendship*.

1833 Argentina, October 31 to November 15. A force was sent ashore at Buenos Aires to protect the interests of the United States and other countries during an insurrection.

1835–1836 Peru, December 10, 1835, to January 24, 1836, and August 31 to December 7, 1836. Marines protected American interests in Callao and Lima during an attempted revolution.

1838–1839 Sumatra, December 24, 1838, to January 4, 1839. A naval force landed to punish natives of the towns of Quallah Battoo and Muckie (Mukki) for depredations on American shipping.

1840 Fiji Islands, July. Naval forces landed to punish natives for attacking American exploring and surveying parties.

1841 Drummond Island, Kingsmill Group. A naval party landed to avenge the murder of a seaman by the natives.

1841 Samoa, February 24. A naval party landed and burned towns after the murder of an American seaman on Upolu Island.

1843 China. Sailors and Marines from the *St. Louis* were landed after a clash between Americans and Chinese at the trading post in Canton.

1843 Africa, November 29 to December 16. Four United States vessels demonstrated and landed various parties (one of two hundred marines and sailors) to discourage piracy and the slave trade along the Ivory Coast, and to punish attacks by the natives on American seamen and shipping.

1849 Smyrna. In July a naval force gained release of an American seized by Austrian officials.

1851 Turkey. After a massacre of foreigners (including Americans) at Jaffa in January, a demonstration by the Mediterranean Squadron was ordered along the Turkish (Levant) coast.

1851 Johanns Island (east of Africa), August.   Forces from the U.S. sloop of war *Dale* exacted redress for the unlawful imprisonment of the captain of an American whaling brig.

1852–1853 Argentina, February 3 to 12, 1852; September 17, 1852, to April 1853.   Marines were landed and maintained in Buenos Aires to protect American interests during a revolution.

1853 Nicaragua, March 11 to 13.   U.S. forces landed to protect American lives and interests during political disturbances.

1853–1854 Ryukyu and Bonin Islands.   Commodore Perry on three visits before going to Japan, and while waiting for a reply from Japan, made a naval demonstration, landing marines twice, and secured a coaling concession from the ruler of Naha on Okinawa; he also demonstrated in the Bonin Islands with the purpose of securing facilities for commerce.

1854 China, April 4 to June 15 to 17.   American and English ships landed forces to protect American interests in and near Shanghai during Chinese civil strife.

1854 Nicaragua, July 9 to 15.   Naval forces bombarded and burned San Juan del Norte (Greytown) to avenge an insult to the American Minister to Nicaragua.

1855 China, May 19 to 21.   U.S. forces protected American interests in Shanghai and, from August 3 to 5 fought pirates near Hong Kong.

1855 Fiji Islands, September 12 to November 4. An American naval force landed to seek reparations for depredations on American residents and seamen.

1855 Uruguay, November 25 to 29. U.S. and European naval forces landed to protect American interests during an attempted revolution in Montevideo.

1856 Panama, Republic of New Grenada, September 19 to 22. U.S. forces landed to protect American interests during an insurrection.

1856 China, October 22 to December 6. U.S. forces landed to protect American interests at Canton during hostilities between the British and the Chinese, and to avenge an assault upon an unarmed boat displaying the U.S. flag.

1857 Nicaragua, April to May, November to December. In May Commander C. H. Davis of the United States Navy, with some Marines, received the surrender of William Walker, who had been attempting to get control of the country, and protected his men from the retaliation of native allies who had been fighting Walker. In November and December of the same year, U.S. vessels *Saratoga*, *Wabash*, and *Fulton* opposed another attempt of William Walker on Nicaragua. Commodore Hiram Paulding's act of landing Marines and compelling the removal of Walker to the United States, was tacitly disavowed by Secretary of State Lewis Cass, and Paulding was forced into retirement.

1858 Uruguay, January 2 to 27. Forces from two United States warships landed to protect American property during a revolution in Montevideo.

1858 Fiji Islands, October 6 to 16. A marine expedition chastised natives for the murder of two American citizens at Waya.

1858–1859 Turkey. The Secretary of State requested a display of naval force along the Levant after a massacre of Americans at Jaffa and mistreatment elsewhere "to remind the authorities (of Turkey) of the power of the United States."

1859 Paraguay. Congress authorized a naval squadron to seek redress for an attack on a naval vessel in the Parana River during 1855. Apologies were made after a large display of force.

1859 China, July 31 to August 2. A naval force landed to protect American interests in Shanghai.

1860 Colombia, Bay of Panama, September 27 to October 8. Naval forces landed to protect American interests during a revolution.

1864 Japan, July 14 to August 3. Naval forces protected the U.S. Minister to Japan when he visited Yedo to negotiate concerning some American claims against Japan, and to make his negotiations easier by impressing the Japanese with American power.

1864 Japan, September 4 to 14. Naval forces of the United States, Great Britain, France, and The Netherlands compelled Japan and the Prince of

Nagato in particular to permit the Straits of Shimonoseki to be used by foreign shipping in accordance with treaties already signed.

1865 Panama, March 9 and 10. U.S. forces protected the lives and the property of American residents during a revolution.

1866 China. From June 20 to July 7, U.S. forces punished an assault on the American consul at Newchwang.

1867 Nicaragua. Marines occupied Managua and Leon.

1867 Formosa, June 13. A naval force landed and burned a number of huts to punish the murder of the crew of a wrecked American vessel.

1868 Japan (Osaka, Hiolo, Nagasaki, Yokohama, and Negata), February 4 to 8, April 4 to May 12, June 12 and 13. U.S. forces were landed to protect American interests during the civil war in Japan over the abolition of the Shogunate and the restoration of the Mikado.

1868 Uruguay, February 7 and 8, 19 to 26. U.S. forces protected foreign residents and the customhouse during an insurrection at Montevideo.

1868 Colombia, April. Japan, September 4 to 14. U.S. forces protected passengers and treasure in transit at Aspinwall during the absence of local police or troops on the occasion of the death of the President of Colombia.

1870 Hawaiian Islands, September 21. U.S. forces placed the American flag at half mast upon the death of Queen Kalama, when the American consul at Honolulu would not assume responsibility for so doing.

1871 Korea, June 10 to 12.   A U.S. naval force attacked and captured five forts to punish natives for depredations on Americans, particularly for murdering the crew of the *General Sherman* and burning the schooner, and for later firing on other American small boats taking soundings up the Salee River.

1873 Colombia (Bay of Panama), May 7 to 22, September 23 to October 9.   U.S. forces protected American interests during hostilities over possession of the government of the State of Panama.

1874 Hawaiian Islands, February 12 to 20.   Detachments from American vessels were landed to preserve order and protect American lives and interests during the coronation of a new king.

1876 Mexico, May 18.   An American force was landed to police the town of Matamoras temporarily while it was without other government.

1882 Egypt, July 14 to 18.   American forces landed to protect American interests during warfare between British and Egyptians and looting of the city of Alexandria by Arabs.

1885 Panama (Colon), January 18 and 19.   U.S. forces were used to guard the valuables in transit over the Panama Railroad, and the safes and vaults of the company during revolutionary activity. In March, April, and May in the cities of Colon and Panama, the forces helped reestablish freedom of transit during revolutionary activity.

1888 Korea, June.   A naval force was sent ashore to protect American residents in Seoul during unsettled political conditions, when an outbreak of the populace was expected.

1888 Haiti, December 20. A display of force persuaded the Haitian government to give up an American steamer that had been seized on the charge of breach of blockade.

1888–1889 Samoa, November 14, 1888, to March 20, 1889. U.S. forces were landed to protect American citizens and the consulate during a native civil war.

1889 Hawaiian Islands, July 30 and 31. U.S. forces protected American interests at Honolulu during a revolution.

1890 Argentina. A naval party landed to protect U.S. consulate and legation in Buenos Aires.

1891 Haiti. U.S. forces sought to protect American lives and property on Navassa Island.

1891 Chile, August 28 to 30. U.S. forces protected the American consulate and the women and children who had taken refuge in it during a revolution in Valparaiso.

1893 Hawaii, January 16 to April 1. Marines were landed ostensibly to protect American lives and property, but many believed actually to promote a provisional government under Sanford B. Dole. This action was disavowed by the United States.

1894 Nicaragua, July 6 to August 7. U.S. forces sought to protect American interests at Bluefields following a revolution.

1894–1895 China.   Marines were stationed at Tientsin and penetrated to Peking for protection purposes during the Sino–Japanese War.

1894–1895 China.   A naval vessel was beached and used as a fort at New-chwang for protection of American nationals.

1894–1896 Korea, July 24, 1894, to April 3, 1896.   A guard of marines was sent to protect the American legation and American lives and interests at Seoul during and following the Sino–Japanese War.

1895 Colombia, March 8 to 9.   U.S. forces protected American interests during an attack on the town of Bocas del Toro by a bandit chieftain.

1896 Nicaragua, May 2 to 4.   U.S. forces protected American interests in Corinto during political unrest.

1898 Nicaragua, February 7 and 8.   U.S. forces protected American lives and property at San Juan del Sur.

1898–1899 China, November 5, 1898, to March 15, 1899.   U.S. forces provided a guard for the legation at Peking and the consulate at Tientsin during a contest between the Dowager Empress and her son.

1899 Nicaragua.   American and British naval forces were landed to protect national interests at San Juan del Norte, February 22 to March 5, and at Bluefields a few weeks later in connection with the insurrection of Gen. Juan P. Reyes.

1899 Samoa, February to May 15.   American and British naval forces were landed to protect national interests and to take part in a bloody contention over the succession to the throne.

1899–1901 Philippine Islands.   U.S. forces protected American interests following the war with Spain and conquered the islands by defeating the Filipinos in their war for independence.

1900 China, May 24 to September 28.   American troops participated in operations to protect foreign lives during the Boxer rising, particularly at Peking. For many years after this experience a permanent legation guard was maintained in Peking, and was strengthened at times as trouble threatened.

1901 Colombia (State of Panama), November 20 to December 4.   U.S. forces protected American property on the Isthmus and kept transit lines open during serious revolutionary disturbances.

1902 Colombia, April 16 to 23.   U.S. forces protected American lives and property at Bocas del Toro during a civil war.

1902 Colombia (State of Panama), September 17 to November 18.   The United States placed armed guards on all trains crossing the Isthmus to keep the railroad line open, and stationed ships on both sides of Panama to prevent the landing of Colombian troops.

1903 Honduras, March 23 to 30 or 31.   U.S. forces protected the American consulate and the steamship wharf at Puerto Cortez during a period of revolutionary activity.

1903 Dominican Republic, March 30 to April 21.   A detachment of

Marines was landed to protect American interests in the city of Santo Domingo during a revolutionary outbreak.

1903 Syria, September 7 to 12.   U.S. forces protected the American consulate in Beirut when a local Muslim uprising was feared.

1903–1904 Abyssinia.   Twenty-five marines were sent to Abyssinia to protect the U.S. Consul General while he negotiated a treaty.

1903–1914 Panama.   U.S. forces sought to protect American interests and lives during and following the revolution for independence from Colombia over construction of the Isthmian Canal. With brief intermissions, U.S. Marines were stationed on the Isthmus from November 4, 1903, to January 21, 1914, to guard American interests.

1904 Dominican Republic, January 2 to February 11.   American and British naval forces established an area in which no fighting would be allowed and protected American interests in Puerto Plata and Sosua and Santo Domingo City during revolutionary fighting.

1904 Tangier, Morocco.   "We want either Perdicaris alive or Raisula dead." A squadron demonstrated to force release of a kidnapped American. A Marine guard was landed to protect the Consul General.

1904 Panama, November 17 to 24.   U.S. forces protected American lives and property at Ancon at the time of a threatened insurrection.

1904–1905 Korea, January 5, 1904, to November 11, 1905.   A Marine guard was sent to protect the American legation in Seoul during the Russo-Japanese War.

1906–1909 Cuba, September 1906 to January 23, 1909.   U.S. forces sought to restore order, protect foreigners, and establish a stable government after serious revolutionary activity.

1907 Honduras, March 18 to June 8.   To protect American interests during a war between Honduras and Nicaragua, troops were stationed in Trujillo, Ceiba, Puerto Cortez, San Pedro Laguna, and Choloma.

1910 Nicaragua, May 19 to September 4.   U.S. forces protected American interests at Bluefields.

1911 Honduras, January 26.   American naval detachments were landed to protect American lives and interests during a civil war in Honduras.

1911 China.   As the nationalist revolution approached, in October an ensign and ten men tried to enter Wuchang to rescue missionaries, but they retired on being warned away, and a small landing force guarded American private property and consulate at Hankow. A marine guard was established in November over the cable stations at Shanghai; landing forces were sent for protection in Nanking, Chinkiang, Taku, and elsewhere.

1912 Honduras.   A small force landed to prevent seizure by the government of an American-owned railroad at Puerto Cortez. The forces were withdrawn after the United States disapproved the action.

1912 Panama.   Troops, on request of both political parties, supervised elections outside the Canal Zone.

1912 Cuba, June 5 to August 5.   U.S. forces protected American interests in the Province of Oriente, and in Havana.

1912 China, August 24 to 26, on Kentucky Island, and August 26 to 30 at Camp Nicholson.   U.S. forces protect Americans and American interests during revolutionary activity.

1912 Turkey, November 18 to December 3.   U.S. forces guarded the American Legation at Constantinople during a Balkan War.

1912–1925 Nicaragua, August to November 1912.   U.S. forces protected American interests during an attempted revolution. A small force, serving as a legation guard and seeking to promote peace and stability, remained until August 5, 1925.

1912–1941 China.   The disorders that began with the Kuomintang rebellion in 1912, which were redirected by the invasion of China by Japan and finally ended by war between Japan and the United States in 1941, led to demonstrations and landing parties for the protection of U.S. interests in China continuously and at many points from 1912 to 1941. The guard at Peking and along the route to the sea was maintained until 1941. In 1927, the United States had 5,670 troops ashore in China and forty-four naval vessels in its waters. In 1933 the United States had 3,027 armed men ashore. The protective action was generally based on treaties with China concluded from 1858 to 1901.

1913 Mexico, September 5 to 7. A few marines landed at Ciaris Estero to aid in evacuating American citizens and others from the Yaqui Valley, made dangerous for foreigners by civil strife.

1914 Haiti, January 29 to February 9, February 20 to 21, October 19. Intermittently U.S. naval forces protected American nationals in a time of rioting and revolution.

1914 Dominican Republic, June and July. During a revolutionary movement, U.S. naval forces by gunfire stopped the bombardment of Puerto Plata, and by threat of force maintained Santo Domingo City as a neutral zone.

1915–1934 Haiti, July 28, 1915, to August 15, 1934. U.S. forces maintained order during a period of chronic and threatened insurrection.

1916 China. American forces landed to quell a riot taking place on American property in Nanking.

1916–1924 Dominican Republic, May 1916 to September 1924. American naval forces maintained order during a period of chronic and threatened insurrection.

1917 China. American troops were landed at Chungking to protect American lives during a political crisis.

1917–1922 Cuba. U.S. forces protected American interests during insurrection and subsequent unsettled conditions. Most of the U.S. armed forces left Cuba by August 1919, but two companies remained at Camaguey until February 1922.

1918–1919 Mexico. After withdrawal of the Pershing expedition, U.S. troops entered Mexico in pursuit of bandits at least three times in 1918 and six times in 1919. In August 1918 American and Mexican troops fought at Nogales.

1918–1920 Panama. U.S. forces were used for police duty according to treaty stipulations, at Chiriqui, during election disturbances and subsequent unrest.

1918–1920 Soviet Russia. Marines were landed at and near Vladivostok in June and July to protect the American Consulate and other points in the fighting between the Bolshevik troops and the Czech Army, which had traversed Siberia from the western front. A joint proclamation of emergency government and neutrality was issued by the American, Japanese, British, French, and Czech commanders in July. In August seven thousand men were landed in Vladivostok and remained until January 1920, as part of an allied occupation force. In September 1918, five thousand American troops joined the allied intervention force at Archangel and remained until June 1919. These operations were in response to the Bolshevik revolution in Russia and were partly supported by Czarist or Kerensky elements.

1919 Dalmatia. U.S. forces were landed at Trau at the request of Italian authorities to police order between the Italians and the Serbs.

1919 Turkey. Marines from the USS *Arizona* were landed to guard the U.S. Consulate during the Greek occupation of Constantinople.

1919 Honduras, September 8 to 12. A landing force was sent ashore to maintain order in a neutral zone during an attempted revolution.

1919 China, March 14. A landing force was sent ashore for a few hours to protect lives during a disturbance at Kiukiang.

1920 Guatemala, April 9 to 27. U.S. forces protected the American Legation and other American interests, such as the cable station, during a period of fighting between Unionists and the Government of Guatemala.

1920–1922 Russia (Siberia), February 16, 1920, to November 19, 1922. A Marine guard was sent to protect the U.S. radio station and property on Russian Island, Bay of Vladivostok.

1921 Panama, Costa Rica. American naval squadrons demonstrated in April on both sides of the Isthmus to prevent war between the two countries over a boundary dispute.

1922 Turkey, September and October. A landing force was sent ashore with consent of both Greek and Turkish authorities, to protect American lives and property when the Turkish Nationalists entered Smyrna.

1922–1923 China. Between April 1922 and November 1923 Marines were landed five times to protect Americans during periods of unrest.

1924 Honduras, February 28 to March 31, September 10 to 15. U.S. forces protected American lives and interests during election hostilities.

1924 China, September. Marines were landed to protect Americans and other foreigners in Shanghai during Chinese factional hostilities.

1925 China, January 15 to August 29. Fighting of Chinese factions accompanied by riots and demonstrations in Shanghai brought the landing of American forces to protect lives and property in the International Settlement.

1925 Honduras, April 19 to 21.   U.S. forces protected foreigners at La Ceiba during a political upheaval.

1925 Panama, October 12 to 23.   Strikes and rent riots led to the landing of about six hundred American troops to keep order and protect American interests.

1926 China, August and September.   The Nationalist attack on Hankow brought the landing of American naval forces to protect American citizens. A small guard was maintained at the Consulate General even after September 16, when the remaining forces were withdrawn. Likewise, when Nationalist forces captured Kiukiang, naval forces were landed for the protection of foreigners November 4 to 6.

1926–1933 Nicaragua, May 7 to June 5, 1926; August 27, 1926, to January 1933.   The coup d'etat of General Chamorro aroused revolutionary activities leading to the landing of American Marines to protect U.S. interests. U.S. forces came and went intermittently until January 3, 1933. Their work included activity against the outlaw leader Sandino in 1928.

1927 China, February.   Fighting at Shanghai caused American naval forces and Marines to be increased. In March a naval guard was stationed at the American Consulate at Nanking after Nationalist forces captured the city. American and British destroyers later used shell fire to protect Americans and other foreigners. Subsequently additional forces of Marines and naval forces were stationed in the vicinity of Shanghai and Tientsin.

1932 China. American forces were landed to protect American interests during the Japanese occupation of Shanghai.

1933 Cuba. During a revolution against President Gerardo Machada, naval forces demonstrated but no landing was made.

1934 China. Marines landed at Foochow to protect the American Consulate.

1945 China. In October fifty thousand U.S. Marines were sent to North China to assist Chinese Nationalist authorities in disarming and repatriating the Japanese in China and in controlling ports, railroads, and airfields. This was in addition to approximately sixty thousand U.S. forces remaining in China at the end of World War II.

1948 Palestine. A Marine Consular Guard was sent to Jerusalem to protect the U.S. Consul General.

1948–1949 China. Marines were dispatched to Nanking to protect the American Embassy when the city fell to Communist troops, and to Shanghai to aid in the protection and evacuation of Americans.

1954–1955 China. Naval units evacuated U.S. civilians and military personnel from the Tachen Islands.

1956 Egypt. A Marine battalion evacuated U.S. nationals and other persons from Alexandria during the Suez crisis.

1958 Lebanon. Marines were landed in Lebanon at the invitation of its government to help protect against threatened insurrection supported from the outside.

1959–1960 The Caribbean. The 2nd Marine Ground Task Force was deployed to protect U.S. nationals during the Cuban crisis.

1962 Thailand. The 3rd Marine Expeditionary Unit landed on May 17, 1962, to support that country during the threat of Communist pressure from outside; by July 30 the five thousand Marines had been withdrawn.

1965 Dominican Republic. The United States intervened to protect lives and property during a Dominican revolt and sent more troops as fears grew that the revolutionary forces were coming increasingly under Communist control.

1974 Evacuation from Cyprus. United States naval forces evacuated U.S. civilians during hostilities between Turkish and Greek Cypriot forces.

1975 Evacuation from Vietnam. On April 3, 1975, President Gerald R. Ford reported U.S. naval vessels, helicopters, and Marines had been sent to assist in evacuation of refugees and U.S. nationals from Vietnam.

1975 Evacuation from Cambodia. On April 12, 1975, President Ford reported that he had ordered U.S. military forces to proceed with the planned evacuation of U.S. citizens from Cambodia.

1975 South Vietnam. On April 30, 1975, President Ford reported that a force of seventy evacuation helicopters and 865 Marines had evacuated about 1,400 U.S. citizens and 5,500 third-country nationals and South Vietnamese from landing zones near the U.S. Embassy in Saigon and the Tan Son Nhut Airfield.

1975 *Mayaguez* Incident.   On May 15, 1975, President Ford reported he had ordered military forces to retake the SS *Mayaguez*, a merchant vessel en route from Hong Kong to Thailand, with U.S. citizen crew, which was seized from Cambodian naval patrol boats in international waters and forced to proceed to a nearby island.

1976 Lebanon.   On July 22 and 23, 1974, helicopters from five U.S. naval vessels evacuated approximately 250 Americans and Europeans from Lebanon during fighting between Lebanese factions after an overland convoy evacuation had been blocked by hostilities.

1980 Iran.   On April 26, 1980, President James E. Carter reported the use of six U.S. transport planes and eight helicopters in an unsuccessful attempt to rescue American hostages being held in Iran.

1982 Lebanon.   On August 21, 1982, President Ronald W. Reagan reported the dispatch of eighty marines to serve in the multinational force to assist in the withdrawal of members of the Palestine Liberation force from Beirut. The Marines left September 20, 1982.

1982 Lebanon.   On September 29, 1982, President Reagan reported the deployment of twelve hundred marines to serve in a temporary multinational force to facilitate the restoration of Lebanese government sovereignty.

On September 29, 1983, Congress passed the Multinational Force in Lebanon Resolution (P.L. 98-119) authorizing the continued participation for eighteen months.

1983 Grenada. On October 25, 1983, President Reagan reported a landing on Grenada by Marines and Army airborne troops to protect lives and assist in the restoration of law and order and at the request of five members of the Organization of Eastern Caribbean States.

1987–1988 Persian Gulf. After the Iran-Iraq War resulted in several military incidents in the Persian Gulf, the United States increased U.S. Navy forces operating in the Persian Gulf and adopted a policy of reflagging and escorting Kuwaiti oil tankers through the Gulf. President Reagan reported that U.S. ships had been fired upon or struck mines or taken other military action on September 23, October 10, and October 20, 1987, and April 19, July 4, and July 14, 1988. The United States gradually reduced its forces after a cease-fire between Iran and Iraq on August 20, 1988.

1988 Panama. In mid-March and April 1988, during a period of instability in Panama and as pressure grew for Panamanian military leader Gen. Manuel Noriega to resign, the United States sent one thousand troops to Panama, to "further safeguard the canal, U.S. lives, property and interests in the area." The forces supplemented ten thousand U.S. military personnel already in Panama.

1989 Panama. On May 11, 1989, in response to General Noriega's disregard of the results of the Panamanian election, President George H.W. Bush ordered a brigade-sized force of approximately nineteen hundred troops to augment the estimated eleven thousand U.S. forces already in the area.

1989 Panama. On December 21, 1989, President Bush reported that he had ordered U.S. military forces to Panama to protect the lives of American citizens and bring General Noriega to justice. By February 13, 1990, all the invasion forces had been withdrawn.

1990 Liberia. On August 6, 1990, President Bush reported that a reinforced rifle company had been sent to provide additional security to the U.S. Embassy in Monrovia, and that helicopter teams had evacuated U.S. citizens from Liberia.

1993 Somalia. On June 10, 1993, President William J. Clinton reported that in response to attacks against UN forces in Somalia by a factional leader, the U.S. Quick Reaction Force in the area had participated in military action to quell the violence. The quick reaction force was part of the U.S. contribution to a success. On July 1, President Clinton reported further air and ground military operations on June 12 and June 17 aimed at neutralizing military capabilities that had impeded UN efforts to deliver humanitarian relief and promote national reconstruction, and additional instances occurred in the following months.

FAMOUS MARINES

As will be obvious by now, the story of the United States Marine Corps is the story of its members. Any number of books could be written about the enormous number who have excelled. But here are short looks at a very few of the best known.

Major Gregory "Pappy" Boyington. Pappy led the legendary Black Sheep squadron, spent a year and a half as a Japanese POW, and was awarded the Medal of Honor. Born on December 4, 1912, in St. Maries, Idaho, he enlisted in the Marine Corps in 1935. Boyington began flight training at Pensacola Naval Air Station in January 1936, with class 88-C. Here he flew a floatplane version of the Consolidated NY-2. The next year he was assigned to VMF-1 at Quantico, Virginia. In 1939 and 1940, he flew with VMF-2, stationed at San Diego. Boyington joined the American Volunteer Group (AVG), also known as the "Flying Tigers," in Burma on November 13, 1941. He flew several missions during the defense of that country. After Burma fell to the Japanese, he returned to Kunming, and flew from there until the Flying Tigers were incorporated into the USAAF. He clashed with the leader of the Flying Tigers, Claire Chennault. He quit the AVG in April 1942; Chennault gave him a dishonorable discharge and Boyington went back to the United States.

Boyington was reappointed to the Marines in November 1942, with the rank of Major. In January of the next year, he embarked on the *Lurline*, bound for New Caledonia, where he would spend a few months on the staff of Marine Air Group (MAG)-11. In the summer of 1943, he was given the assignment to pull together an ad hoc squadron from available men and planes. Originally, they formed the rear echelon of VMF-124.

Under Boyington as commanding officer and Maj. Stan Bailey as Exec, they trained hard at Turtle Bay on Espritu Santo. In early September 1943, the new VMF-214 moved up to their new forward base in the Russells, staging through Guadalcanal's famed Henderson Field. The "Black Sheep" fought their way to fame in just eighty-four days, piling up a record 197 enemy planes destroyed or damaged, troop transports and supply ships sunk, and ground installations destroyed in addition to numerous other victories. They flew their first combat mission on September 14, 1943, escorting Dauntless dive bombers to Ballale, a small island west of Bougainville, where the Japanese had a heavily fortified airstrip. They encountered heavy opposition from the enemy Zeros. Two days later, in a similar raid, Pappy claimed five kills, his best single day total. In October VMF-214 moved up from their orginal base in the Russells to a more advanced location at Munda. From here they were closer to the next big objective—the Japanese bases on Bougainville. On one mission over Bougainville, according to Boyington's autobiography, the Japanese radioed him in English, asking him to report his position and so forth. Pappy played along, but stayed five thousand feet higher than he had told them, and when the Zeros came along, the Black Sheep blew twelve of them away.

On January 3, 1944, Boyington was shot down in a large dogfight in which he claimed three enemy aircraft, and was captured. After about six weeks, the Japanese flew him to Truk. As he landed there, he experienced one of the early carrier strikes against Truk in February 1944. Eventually he was moved to a prison camp at Ofuna, outside of Yokohama. When he was repatriated, he found he had been awarded the Medal of Honor and the Navy Cross. In 1958, he published his memoirs, *Baa Baa Black Sheep*. In the mid-1970s, a television show based loosely on his memoirs appeared, entitled *Baa Baa Black Sheep*, starring Robert Conrad. After a long battle with cancer, Pappy Boyington died in 1988.

Major Smedley Butler. Known as "Old Gimlet Eye," Butler was the first officer to win the Medal of Honor twice, one in Vera Cruz in 1914 and the other in Haiti in 1915. Butler was born in Pennsylvania on July 30, 1881, and raised a Quaker. He served in the Spanish–American War, the Philippines, the siege of the Legations at Beijing, Culebra (off Puerto Rico), Honduras, Panama, Vera Cruz, and Haiti, as well as police commissioner of Philadelphia from 1924–1925 (on loan from the Marines). Butler's final service was as Commander of all Marines in China, at last retiring on October 1, 1931. A Republican candidate for the Senate in 1932, he was instrumental in foiling an attempted coup against President Franklin D. Roosevelt two years later.

In 1935, he authored a book, *War Is a Racket* (New York: Round Table Press). In it he wrote a now-famous passage, often quoted by himself and others since:

I helped make Mexico and especially Tampico safe for American oil interests in 1914. I helped make Haiti and Cuba a decent place for the National City Bank boys to collect revenues in. I helped in the raping of half a dozen Central American republics for the benefit of Wall Street. The record of racketeering is long. I helped purify Nicaragua for the international banking house of Brown Brothers in 1909–12. I brought light to the Dominican Republic for American sugar interests in 1916. I helped make Honduras "right" for American fruit companies in 1903. In China in 1927 I helped see to it that Standard Oil went its way unmolested. . . . Looking back on it, I felt I might have given Al Capone a few hints. The best he could do was to operate his racket in three city districts. We Marines operated on three continents.

Butler argued in the book for a powerful Navy, which would be prohibited from traveling more than two hundred miles from the U.S. coastline. Likewise, military aircraft would be allowed to travel no more than five hundred miles from the U.S. coast, and the Army would be prohibited from leaving the United States. He further counseled that all workers in defense industries, from the lowest laborer to the highest executive, be limited to "$30 a month, the same wage as the lads in the trenches get." He also proposed that "a declaration of war should be passed by a plebiscite in which only those subject to conscription would be eligible to vote."

From 1935 through 1937, Butler was a spokesman for the League Against War and Fascism, a Communist-dominated organization of the time. He also participated in the Third U.S. Congress Against War and Fascism, sharing the platform with well-known leftists of the era, including Langston Hughes, Heywood Broun, and Roger Baldwin. When the Spanish Civil War (1936–1939) threatened the collapse of the Soviet-supported Spanish government, the League's pacifism evaporated, and they supported intervention. Butler, however, remained true to his belief in non-interventionism: "What the hell is it our business what's going on in Spain?" He died at the Naval Hospital, Philadelphia, June 21, 1940.

Brigadier General Evans F. Carlson. A Marine officer who led guerrilla fighters (Carlson's Raiders) on daring military incursions in the Pacific area during World War II, Carlson was born in Vermont in 1896. He enlisted in the Army at age sixteen. In 1922, Carlson joined the Marines after a short stint in civilian life. Commissioned a few months later, in 1927 Carlson deployed to Shanghai with the 4th Marines. There he developed a deep interest in China that would shape his career. He served in Nicaragua, and then back to China with the Legation Guard. Captain Carlson arrived in Shanghai for his third China tour in July 1937. After that, Carlson received permission to accompany the Chinese Communist Party's 8th Route Army, in their combat against the Japanese. During that time, he developed his ideas on guerrilla warfare and ethical indoctrination. When a senior naval officer censured him for granting newspaper interviews, Carlson returned to the States and resigned so that he could speak out about the situation in China. With war looming for the United States, he sought to rejoin the Corps in April 1941. The Commandant granted his request, made him a Major in the reserves, and promptly brought him on to active duty. Ten months later he created the 2nd Raider Battalion.

After his departure from the Raiders in 1943, Carlson served as operations officer of the 4th Marine Division. Serving at Tarawa landing as an observer, he participated with his division in the assaults on Kwajalein and Saipan. In the latter battle he received severe wounds in the arm and leg while trying to pull his wounded radio operator out of the line of fire of an enemy machine gun. He popularized the term "gung ho." After the war Carlson retired from the Marine Corps and made a brief run in the 1946 California Senate race before a heart attack forced him out of the campaign. He died in May 1947.

Colonel Donald G. Cook. This Marine pilot and career military officer was awarded the Medal of Honor posthumously for his courage as a POW in North Vietnam from December 1964 to December 1967, when he died in captivity. His rigid adherence to the Code of Conduct won him the respect of his fellow prisoners and his Communist captors. Born in Brooklyn, New York, August 9, 1934, Cook was reported missing in action on December 8, 1967. He had been seriously wounded and reported dead while, in fact, he had been captured by the Viet Cong on December 31, 1964, while on a temporary three-day assignment in Vietnam.

Cook subsequently died in a POW camp on December 8, 1967, and was buried in the jungle by his fellow prisoners. On February 26, 1980, he was officially declared dead and the Medal of Honor was presented to his wife by the Secretary of the Navy. He was a Captain when captured but continued to receive promotions while in captivity. He has an "In Memory Of" stone in Memorial Section MI of Arlington National Cemetery. Mrs. Laurette A.

Cook, widow of Colonel Cook, received the Medal of Honor on behalf of her husband, May 16, 1980, during ceremonies at the Hall of Heroes in the Pentagon. The Honorable Edward Hidalgo, Secretary of the Navy, presented the Medal to Mrs. Cook while Colonel Cook's parents and four children looked on along with Gen. Robert H. Barrow, Commandant of the Marine Corps.

A list of Colonel Cook's medals and decorations includes the Medal of Honor, the Purple Heart with one bronze star, the Combat Action Ribbon, the National Defense Service Medal, the Armed Forces Expeditionary Medal, and the Republic of Vietnam Campaign Medal. On July 11, 1997, the United States Navy launched the USS *Donald Cook*, DDG-75, an Arleigh Burke Class Aegis guided missile destroyer, named in honor of Colonel Cook.

Gunnery Sergeant Dan Daly. Daly is the only enlisted Marine to win the Medal of Honor twice—one in the Boxer Rebellion in 1900 and the other in Haiti in 1915. In the WWI battle of Belleau Wood, Daily uttered the famous phrase, "Come on, you sons of bitches! Do you want to live forever?" Born on November 11, 1873, at Glen Cove, Long Island, New York, Daly enlisted in the Corps on January 10, 1899, at the age of twenty-five. His professed reason for enlisting was to participate in the Spanish–American War. However, soon after completing boot camp, he was transferred to the Asiatic Fleet. In addition to Beijing, Haiti, and France, Daly served at Vera Cruz and elsewhere. He remained single his entire life and retired from the Corps on February 6, 1929, as a Sergeant Major. At age sixty-five, on April 28, 1937, Daly died in Glenade L.I., New York.

Master Gunnery Sergeant Leland "Lou" Diamond. Diamond served in France with the famous 6th Marines in World War I and with H Company, 2nd Battalion, 5th Marines, 1st Division, on Guadalcanal and Tulagi at the age of fifty-two in World War II. He single-handedly drove a Japanese cruiser from the bay with his harassing near misses. Called "Mr. Marine" and "Mr. Leatherneck," his dedication in training young Marine recruits earned him Corpswide recognition. Commandant of the Marine Corps A. A. Vandegrift called Diamond "the perfect Marine."

Diamond was born May 30, 1890, in Bedford, Ohio, and enlisted in the Marine Corps July 25, 1917, at the age of twenty-seven. He saw action during World War I with the 6th Marines at Chateau Thierry, Belleau Wood, the Aisne-Marne, St. Mihiel, and the Meuse Argonne. By then a sergeant, Diamond marched to the Rhine with the Army of Occupation. At war's end, he returned to the United States and received an Honorable Discharge from the Corps. He returned to the Corps September 23, 1921, and became an assistant armorer at Parris Island, South Carolina. By 1925, he had regained his sergeant's stripes. Diamond became a gunnery sergeant in 1933 and master gunnery sergeant in 1939, at which time he was assigned to the Depot of Supplies at Philadelphia to help design a new infantry pack for Marines.

Following the Japanese attack on Pearl Harbor, Diamond shipped out to Guadalcanal with H Company, 2nd Battalion, 5th Marines, 1st Marine Division. He was fifty-two years old. During World War II, Diamond, an expert with both 60-mm and 81-mm mortars, led a team of Marines whose accurate fire was credited as the strength behind many engagements in the

Pacific. During Diamond's final years in the Corps, he served as an instructor at the Recruit Depot, Parris Island. He then transferred to Camp Lejeune and joined the 5th Training Battalion with the same duties. Diamond retired November 23, 1945, and returned to his home in Toledo, Ohio. He died at the Great Lakes, Illinois, Naval Training Center Hospital in September 1951 and is buried in Sylvania, Ohio.

Major General Merritt "Red Mike" Edson. This Major General earned the Medal of Honor during a desperate, two-day defense of Guadalcanal's vital airfield (a World War II battle that immediately became known as one of the epic struggles in Marine Corps history—the Battle of Edson's Ridge).

Born in Rutland, Vermont, on April 25, 1897, and reared in Chester, Vermont, Edson attended the University of Vermont for two years, and on June 27, 1916, he joined the First Vermont National Guard Regiment. Sent to Eagle Pass, Texas, for duty on the Mexican border with his regiment, Edson returned to the university in September 1916. He joined the Marine Corps Reserve on June 26, 1917.

Edson was commissioned a Second Lieutenant in the Regular Marine Corps on October 9, 1917. He sailed for France but saw no combat. As a First Lieutenant, he spent the two years at Marine Barracks, Quantico, Virginia, as the Adjutant-Registrar of the fledgling Marine Corps Institute. His efforts greatly contributed to the organization and establishment of this "University for Marines." This was followed by a short tour in Louisiana guarding the mails. He applied for flight training at Pensacola, Florida, winning his gold wings in 1922. Soon after, Edson was ordered to the Marine Air

Station at Guam, where he had his introduction to the semitropical islands of the Marianas with which his name was later to become so closely linked.

Upon his return to the United States in 1925, Edson first took an extensive course in advanced aviation tactics at Kelly Field, Texas, and then attended the Company Officers' Course at Quantico, Virginia. He graduated with the highest grades ever attained by any student up to that time. For physical reasons, however, Edson had to give up his flying status in 1927 and revert to ground duty. He was then assigned as Ordnance Officer at the Philadelphia Navy Yard.

Late in the same year, he was ordered to sea duty as Commanding Officer of the Marine Detachment on the USS *Denver*. During the *Denver*'s service in Central American waters, Captain Edson's detachment was ashore in Nicaragua during the period from February 1928 to 1929. In command of 160 picked and specially trained Marines, he fought twelve separate engagements with the Sandino-led bandits and denied them the use of the Poteca and Coco River valleys. Here Edson received his first Navy Cross for actions in which "his exhibition of coolness, intrepidity, and dash so inspired his men that superior forces of bandits were driven from their prepared positions and severe losses inflicted upon them." From a grateful Nicaraguan government, Captain Edson was also awarded the Nicaraguan Medal of Merit with Silver Star.

After a number of stateside assignments, he drew foreign duty as operations officer with the 4th Marines in Shanghai, China, from 1937 to 1939. This enabled Edson to observe closely Japanese military operations. Edson was given command of the 2nd Battalion, 5th Marine Regiment, at the beginning of 1941. Edson's Raiders were sent to join the fight against Japanese in the Pacific. "Red Mike" (Edson's nickname, which originated from the red beard he wore in Nicaragua) and his unit made a stop on Tulagi, where they flushed the Japanese from their caves and utterly routed the enemy. Edson earned his second Navy Cross for this action. Soon, the Raiders were called to Guadalcanal to help control Henderson Field, an airstrip that held great tactical importance for success in the Pacific. Here the battle of Edson's Ridge was fought. In recognition of his leadership on that ridge, Edson was awarded the Medal of Honor. After that battle, he was promoted to Colonel and given command of the 5th Marine Regiment. Edson was soon promoted to Brigadier General and fought in Saipan and Tinian, earning such honors as the Legion of Merit and Silver Star.

Following World War II, Congress and the other services were threatening to dissolve the Marine Corps. Major General Edson sacrificed his career and an opportunity to become Commandant by retiring in 1947 to fight to retain the Corps as an individual service. He contacted members of Congress personally and as a civilian. General Edson achieved his goal, but at the expense of his career. The National Security Act of 1947 provided for the status and mission of the Marine Corps within the Department of Defense.

Maj. Gen. Merritt Austin Edson died on August 14, 1955, in Washington, D.C. He completed more than thirty years in the military service of his country.

Corporal Ira Hamilton Hayes. Ira Hayes, a full-blooded Pima Indian, was born on the Gila River Indian Reservation, just a few miles south of Chandler, Arizona, on January 12, 1923. Feeling that after Pearl Harbor it was his duty to serve, in August of 1942 Hayes quit school and enlisted in the Marines. He applied for parachute training and was accepted. On February 23, 1945, forty Marines climbed atop Mount Suribachi to plant the American Flag. Joe Rosenthal, an AP photographer, took several shots of the event. The six men planting the flag in the photo were Mike Strank from Pennsylvania, Harlon Block from Texas, Franklin Sousley from Kentucky, John Bradley from Wisconsin, Rene Gagnon from New Hampshire, and Ira Hayes from Arizona. Strank, Harlon, and Sousley died in combat.

On January 24, 1955, Ira Hayes was found dead just a short distance from his home. The coroner said it was an accident. Ira Hamilton Hayes was buried in Arlington National Cemetery with customary pomp and circumstance. He was thirty-two years old.

Marine Corporal John F. Mackie. Born in New York, New York, in 1836, Mackie was the first Marine to win the Medal of Honor for his acts of heroism during the Civil War. Four days after the destruction of the *Virginia* had opened the James River, Union warships approached Drewry's Bluff on the James about eight miles below Richmond. Here they came under fire from Confederate shore batteries mounted on the bluff. Marine Corporal Mackie was on board the USS *Galena*, which was returning their fire when the warship received a hit that caused an explosion. Mackie rallied the survivors, carried off the dead and wounded, and got three of the Galena's guns back in action. As a result of Mackie's heroic action, he became the first Marine to win the Medal of Honor. By the time the war had ended, seventeen Marines had won such an honor.

Lieutenant Presley Neville O'Bannon. Presley Neville O'Bannon was born in 1776, in Fauquier County, Virginia. First appointed a Second Lieutenant in the U.S. Marine Corps on January 18, 1801, he served in various stations in the United States prior to assignment on board the USS *Adams*. Following a deployment to the Mediterranean on the *Adams*, First Lieutenant O'Bannon returned to the United States in November 1803, where he was assigned to duty at Marine Barracks, Washington, D.C. This was followed by sea duty and the famed Tripoli adventure (as a result of which he won the Mameluke Sword). Hailed as "the hero of Derna," O'Bannon resigned from the Marine Corps on March 6, 1807. He went to Kentucky and served in the State Legislature. He died on September 12, 1850, at the age of seventy-four. A monument to his memory was erected over his grave in the state cemetery in Frankfort, Kentucky.

Lieutenant General Louis B. "Chesty" Puller. The most decorated Marine in the history of the Corps—General Puller won fifty-two ribbons in all, including five Navy Crosses, the second highest award a Marine can win, and a Distinguished Service Cross (the U.S. Army equivalent of the Navy Cross). He was a veteran of the Korean War, four WWII campaigns, and expeditionary service in China, Nicaragua, and Haiti. Puller was the only Marine to win the Navy Cross five times for heroism and gallantry in combat.

A Marine officer and enlisted man for thirty-seven years, General Puller served at sea or overseas for all but ten of those years, including a hitch as Commander of the "Horse Marines" in China. Excluding medals from foreign governments, he won fourteen personal decorations in combat, plus a long list of campaign medals, unit citation ribbons, and other awards.

Born June 26, 1898, at West Point, Virginia, the general attended Virginia Military Institute until enlisting in the Marine Corps in August 1918. He was appointed a Marine Reserve Second Lieutenant June 16, 1919, but due to force reductions after World War I was placed on inactive duty ten days later. He rejoined the Marines as an enlisted man to serve with the *Gendarmerie d'Haiti*, a military force in that country under a treaty with the United States. Most of its officers were U.S. Marines, while its enlisted personnel were Haitians. In his career, he served in Nicaragua, China (commanding the Horse Marines), Guadalcanal, Peleliu, Inchon, Korea, and, of course, Chosin Reservoir.

In 1966, General Puller's request to return to active duty to serve in Vietnam was turned down because of his age. He died October 11, 1971, in Hampton, Virginia, after a long illness. He was seventy-three.

Major General Ray "E-tool" Smith. General Smith is one of the most decorated Marines since World War II. He was commanding a company in the fight for Hue City during the Tet Offensive of 1968 when three U.S. Marine battalions, consisting of fewer than 2,500 men, defeated more than 10,000 entrenched enemy troops to liberate the City of Hue for South Vietnam. Smith began the battle with 146 men. Thirty-four days later, only 7 of his men had not been killed or wounded. He was an adviser to the South Vietnamese Marines during the 1972 Easter Offensive. He commanded a battalion during the Grenada operation and later a division.

"E-tool" is of course an abbreviation for "entrenching tool," the small shovel that soldiers and Marines carry for digging their fighting holes. During battle, General Smith used his e-tool to kill a number of NVA soldiers. To quote him, "Unlike a rifle, a shovel doesn't jam."

Smith is also the co-author, with Bing West, of the critically acclaimed book, *The March Up: Taking Baghdad with the 1st Marine Division* (Bantam, September 2003).

Marine Sergeant Kirk Allen Straseskie. Sgt. Kirk Allen Straseskie, twenty-three, drowned on May 19, 2003, while trying to rescue four Marines on board a helicopter that crashed in a canal in central Iraq. The four others also died in the accident. Straseskie, of Beaver Dam, Wisconsin, was assigned to the 1st Battalion, 4th Marine Regiment, from Camp Pendleton. He joined the Marines in 1998, following in the footsteps of his father, grandfather, and older brother—all Army men. He had planned to make the military a career, his father said, but then met a woman and fell in love. They had hoped to marry.

His fearlessness was evident both at home, with his brothers, and in school. He often wrestled, even though, at 171 pounds, he was almost always lighter than his opponents. He also called the defensive alignments as a linebacker for the football team. Here is the text of a letter sent by U.S. Marine Sgt. Kirk Straseskie to his friend Nick Neuman on September 19, 2001. The letter was read at Straseskie's funeral. It also was published with his obituary in the *Daily Citizen*, Beaver Dam. Straseskie was the first of two people from Wisconsin to die in military operations in Iraq:

I suppose now is as good a time as any to go ahead and get this off my chest. With all that's happened in the past weeks the possibility of war seems high. Well, in the long run or the big picture, what does that mean for me? Quite possibly Nick, I could die. Plain and simple.

I do not want to die, it saddens me to think of what I would miss if I were killed. But don't confuse that with fear. I am not afraid to die, and I am prepared to in both my heart and soul. It is my belief that there are greater causes to live and fight for than one's self. That is why I serve. To all I have known and been friends with, I thank you for the experiences and lessons I've had while living my life. I have had friends who have been so important to me, friends that have been with me wherever the Corps has taken me. The most miserable times have been eased by the memories of our times together.

Nick, I ask you to pass these thoughts of mine on to any you think should hear them. To my family I have this: To my parents, Dad and Barb, thank you for being there for me. Dad, I know you've told me not to take chances, and to push myself hard, but for me that would not have been living. Life was something for me to grab by the throat and squeeze, demanding all I could get from it. When the time comes for me, it will find me ready and standing tall. My life was not wasted and I died for what I believe in. I ask you to take comfort in that, and do not mourn me, for now I wear my Dress Blues and stand guard at the gates of heaven.

My brothers, you all have had my back in the biggest way as I grew up. There had been nothing that I would not have done for you at any time. As I served my country I truly believed that I had your backs in the biggest way I could. I love you guys and hope for the best to come your way in the years to follow. Good health, and God willing, freedom to you and your families.

This here, is the most important thing I have, this for my nieces and nephews. Make sure they know and understand as they grow older, how much they meant to me. They were the biggest cause of my desire to serve our nation. I would have loved to be there and watch them grow. Devon, Nate, Katy, Maddy, Hannah, Sydney and any others that might have come along since I wrote this, you all were so special to me. Just knowing that you are my family, that my actions have helped to secure your safety and freedom, is more reward to me than any dollar sign, the time I spent watching you grow has given me years of happiness. So many smiles to last three lifetimes. If there is only one thing you could do for me, do not let my nieces and nephews forget about me, but above all, let them know I loved them, and I pray my sacrifice to them will be all they ever have to pay for happiness in life.

Nick, I have many more family members and friends to which I could write, but to keep it as simple as possible, tell them I was at peace with myself when I died, and I fought with everything I had. Take care of yourself buddy, and a happy life to you and Ray, my two best friends in life.

Godspeed and Semper Fidelis,

Kirk A. Straseskie.

General Alexander Archer Vandegrift. Vandegrift led the first large-scale U.S. offensive against the Japanese on Guadalcanal in the Solomon Islands during World War II, and the first Marine to be awarded both the Navy Cross and the Medal of Honor. Vandegrift was the 18th Commandant from 1944 to 1948, and the first Marine to hold the rank of Four-Star General while still on active duty.

Born on March 13, 1887, in Charlottesville, Virginia, Vandegrift attended the University of Virginia and was commissioned in the Marine Corps as a Second Lieutenant on January 22, 1909. He went to foreign shore duty in the Caribbean area where he participated in the bombardment, assault, and capture of Coyotepe in Nicaragua and the seizure of Vera Cruz, Mexico. He sailed for Haiti with the First Brigade and participated in action against hostile Cacos bandits at LeTrou and Fort Capois. In August 1916, Vandegrift was promoted to captain and became a member of the Haitian Constabulary at Port Au Prince where he remained until detached to the United States in December 1918. He returned to Haiti again in July 1919, to serve with the *Gendarmerie d'Haiti* as an Inspector of Constabulary. He was promoted to Major in June 1920.

After serving in the United States in various capacities, Vandegrift sailed for China in February 1927. There he served as Operations and Training Officer of the 3rd Marine Brigade with Headquarters at Tientsin. After a staff stint in Washington, he was ordered back to China in June 1935. Vandegrift served successively as Executive Officer and Commanding Officer of the Marine detachment at the American Embassy, being promoted to Colonel in September 1936.

He was promoted to Major General in March 1942, and in May sailed for the South Pacific area as commanding general of the 1st Marine division to ever leave the shores of the United States. On August 7, 1942, in the Solomon Islands, he led ashore the First Marine Division in the first large-scale offensive action against the Japanese. Vandegrift assumed command of the 1st Marine Amphibious Corps in July of 1943, and commanded this organization in the landing at Empress Augusta Bay, Bougainville, Northern Solomon Islands, on November 1, 1943. Upon establishing the initial beach-head, he relinquished command and returned to Washington, D.C., as Commandant-designate. On January 1, 1944, as a Lieutenant General, he was sworn in as the 18th Commandant of the Marine Corps. On April 4, 1945, he was appointed General, with date of rank from March 21, 1945, the first Marine officer on active duty to attain four-star rank.

For outstanding services as Commandant of the Marine Corps from January 1, 1944, to June 30, 1946, General Vandegrift was awarded the Distinguished Service Medal. He left active service on December 31, 1947, and was placed on the retired list, April 1, 1949.

NOTABLE WOMEN MARINES

Brigadier General Margaret A. Brewer. Appointed to a general officer's billet as Director of Information with the rank of Brigadier General in May 1978, Brewer became the first female general officer in the Marine Corps. She retired on July 1, 1980, after having served as the Director of Public Affairs, Headquarters Marine Corps, Washington, D.C.

Born in Durand, Michigan, in 1930, Brewer received her primary education in Durand schools but graduated from the Catholic High School in Baltimore, Maryland, prior to entering the University of Michigan at Ann Arbor. She received a bachelor's degree in geography in January 1952 and was commissioned a Marine Second Lieutenant in March of that year. Her first assignment was at the Marine Corps Air Station in El Toro, California, where she served as Communications Watch Officer from 1952 to 1953. From 1953 to 1955, she served as Inspector-Instructor of a woman Marine reserve unit in Brooklyn, New York. From 1955 to 1958, Captain Brewer served successively as Commanding Officer of the woman Marine companies at Norfolk, Virginia, and Camp Lejeune, North Carolina. From 1958 to 1960, she served as Platoon Commander for woman officer candidates at Quantico, Virginia, during summer training sessions, and for the balance of the time, a woman officer selection officer with headquarters in Lexington, Kentucky. In 1959, Brewer was transferred to Camp Pendleton, California, for duty with the Commissioned Officers Mess (Open). She was promoted to Major in September 1961 and in April 1963 returned to Quantico to serve as executive officer and later as commanding officer of the Woman Officer School.

From 1966 to 1968, she served as Public Affairs Officer for the 6th Marine Corps District in Atlanta, Georgia, where she was promoted to Lieutenant Colonel in December 1966. While serving as the Deputy Director of the Division of Information, Brewer was nominated during April 1978 for appointment to the grade of Brigadier General, making her the first female general officer in the United States.

Major Sarah Deal. On July 23, 1993, Deal was the first woman to be selected for Naval aviation training; she became the Marine Corps' first female pilot in April 1995; she is a CH-53E Super Stallion helicopter pilot.

Master Sergeant Barbara J. Dulinsky. On March 18, 1967, in Saigon, Dulinsky became the first woman Marine ordered to a combat zone.

Lieutenant Colonel Robin Higgins. Her final assignments during her twenty years of service were as chief spokesman for the Commandant and head of the Public Affairs Division's media branch. Higgins became an internationally known speaker and author after the capture of her husband, Col.

William R. Higgins, by Lebanese terrorists in 1988. He was later murdered by the terrorists in 1990. A destroyer, the USS *Higgins* (DDG-76), is named after him. Robin served as Executive Director of Florida's Department of Veteran's Affairs and was appointed by President George W. Bush to serve as the Under Secretary of the Department of Veteran's Affairs for Memorial Affairs. The Senate unanimously confirmed her in March 2001. Robin Higgins (then Ross) was born in 1950, in the Bronx, New York. She graduated from high school in 1968. Robin then attended the State University of New York (SUNY) at Oneonta. She spent her junior year in Israel from August 1970 to May 1971. She graduated from SUNY Oneonta in 1972. Afterward, she spent a short time teaching and then enlisted in the U.S. Marine Corps, where she was commissioned as an officer.

Robin originally chose the MOS (Military Occupational Specialty) of the military police. She completed her training in this field and then became an English teacher at the Basic School in Quantico, Virginia. Her MOS title then became Effective Communication Specialist. During her time in the Marines, Robin also served as head of the media branch of the Public Affairs Division and as chief spokeswoman for the Commandant.

In December 1977, she married Col. Rich Higgins, in Jacksonville, North Carolina. Her husband was one of seven U.S. Marine Corps officers assigned to the United Nations peacekeeping force in Lebanon in 1987. Colonel Higgins was taken hostage in February 1988 and was later murdered by Iranian-backed Hezbollah terrorists in Lebanon. Hezbollah released a videotape claiming to have hanged Colonel Higgins in July 1989. However, the U.S. military confirmed that he actually died on July 6, 1990.

Colonel Higgins's remains were returned to the United States on December 30, 1991, for burial at Quantico National Cemetery in Quantico, Virginia. The destroyer named after Colonel Higgins, the USS *Higgins*, DDG-76, was launched on October 4, 1997. Throughout the time that Robin's husband was in captivity, she worked for his release. She hid her Jewish heritage so that the Hezbollah would not torture or kill her husband. She is the author of a book, *Patriot Dreams*, which deals with the murder of her husband.

Opha Mae Johnson. Enlisting on August 13, 1918, Johnson became the first woman Marine. Her enlistment reflected the dramatic changes in the status of women brought about by the entry of the United States into World War I. Marine Reserve (F) was the official title by which the Marine Corps' first enlisted women were known. They were better known as "skirt Marines" and "Marinettes." During the WWI period, 305 women served as Marines. These women performed administrative duties at Headquarters, Marine Corps until August 11, 1919, when the Commandant ordered them to inactive status. On June 30, 1919, Maj. Gen. Commandant Barnett said of the Woman Reservists, "It is a pleasure . . . to be able to state that the service rendered by the reservists [female] has been uniformly excellent."

Lieutenant General Carol A. Mutter. Lt. Gen. Carol A. Mutter is the most senior woman officer in the U.S. Marine Corps and the first woman to receive the rank of Lieutenant General. Today, Lieutenant General Mutter serves as Deputy Chief of Staff for Manpower and Reserve Affairs at Headquarters Marine Corps.

The road to this important position began when Mutter received her Second Lieutenant bars in 1967 after graduating from the University of Northern Colorado with a B.A. degree in Mathematics Education. Since then, General Mutter has received her M.A. degree in National Security and Strategic Services from the Naval War College and has both an M.S. degree and an honorary doctorate. She also attended the Amphibious Warfare School and the Marine Corps Command and Staff College.

Capitalizing on her knowledge and expertise in both data processing and financial management, General Mutter was assigned as program manager for the development of new Marine Corps automated pay and personnel systems for active duty, retired and reserve Marines.

She then joined the U.S. Space Command, becoming Division Chief responsible for the operation of Commander in Chief's Command Center.

In 1990, General Mutter was assigned to the III Marine Expeditionary Force on Okinawa, Japan, as the assistant Chief of Staff, Comptroller. In 1991, she assumed duties as Deputy Commanding General, Marine Corps Systems Command, and the Program Manager for Marine Air Ground Task Force Command and Control in Quantico, Virginia. She returned to Okinawa to command the 3rd Force Service Support Group, U.S. Marine Forces, Pacific. Upon advancement to Lieutenant General on September 1, 1996, she resumed her present position.

Her medals and decorations include the Defense Superior Service Medal, National Defense Service Medal with bronze star, and the Sea Service Deployment Ribbon with four bronze stars. She retired on January 1, 1999, after more than thirty years of service starting in 1967.

Brigadier General Gail M. Reals. Selected to the rank of Brigadier General in February 1985, Reals became the first woman Marine selected to general grade. She also served as the Commanding General of the Marine Corps Base in Quantico, Virginia.

Colonel Ruth Cheney Streeter (1895–1990). In January 1943, Streeter was sworn in as a Major in the United States Marine Corps Women's Reserve (USMCWR) and was sworn in as the first Director of the Women's Reserve, which was formed on November 7, 1942. She served until December 1945. Streeter lived most of her adult life in Morristown where she was active in civic affairs. She was serving as the first woman President of the Morris County Welfare Board when she was appointed Director of the United States Marine Corps Women's Reserve in 1943. In 1947, after returning to civilian life, she was a member of the New Jersey Constitutional Convention.

Colonel Katherine Amelia Towle (April 30, 1898–March 1, 1986). Second Director of the Women's Reserve, Towle was discharged from the Marine Corps Reserve on November 3, 1948, and accepted a Regular commission as a permanent Lieutenant Colonel. The next day, she was appointed the first Director of Women Marines, with the temporary rank of Colonel. Born April 30, 1898, in Towle, California, Katherine Towle graduated from the University of California at Berkeley in 1920. After several years as an administrator at Berkeley and at a private girls' school, she resumed her studies in political science at Berkeley in 1933, receiving a master's degree in 1935. From that year to 1942 she was assistant to the manager and a senior editor of the University of California Press.

In February 1943 Towle took a commission as Captain in the newly established Women's Reserve (WR) of the U.S. Marine Corps. Until September 1944, her duties were divided between corps headquarters in Washington, D.C., and the women's training centers at Hunter College, New York City, and, from June 1943, at Camp Lejeune, North Carolina. Promoted to Major in February 1944, she became assistant director of the WR in September, advancing to Lieutenant Colonel in March 1945, and in December 1945 she was promoted to Colonel and named director to succeed Colonel Ruth C. Streeter. Towle remained in that post until June 1946, when the WR was inactivated.

During 1946 to 1947, she served as administrative assistant to the vice president and provost of the University of California, and in July 1947 she was appointed assistant dean of women. With the passage of the Women's Armed Forces Integration Act of June 12, 1948, the women's reserve of the Marine Corps, like those of the other branches of the armed services, was integrated into the active line. Colonel Towle was recalled to active duty as Director in October. Retiring from that post in May 1953, she then served as dean of women and Associate Dean of Students at the University of California at Berkeley from 1953 to 1962 and as Dean of Students from 1962 to her retirement in 1965. During her tenure as dean of students, she ordered that political activity on the campus be limited. The students reacted with sit-ins and demonstrations and formed a protest group—the Free Speech Movement—which kept student involvement and activism high for months. Towle died on March 1, 1986, in Pacific Grove, California.

OTHER NOTABLE MARINES

As mentioned, outstanding Marines are innumerable. Here are several more—some of whom may surprise you!

Bernice Frankel "Bea Arthur" (b. 1923). Frankel served during World War II. She was best known for her roles in *Maude, All in the Family*, and *The Golden Girls*.

F. Lee Bailey (b. 1933). A Marine pilot; Bailey went on to become a well-known attorney.

Lieutenant James Addison Baker III (b. 1930). Baker served from 1952 to 1954. He was an expert marksman and member of the Camp Lejeune rifle and pistol team. He was appointed Undersecretary of Commerce in 1975, campaign manager for Gerald Ford in his unsuccessful bid for reelection in 1976, and campaign manager for George H. W. Bush in his unsuccessful bid for the Republican presidential nomination in 1980 and his successful election in 1988. Under Ronald Reagan, Baker served first as Chief of Staff and then as Secretary of the Treasury. He served as Secretary of State from 1989 to 1992.

James Lee Barrett. This Marine became a screenwriter for a large number of films, including *The D.I.* (1957), *The Greatest Story Ever Told* (1965), *Shenandoah* (1965), *The Green Berets* (1968), and *Smokey and the Bandit* (1977).

Robert Bork. Serving from 1945 to 1946, Bork was then called back during the Korean War. He earned his law degree and practiced law in the Chicago area until the 1960s and taught constitutional law at Yale Law School as the Alexander M. Bickel Professor of Public Law—two of his students were Bill and Hillary Clinton. During the Nixon presidency he served as Solicitor General and Acting Attorney General; President Reagan appointed him Circuit Judge of the U.S. Court of Appeals for the District of Columbia (D.C.) in 1981. Bork authored *The Antitrust Paradox* (1978) and *The Tempting of America: The Political Seduction of the Law* (1990). He was an unsuccessful candidate for the Supreme Court.

Jesse Brown. Serving from 1963 to 1966, Brown's right arm was partially paralyzed by sniper fire in Vietnam in 1965. He served on the staff of the Disabled American Veterans for twenty-six years. President Clinton appointed him United States Secretary of Veterans Affairs in 1993.

Staff Sergeant Dale Bumpers. Bumpers served twenty-four years as U.S. Senator (D) from Arkansas, two terms as Arkansas Governor.

Corporal Conrad Burns (b. 1935). Burns is a U.S. Senator (R) from Montana.

Rod Carew (b. 1945). Baseball Hall-of-Famer Carew led the AL in batting seven times (1969, 1972–1975, 1977–1978) with Minnesota. He won MVP in 1977 and had 3,053 career hits.

Drew Carey (b. 1958). Carey served in the USMCR from 1981 to 1986. As an actor and comedian, he has appeared on many shows. Carey has his own show, *The Drew Carey Show* (1995 to present) and hosts *Who's Line is it Anyway?*

Lieutenant John H. Chaffee (b. 1922). Chaffee is a U.S. Senator (R) from Rhode Island.

Ronnie Walter Cunningham (b. 1932). Marine fighter pilot from 1953 to 1956, Cunningham was an American astronaut. He participated in the Apollo 7 mission as a civilian.

Brian Dennehy. Serving five years in the Corps, and contrary to some stories, Dennehy did not see combat and was not wounded. He has starred in over forty feature films and numerous TV movies.

David N. Dinkins (b. 1927). Dinkins was the first African American Mayor of New York City.

Andre Dubus (1936–1999). Dubus served six years in the Corps. As a short-story writer and novelist, his works included *The Lieutenant* (1967) and *Andromache* (1977), which is considered to be his best of many stories about the Corps.

David Douglas Duncan (b. 1916). During World War II, Duncan served as photographer to the Marine Corps aviation in the Pacific. He became a staff photographer for *Life* magazine in 1946 and covered the Korean War in 1950. Duncan's photos are featured in the book *This Is War* (1951).

Captain Dale Dye (b. October 8, 1944). This mustang officer served his enlisted time as a combat correspondent in Vietnam in 1965 and 1967 to 1970. He earned numerous decorations including three Purple Hearts. He rose to the rank of Master Sergeant during his thirteen years as an enlisted Marine before going to OCS and being commissioned as a Captain. He retired in 1984. He has been the military technical adviser on numerous movies including *Starship Troopers, Platoon, JFK, Forrest Gump*, and *Born on the Fourth of July*.

Gunnery Sergeant Ronald Lee Ermey (b. March 24, 1944). Ermey served eleven years in the Corps including one and a half tours in Vietnam. He was medically retired from injuries received. He has since appeared in nearly forty movies including *Apocalypse Now, The Boys in Company C, Mississippi Burning*, and *Full Metal Jacket*.

Glenn Ford (b. 1916). This Broadway stage actor entered films in 1939 and starred opposite Rita Hayworth in *Gilda* (1946). He was in many other films including *Battle of the Midway* (1976).

Colonel John Herschel Glenn Jr. (b. 1921). John Glenn served in the Corps from 1943 to 1964. He flew fifty-nine missions in World War II and 90 missions in Korea. He was a test pilot from 1954 to 1959. Glenn became the first American to orbit Earth in his space capsule *Friendship 7* in 1962. Starting in 1974, he was U.S. Senator (D) from Ohio for four terms. Later, he became the oldest person to travel into space in 1998.

Lou Gossett. Actor.

Corporal Gene Hackman (b. 1931). Serving six years from 1946 to 1952 in China, Japan, and Hawaii, Hackman is a two-time Oscar-winning actor.

Corporal Gustav Hasford (November 28, 1947–January 29, 1993). Hasford served as a Marine combat correspondent with the 1st Marine Division in Vietnam from 1966 to 1968. While still in Vietnam he began writing about the experiences he had. The finished novel was finally published in 1979 as *The Short-Timers*. This book became the basis for the movie, *Full Metal Jacket* (1987). He also wrote the screenplay for the movie with Stanley Kubrick and Michael Hess. This resulted in an Academy Award nomination.

I. Michael Heyman (b. 1930). This Marine Corps officer served during the Korean War. Heyman is former editor of the *Yale Law Journal*, former chief law clerk for Chief Justice Earl Warren, and former chancellor of the University of California at Berkeley. He was inducted as the CEO of the Smithsonian Institution in 1994.

Huell Howser. Public Broadcasting personality.

Roberto Walker Clemente (1934–1972). A baseball Hall of Famer, Clemente enjoyed a lifetime batting average of .317 and hit 240 home runs. He died in an airplane crash while attempting to take food and medicine to earthquake victims in Nicaragua in December 1972.

Keith Jackson. The "Voice of the NCAA" (college football announcer).

Bob Keeshan (b. 1927). Keeshan served during World War II. He played

Clarabell the Clown on the *Howdy Doody* show for six years, but is best known as Captain Kangaroo, a role that he played for fifty years.

Harvey Keitel. Keitel served in Lebanon. He first appeared in a movie in 1968 and has since been in more than seventy films. His movie credits include *Mean Streets, Taxi Driver, The Last Temptation of Christ, Reservoir Dogs*, and *Pulp Fiction*.

Mills Lane. This Marine served three years in the Corps from 1956 to 1959 as an infantry rifle instructor and earned the Welterweight Boxing Championship while stationed on Okinawa. Lane was NCAA Welterweight Champion in 1960. He became a boxing referee in 1964 and became most well known for his decision against Mike Tyson during the Holyfield fight when Tyson bit Holyfield's ear. He graduated law school in 1970, and became a trial prosecutor in 1971. Lane worked as chief deputy sheriff and special prosecutor from 1979 to 1982, District Attorney from 1982 to 1990, and District Judge from 1990 to 1998. Since 1998 he has appeared in his own courtroom television series, *Judge Mills Lane*.

Robert Lutz. Former Marine fighter pilot, as vice chairman and president of Chrysler Lutz is largely credited with their revitalization during the company's second turnaround in the 1990s; he retired from Chrysler in 1998 to take over Exide.

Private Lee Marvin (February 19, 1924 to August 28 1987). This popular character actor went from Broadway to television to the big screen. He was in numerous movies including *The Dirty Dozen* and an Academy Award–

winning performance in *Cat Ballou*. He served in the Pacific during World War II. He was wounded in the buttocks during the battle of Saipan and received a Purple Heart. He is buried in Arlington National Cemetery.

Colonel Ed McMahon. McMahon was a Marine fighter pilot in World War II and Korea (eighty-five combat missions). He was also a test pilot for the Corsair. McMahon co-hosted *The Tonight Show* with Johnny Carson for thirty years from 1962 to 1992, then hosted *Star Search* for twelve years.

Terrence Steven "Steve" McQueen (1930–1980). Steve McQueen enlisted and served as a mechanic/tank driver for three years. As a television and film actor he was known for his roles as a cool loner. He appeared in the television series *Wanted—Dead or Alive* (1958–1961). His many film credits include *The Magnificent Seven* (1960), *The Great Escape* (1963), *The Thomas Crown Affair* (1968), *Bullitt* (1968), and *Papillon* (1973).

Lieutenant Colonel Oliver North. North became well known during the Iran-Contra hearings, but has since made a name for himself as a radio talk show host.

Ken Norton. A former Heavyweight Boxing Champion, Norton was a three-time All-Marine Boxing Champion.

Jefferey P. Papows. This former Marine officer earned a Ph.D.; he was a CEO and President of Lotus Development Corporation until February 2000. Papows authored the book *Enterprise.com* and has also been a keynote speaker at COMDEX.

Tyrone Power (1914–1958). Film and stage actor, Power was known for his roles as a romantic swashbuckler. His films include *Mark of Zorro* (1940), *The Razor's Edge* (1946), *Nightmare Alley* (1947), *The Sun Also Rises* (1957), and *Witness for the Prosecution* (1957).

Dan Rather (b. 1931). Rather co-anchored *60 Minutes* (1975–1981) and *CBS Evening News* (1981–present).

Donald Regan. Youngest President of Merrill Lynch.

Lieutenant Colonel Charles S. Robb. U.S. Senator (D) from Virginia, Robb served thirty-four years of active and reserve time in the Corps before retiring in 1991. He was awarded the Bronze Star with Combat V and Vietnamese Cross of Gallantry with Silver Star.

Captain Pat Roberts. U.S. Senator (R) from Kansas.

George Pratt Schultz (b. 1920). Under President Nixon, he served as Secretary of Labor (1969–1970), Director of the Office of Management and Budget (1970–1972), and Secretary of the Treasury (1972–1974). Under President Ronald Reagan, Schultz served as Secretary of State from 1982 to 1989.

George Campbell Scott (1927–1999). Scott served for four years starting in 1945. An actor, he was best known for his Oscar-winning portrayal of Gen. George S. Patton in the film *Patton*.

Bernard Shaw. *CNN Evening News* anchor.

Frederick W. Smith. Founder and CEO of Federal Express.

Jack Smith. Former columnist with the *Los Angeles Times*.

John Philip "The March King" Sousa (1854–1932). The most famous leader of the Marine Band, "The President's Own," Sousa wrote many famous marches, including *Semper Fidelis* and *Stars and Stripes Forever*. His father enlisted him on June 9, 1868, at the age of thirteen for seven and a half years to prevent him from running away with the circus. Sousa left the Marine Corps after that enlistment but returned in 1880 and served as Director of the Marine Band until 1892. He wrote an autobiography called *Marching Along* in 1928.

Leon Spinks (b. 1953). Spinks won the heavyweight crown in a split decision over Muhammad Ali in February 1978; he won a gold medal in light heavyweight division at the 1976 Olympics.

Captain Arthur Sulzberger. This Marine served as a Corporal in World War II and as a Lieutenant in Korea. Publisher of the *New York Times* for twenty-six years.

Charles (Chuck) R. Swindoll (b. 1934). Swindoll is President of Dallas Theological Seminary and chairman of Insight for Living, his radio Bible teaching ministry.

Captain Craig Thomas. U.S. Senator (R) from Wyoming.

John Warner (USMCR). U.S. Senator (R) from Virginia.

Jack Webb. An actor and director, Webb is famous for his roles in *The D.I.* and as LAPD Sergeant Joe Friday in various incarnations of *Dragnet*.

Montel Williams. Williams was the first black Marine selected to the Naval Academy Prep School to go on and graduate from the Naval Academy. He served on board the USS *Sampson* during the U.S. invasion of Grenada. His awards include the Armed Forces Expeditionary Medal, two Navy Expeditionary Medals, two Humanitarian Service Medals, a Navy Achievement Medal, two Navy Commendation Medals, and two Meritorious Service Awards. After the Marines, he became an Emmy award–winning talk show host.

Theodore (Ted) Samuel Williams (b. 1918). This Marine pilot served (1943–1945) in World War II and again (1952–1953) in the Korean War. He is a Baseball Hall-of-Famer with a lifetime batting average of .344 and a total of 521 home runs.

Pete Wilson. Former Governor of California.

Donald James Yarmy "Don Adams" (b. 1926). After enlisting, Yarmy was shot on Guadalcanal in World War II and was medevaced to New Zealand in 1943 suffering from blackwater fever, which was fatal in 90 percent of all cases. Don says that God answered his prayers and saved his life. He was the voice of Tennessee Tuxedo and Inspector Gadget in the cartoons, but he is most well known for his role as bumbling Maxwell Smart, Agent 86, in the TV spy show *Get Smart!* He won three Emmy Awards for that role.

MARINE BOOKS

Many Marines have written books about the Corps. Here are a few—both fact and fiction—which either help the reader feel what it was really like in some of the USMC's most famous struggles, or else illuminate the history and customs of the Marines.

Battle Cry by Leon Uris (April 1953; also a film)

Moving, shocking, tense, and glorious, here is a magnificent saga of men at war—Leon Uris's famous novel about life in the jaws of death, in the U.S. Marine Corps. Based on Uris's own experiences with 2/6 (2nd Battalion, 6th Marine Regiment, 2nd Marine Division), this novel follows the radio section of the battalion from Guadalcanal ("the Canal" in WWII Marine lingo) to Tarawa and climaxes with the bloody invasion of Saipan. There's plenty of combat action to satisfy the most demanding fans of blood-and-guts writing, and enough romance to keep readers of a more gentle nature turning the pages. Many WWII Marines said *Battle Cry* truly echoed their own wartime experiences. Uris's focus is not only combat, but also the training and what the Marines did when they got liberty.

Tarawa by Robert Sherrod (January 1973)

A war correspondent for *Time*, Sherrod waded ashore Tarawa on the afternoon of D-day, November 20, 1943. Aboard his transport ship Sherrod heard fascinating tales of the Gilbert Islands before the war, tales told to him by his shipmates Karl Tschaun and James Forbes. Both of these men had lived and worked among these island paradises and now returned to share their knowledge of the waters with the allies. The reader hears the authentic voice of one who has been there, one who heard firsthand the anticipation that the island would be a cakewalk and then saw men horribly chopped to pieces as they went ashore. But for Sherrod to get to Tarawa he too had to wade seven hundred yards across the reef that surrounded and protected the island. During this march no fewer than five machine guns were firing upon him and the few Marines with him.

A Rumor of War by Philip Caputo (June 1977)

In this autobiographical account of his time as an infantry officer in "the 'Nam," Caputo describes the experience in authoritative terms enhanced by collegiate English studies and time spent as a combat journalist. Caputo takes the reader into the muddy foxhole with him, making you feel the heat and annoyance of the ever-present insects, and the sniper shots that all united to deprive you of the precious commodity of sleep. He takes you on patrol with them down "Purple Heart Trail," where the main enemies were the heat, the insects, and endless mines and booby traps. The reader can feel the rage of the infantrymen who fought endless battles with an enemy that was everywhere, yet nowhere.

Fields of Fire by James Webb (August 1978)

The classic novel of the Vietnam War, it was hailed by the *Philadelphia Inquirer* as "one hell of a good read." In the tradition of *All Quiet on the Western Front, The Naked and the Dead*, and *Platoons*, James Webb's novel is the story of a platoon of tough, young Marines enduring the tropical hell of Southeast Asian jungles; they face an invisible enemy—in a war no one understands. It brilliantly expresses the basic ambiguity of war: the repulsion of war's destruction contrasted with its attraction as the ultimate test of survival.

Goodbye Darkness: A Memoir of the Pacific War by William Manchester (September 1980)

One of the most celebrated biographer/historians of present time looks back at his own early life and gives a remarkable account of World War II in the Pacific, of what it looked like, sounded like, smelled like, and, most of all, what it felt like to one who underwent all but the ultimate of its experiences.

With the Old Breed at Peleliu and Okinawa by E. B. Sledge (1981)

A stirring, personal account of the vitality and bravery of the Marines in the battles at Peleliu and Okinawa. Born in Mobile, Alabama, in 1923 and raised on riding, hunting, fishing, and a respect for history and legendary heroes such as George Washington and Daniel Boone, Eugene Bondurant Sledge (later called "Sledgehammer" by his Marine Corps buddies) joined the Marines the year after the bombing of Pearl Harbor and from 1943 to

1946 endured the events recorded in this book. Sledge still has nightmares about "the bloody, muddy month of May on Okinawa." But, as he also tellingly reveals, the bonds of friendship formed then will never be severed.

Semper Fi, Mac by Henry Berry (September 1982)

Semper Fi, Mac brings to life the Marines of World War II—the tough, battle-trained troops who stormed the beaches of Bougainville, Tarawa, Saipan, Iwo Jima, and Okinawa—in some of the bitterest and bloodiest fighting of the war. Compiled from over seventy-five interviews with surviving officers and enlisted men, these powerful firsthand accounts give a soldier's-eye portrait of the Marine Pacific war experience—the camaraderie, the women, the loneliness, the fear—and the profound emotional as well as spiritual rewards that resulted. Former machine gunners, riflemen, mortarmen, and engineers share the horrifying and humorous stories that defined their days in the Pacific. Through this filter of recollection, one truism is reflected time and again: "There is no such thing as an ex-Marine."

Semper Fidelis: The History of the United States Marine Corps by Allan R. Millett (June 1991)

Traces the history of the Marine Corps from the American Revolution to the present and reveals how the force has adapted to changing times. The ultimate reference book on the subject—it should be on the shelf of anyone interested in the Corps.

Fix Bayonets! by Captain John W. Thomason Jr. (May 1994)

Writer, artist, and U.S. Marine Corps officer Thompson recounts his experiences of the final months of World War I on the western front of France with a chronological narrative and the battlefield sketches and drawings that made him famous. He describes the Marines: "a number of diverse people who ran curiously to type, with drilled shoulders and a bone-deep sunburn, and a tolerant scorn of nearly everything on earth. . . . They drank the eau de vie of Haute-Marne, and reminisced on saki, and vino, and Bacardi Rum—strange drinks in strange cantinas at the far ends of the earth; and they spoke fondly of Milwaukee beer. Rifles were high and holy things to them, and they knew five-inch broadside guns. They talked patronizingly of the war, and were concerned about rations. They were the Leathernecks, the Old Timers."

Flags of Our Fathers: Heroes of Iwo Jima by James Bradley (May 2000)

James Bradley captures the glory, the triumph, the heartbreak, and the legacy of the six men who raised the flag at Iwo Jima. Here is the true story behind the immortal photograph that has come to symbolize the courage and indomitable will of America.

In February 1945, American Marines plunged into the surf at Iwo Jima—and into history. Through a hail of machine-gun and mortar fire that left the beaches strewn with comrades, they battled to the island's highest peak.

And after climbing through a landscape of hell itself, they raised a flag. Now the son of one of the flag raisers has written a powerful account of six very different men who came together in a moment that will live forever.

Warrior Culture of the U.S. Marines by Marion F. Sturkey (February 2002)

This is the authoritative guide to the interior life of the Corps. It describes in detail the history, customs, and mentality of the Marines.

China Marine by E. B. Sledge (May 2002)

China Marine is the sequel to E. B. Sledge's critically acclaimed memoir, *With the Old Breed at Peleliu and Okinawa*. Picking up where his previous memoir left off, Sledge, a young Marine in the 1st Division, traces his company's movements and charts his own "difficult passage to peace" following his horrific experiences in the Pacific. He reflects on his duty in the ancient city of Peiping—now Beijing—and recounts the difficulty of returning to his hometown of Mobile, Alabama, and resuming civilian life haunted by the shadows of close combat.

Jarhead by Anthony Swofford (March 2003)

When the Marines—or "jarheads," as they call themselves—were sent in 1990 to Saudi Arabia to fight the Iraqis, Swofford was there, with a hundred-pound pack on his shoulders and a sniper's rifle in his hands. It was one misery upon another. He lived in sand for six months, his girlfriend back home betrayed him for a scrawny hotel clerk, he was punished by boredom and fear, he considered suicide, he pulled a gun on one of his fellow marines, and he was shot at by both Iraqis and Americans. At the end of the war, Swofford hiked for miles through a landscape of incinerated Iraqi soldiers and later was nearly killed in a booby-trapped Iraqi bunker. He weaves this experience of war with vivid accounts of boot camp (which included physical abuse by his drill instructor), reflections on the mythos of the Marines, and remembrances of battles with lovers and family. As engagement with the Iraqis draws closer, he is forced to consider what it is to be an American, a soldier, a son of a soldier, and a man.

Retreat, Hell by W. E. B. Griffin (September 2003)

It is the fall of 1950. The Marines have made a pivotal breakthrough at Inchon, but a roller coaster awaits them. The bit in his teeth, MacArthur surges across the thirty-eighth parallel toward the Yalu River, only to encounter the Chinese in full force, who drive him back in turn. Back and forth, the bloody tides of war shift, and swept along with them are Capt. Ken McCoy and Master Gunner Ernie Zimmerman, caught in the fight of their lives; Brig. Gen. Fleming Pickering, working desperately to mediate the escalating battle between MacArthur and Truman; and Pickering's daredevil pilot son, Malcolm, lost somewhere behind enemy lines—and maybe lost forever.

MARINE MOVIES

If anything, Hollywood loves the Marines even more than publishers do—that may seem strange considering the politics of so many in the entertainment industry. Nevertheless, the fact is that drama sells movie tickets, and the stories of young men balancing idealism and gritty reality, personal lives and historical events, are nothing if not dramatic. Here is a small selection.

Wake Island (1942)
Director: John Farrow

Wake Island was among Hollywood's earliest responses to America's being attacked and drawn into World War II. The Marine Corps defenders of Wake became instant war heroes, akin to the martyrs of the Alamo. Nothing could be done to rescue or even to reinforce and resupply them, and they fought on through air attacks and naval bombardment for two weeks until, finally overrun, they were wiped out.

Guadalcanal Diary (1942)
Director: Lewis Seiler

Filmed just months after the actual invasion of Guadalcanal late in 1942 and based on Richard Tregaskis's wildly popular (but excessively jingoistic and poorly written) memoir of the same, *Guadalcanal Diary* is interesting for a glimpse at the Hollywood propaganda machine of World War II if not for any other reason. With predictable inflammatory dialogue and plotting and broad burlesque performances by a gaggle of recognizable character actors in familiar stereotypes, *Guadalcanal Diary* is a rush job notable today for an early appearance by Anthony Quinn.

Sands of Iwo Jima (1949)
Director: Allan Dwan

Tough Marine sergeant leads a group of raw recruits on a historic invasion in this highly popular, influential WWII drama. This is an entertaining must-see for war movie buffs. Filmed at Camp Pendleton near San Diego, *Sands of Iwo Jima* begins with the hard-nosed Stryker, played by John Wayne, training new Marines in New Zealand for the island-hopping battles to come. Training proceeds as expected, as the older Stryker works to get the platoon into fighting shape. The battle at Iwo Jima turns anticlimactic because the more interesting scenes take place at the Battle of Tarawa, where Stryker gains credibility with his platoon for heroically taking out a Japanese stronghold, losing only three men in the process.

Halls of Montezuma (1951)
Director: Lewis Milestone

Richard Widmark stars as a Marine platoon leader who, having brought only seven of his men through Guadalcanal, is determined to see them safely through the next island conquest. The Lieutenant was a schoolteacher in civilian life—as we see in flashbacks—and one member of his command is a former student (Richard Hylton) he helped to overcome his fear. Other platoon members include ex-boxer Jack Palance, trigger-happy bad boy Skip Homeier, hardcase veterans Neville Brand and Bert Freed, and Karl Malden as a philosophical corpsman. However, the most arresting performance is given by milestone discovery Richard Boone, making his screen debut as a sympathetic Colonel stuck with fighting the Japanese and fighting off a miserable cold at the same time.

Flying Leathernecks (1951)
Director: Nicholas Ray

Maj. Dan Kirby (John Wayne) is commander of a Marine Corps fighting unit sent to Guadalcanal to give support to the ground troops. He is short of planes and pilots and drives his men to the point of complete breakdown. The executive officer, Griff (Robert Ryan) objects to Kirby's hard treatment of the men, but he lets his human feelings cloud his judgment. For a soldier, that is bad. Kirby is recalled to the States to train pilots in his new low-level attack technique, and before leaving he informs Griff that he does not consider him fit to command. He hasn't yet got the guts to lead. When they are reunited later the hostility between them is intense. An emergency arises, and there is a scramble to get into the air to intercept a formation of Japanese bombers, forcing some hard decisions to be made.

Battle Cry (1955)
Director: Raoul Walsh

The most interesting—and entertaining—aspect of this long, episodic WWII drama is that it marked the debut of one Justus E. McQueen, who subsequently took the name of the good ol' Arkansas boy he played in the movie: L.Q. Jones. He's only one of eight or nine Marine recruits who divide the screen time with commanding officer Van Heflin and James Whitmore—a lifer sergeant named Mac, "just Mac," who ramrods their squad and also delivers the movie's overbearing narration. Unfortunately, the narration is necessary to maintain continuity as the CinemaScope production galumphs its way from rounding up the melting-pot cast, to seeing them through basic training and sundry, mostly amatory misadventures in San Diego, to further training in New Zealand, and finally to a baptism by fire on Guadalcanal.

The D.I. (1957)
Director: Jack Webb

To immerse his men into the world of military discipline, a Marine drill instructor must be relentlessly grim, showing no signs of weakness before his recruits. But what of the drill instructor's private side—his doubts, his needs, his passions? Jack Webb stars as the meanest DI on Parris Island, the man responsible for whipping a series of sorry "boots" into shape. As the film opens, one of his charges, the oversensitive yet ruggedly good-looking Don Dubbins, is giving Webb more trouble than usual. Frequently absenting himself to sick bay with mysterious ailments, and failing to keep up with the other recruits, Dubbins seems determined to get out of the Corps. But Webb sees Dubbins's potential—screw-ups and psychosomatic complaints aside—and what he sees impresses him mightily. "There's a man hidden somewhere under that baby powder."

The Wind and the Lion (1975)
Director: John Milius

Very loosely based on historic events in 1904, the film features Sean Connery as a Berber chieftain who kidnaps the widow of the former American consul at Tangier, Morocco. In response, President Teddy Roosevelt sends in the Marines, paving the way for some pretty inspiring action scenes. Good insight into the place of the United States in the world.

Full Metal Jacket (1987)
Director: Stanley Kubrick

You can't get any more into Marine Boot Camp at Parris Island (without signing up) than you do in the first half of *Full Metal Jacket*. R. Lee Ermey, who plays Senior Drill Instructor Gunnery Sergeant Hartman, was originally the technical adviser for the film. Since he had really been a Marine DI, Stanley Kubrick asked him to give an example of how an SDI would talk to a new platoon of recruits. After some minutes of nonstop invectives without repeating himself, Kubrick was so impressed that he hired Ermey on the spot to play the role on screen. Also, the sample dialogue was incorporated into the script. After a tragic end to training, the film switches to Vietnam on the eve of the Tet Offensive. "Joker" is a military journalist (in the "rear with the gear," working out of DaNang). When Tet begins, he is sent to Hue and finds his old Parris Island buddy "Cowboy" with "Hotel" Company, 2/5.

A Few Good Men (1992)
Director: Rob Reiner

A U.S. soldier is dead, and military lawyers Lt. Daniel Kaffee and Lt. Commander JoAnne Galloway want to know who killed him. "You want the truth?" snaps Colonel Jessup (Jack Nicholson). "You can't handle the truth!" Astonishingly, Jack Nicholson's legendary performance as a military tough guy in *A Few Good Men* really amounts to a glorified cameo: he's only in a few scenes. But they're killer scenes, and the film has much more to offer. Tom Cruise (Kaffee) shines as a lazy lawyer who rises to the occasion, and Demi Moore (Galloway) gives a command performance. Kevin Bacon, Kiefer Sutherland, J.T. Walsh, and Cuba Gooding Jr. (of *Jerry Maguire* fame) round out the superb cast. Director Rob Reiner poses important questions about the rights of the powerful and the responsibilities of those just following orders in this classic courtroom drama.

Rules of Engagement (2000)
Director: William Friedkin

Tommy Lee Jones plays Col. Hays Hodges, whose father and grandfather were Marine generals. He himself was in Vietnam as a platoon leader, where he was shot up rather badly in a battle and had to come home. He now faces a test as tough as any he faced under enemy fire: to defend a friend who saved his life in Vietnam, and who is now charged with a major breach of the Marine Corps's Rules of Engagement that left eighty foreign civilians dead.

OTHER COUNTRIES, OTHER CORPS

The idea of Marines—elite ocean-going soldiers capable of intervening swiftly to defend national interests—long predates the USMC. Indeed, it actually goes back to the time of the Romans. But as the nations of Europe began to carve out empires for themselves around the world in the seventeenth and eighteenth centuries, the need for such soldiers became ever greater. As various modern nations emerged from those empires, they too saw the need. Here are historical descriptions of some of these "other Corps." May they never come in conflict with each other again—especially as all the units concerned have participated in Operation Enduring Freedom.

THE DUTCH MARINES

The Royal Netherlands Marine Corps was established on December 10, 1665, on the initiative of Michiel de Ruyter and Johan de Witt. Almost immediately they were thrust into the Anglo-Dutch War of 1665–1667. Although they fought many bitter battles then, they earned the respect of their then foe, the British. But the Royal Marines from both the Dutch and the British sides joined forces in 1704 in the Battle of Gibraltar. It was here that a long-standing relationship and close cooperation between the two former foes was established. The Corps continue to enjoy close ties and train regularly with the British Royal Marines, thus maintaining a similar operational doctrine with their British cousins.

In the West Indies, Surinam, and the East Indies, the Duth Marines proved their worth in various colonial struggles. But their great moment was certainly World War II. With their Dutch Army counterparts they fought bravely to defend the river bridges of Rotterdam against the invading forces of the Third Reich between May 10 and 15, 1940.

When the Nazis attacked Rotterdam, the Dutch Marines had a regiment stationed in the city that was actually preparing for attachment to the Dutch East Indies. They were immediately ordered to defend the bridges and took up defensive front-line positions armed only with light machine guns. Without sleep and limited food and water supplies, they bravely repelled the German paras from crossing the bridge.

Although suffering heavy losses, the bridges were never captured and no German soldier had managed to set foot on the opposite side during the five days of fighting. Unfortunately, the Dutch relented after ruthless bombardment of the city of Rotterdam. Hundreds of civilians lost their lives and with the threat that other cities would soon follow suit, the Dutch government had no choice but to surrender.

When the surrender was declared and the Dutch soldiers came out of their positions, the German commander who was expecting a full battalion of men was stunned to see only a few Dutch Marines emerge in their black uniforms. He ordered his men to salute them out of respect for their bravery and determination and labeled them "Zwarte duivels" (the Black Devils).

The Dutch Marines played an important part in the defense of the East Indies against the Japanese, and then again in the 1945–1949 war against the Indonesian rebels. Today they perform in many peacekeeping and anti-terror roles. The ceremonial functions of the Corps are to provide the Netherlands Marine Band and to act as ceremonial troops for the Dutch government. Marines are the only troops authorized to have fifes and drums, and this music is the Marine trademark in Holland.

Fulfilling their motto, "Qua Patet Orbis" (Wherever the World Extends), the Marines have performed their duties worldwide and often under adverse circumstances. But whatever may be their background and wherever they were on service, in the "East" or in the "West," in Norway, Cambodia, Haiti, Bosnia, or in Albania, they all share their experiences as Marines.

THE FRENCH MARINES

The French Marines, the *fusiliers marins*, predate the Royal Marines by several decades. In past centuries, on the vessels of the French king, there always were sailors trained in musketry, the ancestors of the present Marine Fusiliers.

The first serious organization of these troops, however, was the work of Cardinal Richelieu, who, in 1627, created the Regiment of the Marine. This was intended to provide ships with troops able to fight on sea or land, commanded by the officers of the vessels. These troops were not temporary: they would be a permanent part of the crew, and even give limited assistance with the sails and rigging. These formations existed under various names until the beginning of the nineteenth century; but in 1825, they were dissolved by Royal decree. It was decided that landing parties would consist only of sailors supervised by naval officers.

These shore parties, however, were insufficiently trained for this mission: so, on June 5, 1856, Napoleon III issued an imperial decree creating the specialty of "sailor fusilier" whose training was undertaken in a battalion organized in Lorient. This specialized corps, to which were entrusted the important functions of the weapons of the fleet, at the same time as the instruction and command of the shore parties, is the direct ancestor of the current fusiliers.

Since that time, whether in such nineteenth-century colonial campaigns as China, Cochin-China, Tonkin, or Madagascar, as in France herself during the world wars, the Marine fusiliers proved, fighting side by side with the other services, their valor and heroism.

During the Franco-Prussian War of 1870–1871, after the disasters undergone by the armies of the Second Empire, the brigades of sailor fusiliers and gunners were covered with glory, especially at Bapaume and Le Bourget. The war of 1914–1918 further heightened the fame of the Marine fusiliers. Their feats of arms in Dixmude, on Yser, in Longewaede, Hailles, and Laffaux marked their esprit. Their flag was decorated with the Legion of Honor, and they were given the right to wear the red fourragère. This fourragère has been worn ever since at the school of the Marine fusiliers, in homage to the heroism of the veterans of the Great War.

In the War of 1939 to 1945, a new war created new exploits. Sailors of the defense of Dunkirk, of Cherbourg, of Lorient, fusiliers of the 1st Regiment of Marine fusiliers (1st R.F.M.), heir to the flag, in Bir Hakeim, in Italy, in the Vosges, and on the Rhine, crews of the tanks of the regiment armoured Marine fusiliers (R.B.F.M.) Leclerc division, in Paris, Dompaire, Baccarat and Strasbourg, men of the commandos with Dieppe, Ouistreham, and Flessingue—everywhere the Marine fusiliers continued the tradition. The cross of the Liberation, the honors acquired by the Marine Brigade of the Far East (B.M.E.O.), by the squadron of tradition of the 1st R.F.M., by the R.B.F.M., by the commandos of the navy, naval divisions of attack, and the amphibian flotillas in Indo-China prove that this tradition endured.

With the half brigade of Marine fusiliers (D.B.F.M.) and the regrouping of Marine commandos, the Marine fusiliers engaged in the operations of Algeria, adding to an already glorious past new pages of heroism and sacrifice.

The Marine commandos are successors to the Free French units created during World War II in Great Britain. They too have proved themselves in many emergencies during the last few decades. The Marine fusiliers and the commandos are units intended

- ★ To take part in operations with ground forces starting from the sea.
- ★ To reinforce the protection of the naval forces.
- ★ To take part in special operations under the orders of the Command of the Special Operations (COS).
- ★ To ensure the protection of the sensitive installations of the navy in metropolitan territory and overseas.

THE ITALIAN MARINES

In 1713, King Victor Amadeus II of Sardinia founded the Marine Regiment, made up of sailors. In the following years, this unit remained part of the Navy, participating in the War of 1848, and in the struggles for Italian reunification, from 1860 to 1870. Finally, in 1878, it was separated from the Navy and renamed the Royal Marine Infantry. But the Marines continued to deploy from naval ships, training at sea with light weapons. The RMI was used in various campaigns (Somalia, Ethiopia, China, Venezuela, and elsewhere) during the end of the nineteenth and the beginning of the twentieth centuries, distinguishing itself for valor and the spirit of sacrifice.

In 1915, the regiment was reconstituted as the Marine Brigade. In addition to a regiment of Artillery, this comprised a rifle regiment of three battalions, later expanding to five during World War I. The Marines lived the tragic epic of the trenches; they distinguished themselves, in particular, during the defense of Venice. Attacked by the Austrians on both land and sea, they fought courageously. The Marines distinguished themselves at the Battle of the Piave, where the enemy advance was stopped. Between 1917 and 1918, the Marine Regiment suffered the highest casualties of any single Italian regiment: 384 dead and more than 1,500 wounded.

In May 1918, the unit received its battle flag; on March 17, 1919, a royal decree established the Marines as a separate branch. Venice, to commemorate the heroic sacrifice of the Marine Infantry on its behalf, gave to the unit the Venetian symbol of the winged lion of St. Mark, patron of the city, in the course of a solemn and moving ceremony. The Marine Infantry took his name for its own, being called the Regiment of St. Mark—San Marco—ever after.

After the Boxer revolt, Italy was given a concession at Tientsin, where the Italian community pursued its various commercial interests. Later, as a result of unrest in China, the Italian government decided to take steps to ensure the concession's safety. In 1925, the Riflemen of Saint Mark were entrusted with the defense of the concession from external threat, the protection of Italian interests, as well as guard and ceremonial duties for the country's legation at Beijing. The Italian contingent of approximately fifteen hundred men was distinguished in every circumstance, serving alongside the troops of other nations (American and British Marines and French and Japanese Naval Infantry).

In September of 1943, when the government in Rome joined the Allies, the St. Mark Infantry in China was stationed in the Carlotto Barracks at Tientsin. Orders came from Rome to destroy secret papers, to embark on ships, and do so in a manner befitting the national honor and dignity. But the barracks were surrounded by the Japanese. The garrison was given the choice of collaborating with the Japanese. This choice was very difficult, given both the distance from home and lack of knowledge of what was happening there. Those who agreed to work with the Japanese were given employment in the shipyards; those who refused were interned in the concentration camps at Shanghai and then moved to Manchuria.

During the Colonial Wars of the 1920s and '30s and World War II, the Naval Riflemen were always present at the front lines, acting heroically; in particular, the St. Mark Regiment fought in the Aegean Islands, Greece, and

Africa, where it distinguished itself defending Tobruk. After the armistice of September 8, 1943, Italy divided into two hostile camps—the Royal Government versus Mussolini's "Italian Social Republic" (called also the "Republic of Salò"). In January, 1944, Naval Headquarters reconstituted the Regiment of St. Mark; its record in the War of Liberation won it such admiration from the Allies that they gave the Regiment the honor of being the first to disembark in the city of Venice. At the same time, however, the Republic of Salò formed the "Division of St. Mark," whose emblem was also the Winged Lion.

After the war, the Regiment was at Udine, assisting in the floods of 1951. Despite this service, they were abolished five years later. They were reconstituted in 1964. Today, called the Regiment of St. Mark, they are described as *Fucilieri di Marina*—"Fusiliers of the Sea." This amphibious force is based on three Italian naval ships: the *San Marco*, the *San Giorgio*, and the *San Giusto*. They are effective at deploying quickly anywhere in the world. In the past few years they have participated in all Italian military missions, from Lebanon to the Persian Gulf, from Somalia to Bosnia, from Kosovo to Eritrean waters during that country's war with Ethiopia.

THE PORTUGUESE MARINES

The Portuguese Marine Corps (*Corpo de Fuzileiros*) is the successor of the eldest military corps in Portugal. Founded in 1618, this first group was designated the *Terço da Armada da Coroa de Portugal* (Battalion of the Armada of the Crown of Portugal). Its name was changed to the *Terço da Armada*

Real do Mar Oceano (Battalion of the Royal Armada of the Ocean) with the Restoration of the Independence in 1640. Its missions included the defense of the coast against the corsairs, forming the king's guard, and guarding the ships of the Royal Portuguese Navy. The unit was sent to combat in the most threatened and more distant points, wherever the sovereignty of Portugal was under attack.

During the seventeenth and eighteenth centuries, this corps operated brilliantly. The interventions in the re-conquest of São Salvador da Baía from the Dutch in 1625, the battle of Montijo, and the attack on Badajoz are the most noteworth achievements of this unit.

In 1797 the *Brigada Real de Marinha* (Royal Navy Brigade) was created. Composed of the *Corpo de Artilheiros-Marinheiros* (Unit of Sailor-Gunners), the *Corpo de Artífices e Lastradores* (Unit of Workers), and the *Corpo de Fuzileiros-Marinheiros* (Unit of Navy Marines), this new unit boasted twelve companies and 2,124 men.

In the Mediterranean Sea, integrated in the squadron commanded by D. Domingos Xavier of Lima, Marquis of Niza, under Nelson's orders, the brigade participated in several actions against the French. In 1808, it accompanied the Portuguese royal family in its flight to Brazil. With the independence of that country, the *Corpo de Fuzileiros Navais da Armada Brasileira* (Marine Corps of Brazilian Navy) was created.

Up to 1926, there were several Marine units in the Portuguese Navy, generally serving on board as naval infantry and on land garrisoning the fortresses of overseas territories. From those units, one became part of the *Batalhão Naval* (Navy Battalion) in 1837. With eight companies and 681 men, this Battalion became part of the *Corpo de Marinheiros Militares* (Sailors Corps) in 1851.

In 1961, before the beginning of the wars in the Portuguese African territories, the Marines were created again in the Portuguese Navy. From 1961 to 1975, sixty-four detachments of Special Marines, forty-six Marine companies, and fifteen Independent Marine platoons rendered service in Angola, Cape Verde, Guinea, and Mozambique; this totaled about 12,250 men, without taking into account the Marines in service in the HQ and Naval Commands. The Marine forces had, during the wars in Africa, a military behavior of extraordinary merit as attested to by the many military medals that were granted to the units: three 1st Class War Crosses. To Marines individually were granted four medals of the Military Order of the Tower and Sword (Portuguese higher medal), seven medals of Military Value, and 133 War Crosses, among many others.

After the April 25 Revolution, in 1974, and the end of the wars in Africa, the role of the Portuguese Armed Forces changed significantly. The coast extension, the diversity and characteristics of the continental and insular territory are factors in the current role of the Marines as part of the Portuguese Navy amphibious component.

THE ROYAL MARINES (GREAT BRITAIN)

On October 28, 1664, King Charles II issued an Order-in-Council calling for twelve hundred soldiers to be recruited for service in the Fleet. This would be called the Duke of York and Albany's Maritime Regiment of Foot.

Since the Duke of York (the King's brother, and later to assume the throne as James II) was the Lord High Admiral, the new unit became known as the Admiral's Regiment. The Regiment was paid by the Admiralty, it and its successors being the only long service troops in the seventeenth and eighteenth century Navy.

Not only soldiers but seamen as well, all warships carried a detachment of them. In 1704, during the war with France and Spain, the British attacked the Rock of Gibraltar: nineteen hundred British and four hundred Dutch Marines prevented Spanish reinforcements from reaching the fortress. Later, British ships bombarded the city while Marines and seamen stormed the defenses. These later withstood nine months of siege. Today the Royal Marines display only the battle honour "Gibraltar," and their close relationship with the Royal Netherlands Marine Corps continues. They were, of course, the inspiration for the United States Marine Corps.

Throughout the eighteenth and nineteenth century the Corps played a major part in fighting to win Britain the largest empire ever created. Marines were aboard the first ships to arrive in Australia in 1788. The policy of "Imperial Policing" took the Marines to the bombardment of Algiers in 1816, to the Ashantee Wars, and to the destruction of the Turkish Fleet at Navarino in 1827. In 1805, some twenty-seven hundred Royal Marines took part in the great victory at Trafalgar. Closer to home, they maintained civil order in Northern Ireland and in Newcastle during the coal dispute of 1831. By the outbreak of war in 1914, Britain had the largest fleet in commission in the world, with all ships above that of destroyer size having Royal Marine detachments. On board ship, Marines were required to operate one of the

main gun turrets, as well as secondary armament. Royal Marines also fought on land, notably in the amphibious assault at Gallipoli in 1915, together with ANZAC (Australian and New Zealand Army Corps) forces, and led the famous assault on the harbor at Zeebrugge in 1918.

During World War II, some eighty thousand men served in the Royal Marines, and they continued to operate at sea and in land formations, but 1942 saw the formation of the first Royal Marines Commandos. Five RM Commandos were among the first to land on D-day, and two-thirds of all the landing craft involved were crewed by Royal Marines. Sixty thousand members of the Corps took part in Operation "Overlord" in many roles, some even manning tanks.

After the war the Royal Marines spent much time in action in the Far East, including involvement in the Malayan emergency and in Borneo, as well as in Korea, Suez, Aden, and Cyprus. In 1982, the Royal Marines played a major part in recapturing the Falkland Islands from the Argentinians, and in 1991 they participated in the Gulf War, mounting a sizable humanitarian task force—Operation HAVEN, in support of the Kurdish people of northern Iraq.

This was the start of a particularly busy decade for the Royal Marines. In 1994, a commando unit flew to Kuwait following threats by Iraq. The next year the Royal Marines provided the commander and staff for the Rapid Reaction Force in Bosnia, and in 1997 and 1998 a Commando unit flew to the Congo Republic to protect British interests. In the same period help was provided to the local populations of Montserrat in the West Indies following a volcano eruption, and in Central America following a hurricane. Recent years have seen elements of the Royal Marines on operations in Northern Ireland (where they have completed some thirty-nine tours of duty since 1969), Kosovo, and Sierra Leone. In addition, while few ships now have the traditional RM detachment aboard, Royal Marines Protection Parties join ships as necessary, and have served in such diverse places as Albania and East Timor, where they worked closely with Australian forces. The Royal Marines have played an important part in Operation Iraqi Freedom.

The Royal Marines are U.K. "go anywhere" amphibious forces and a key component of the government's Rapid Reaction Force. As such, they are required to be trained to work in different terrains and environments, from the cold, mountainous conditions in Northern Europe, to the hot arid regions of the Middle East and Africa and to the dense tropical jungles of the Far East.

THE SPANISH MARINES

The Spanish Marines were born in 1537, which makes them the oldest Marine Corps in the world. Among their ranks, great men (such as D. Miguel de Cervantes Saavedra, author of *Don Quixote*) have been found in every age. The *Infanteria de Marina* is part of the *Armada Espanola* (Spanish Navy). The Spanish Marines are Sea Soldiers. They belong to the Navy, have Navy regulations, and their budget comes from the Navy; but they will always be Marines, serving in Marine units and performing Marine tasks. They are tankers, artillerymen, sappers, soldiers . . . inside the Navy.

It is an elite corps, highly specialized in amphibious operations. Its ability to embark on short notice with the Navy's land, air, and naval assets makes it a unit with a high strategic value.

One of the main characteristics of the Spanish Marines are the uniforms they wear. On the sleeve are the three *sardinetas*, which means they belong to a Royal House Corps. This was earned in 1763 by defending Castillo del Morro, as were the red stripes in the trousers. The only units today to wear sardinetas and red stripes are the Royal Guard and the Spanish Marines.

The *Infantera de Armada* (Navy Infantry) was created by Carlos I (Emperor Charles V) in 1537, when he permanently assigned the Naples Maritime Companies to the *Escuadras de Galeras del Mediterraneo* (Mediterranean Galley Squadrons). But it was Philip II who originated today's concept of a landing force. This was military power that was projected ashore by forces coming from ships and able to fight, unweakened by having been based on board. This is the period of the famous *Tercios* (literally "One Third", due to its organization: one third of musketeers, one third of spearmen, and the left third of pike men), the feared Spanish infantry, renowned for valor and ferocity.

In 1704, the Tercios became *Regimientos de Bajeles* (Vessel's Regiments), *Armada* (Navy Regiment), *Mar de Napoles* (Naples' Sea Regiment), and *Marina de Sicilia* (Sicily's Navy Regiment). Detached to the Army were some small units, while the main body remained in the Navy, becoming the *Cuerpo de Batallones de Marina* (Navy Battalions Corps).

In these early days, the Spanish Marines participated in many famous campaigns: the Algiers expedition in 1541; the Lepanto Naval Battle in 1571; the Tunisia expedition in 1573; the Terceras and Azores islands conquest in 1582; the Great Britain expedition in 1599; and the San Salvador (Brazil) expedition in 1625.

In 1717, the Cuerpo de Batallones de Marina was definitively organized. Their mission was to form the "main body of landing columns and ship's soldiers tasks" in a time when boarding was the way to fight among vessels; they also served as gun crews. Some of the actions they took part in were the Sardinia Conquest in 1717; the Naples and Sicily Conquest in 1732; the Pensacola (Florida) expedition in 1770; the La Habaña defense in 1762; the Algiers expedition in 1775; the Toulon Landing in 1793; the Ferrol defense in 1800; and the reconquest of Buenos Aires in 1806.

Spain's colonial conflicts gave a new mission to the Spanish Marines, making them a permanent expeditionary force. The *Batallones Expedicionarios* (Expeditionary Battalions) conducted campaigns in Cochin-China

(1858), Mexico (1862), Santo Domingo (1864), Cuba and Filipinas (1898), Africa (1911), some of them lasting as long as ten years.

At the end of World War I, the battle at Gallipoli led most countries to abandon the idea of amphibious assault. The entire world's marine corps fell into a deep crisis, and the Infantera de Marina was no exception (despite the successful Alhucemas amphibious assault in 1925, in which it first employed air and naval gunfire support). Indeed, the "Expeditionary Mission" came to be considered a "colonial force"; thus in 1931, the Marines were condemned to extinction by the Spanish Republican Government. During the Spanish Civil War, the Corps split, with Marines fighting on both sides—they acted as garrisons, landing parties, and gun and machine gun crews. After the Civil War, the Marines' death sentence was revoked, and their strength increased again.

In 1957, the *Grupo Especial Anfibio* (Amphibious Special Group) was created, and the Infantera de Marina regained its landing force mission as its main purpose. This was just in time; in 1958, Marines established a beach-head in Spanish Sahara and Ifni. The beach was open and fully operational for one year despite the conflict that motivated the action. From that year on, the capabilities and strength of the Marines was increased—new amphibious vehicles, anti-tank weapons, individual gear, artillery.

The Spanish Marines have been present in Bosnia, Albania, Central America, and serve as an "emergency force" ready to evacuate civilians in conflict areas or as deterrence force covering the action of friendly forces. They have also served in Angola, Mozambique, El Salvador, Nicaragua,

Guatemala, and Bosnia. They also participated in relief operations after the catastrophe caused in Central America by Hurricane Mitch, when three helicopters and a reinforced company were sent on board LPD *Galicia* in a humanitarian mission.